MARÍA OF ÁGREDA

MARÍA OF ÁGREDA
Mystical Lady in Blue

MARILYN H. FEDEWA

UNIVERSITY OF NEW MEXICO PRESS
ALBUQUERQUE

Library of Congress Cataloging-in-Publication Data

Fedewa, Marilyn H.
  María of Ágreda : mystical lady in blue / Marilyn H. Fedewa.
    p. cm.
  Includes bibliographical references and index.
  isbn 978-0-8263-4643-8 (hardcover : alk. paper)
  1. María de Jesús, de Agreda, sor, 1602–1665.
  2. Abbesses, Christian—Spain—Biography.
  I. Title.
  bx4705.m3255f343 2009
  271'.97302—dc22
  [B]
                              2008049080

Imprimatur 2008
Most Rev. Earl Boyea, Bishop of the Diocese of Lansing, Michigan

Excerpts from *The Visions of Sor María de Agreda: Writing Knowledge and Power* by Clark Colahan © 1994 The Arizona Board of Regents. Reprinted by permission of the University of Arizona Press.

Excerpts from *Mary of Ágreda: The Life and Legend of a Spanish Nun* by Sir Thomas Downing Kendrick © 1967 T. D. Kendrick. Reprinted by permission of Taylor and Francis Books UK.

All photographs, maps, and diagrams, unless otherwise stated, are by—and remain the copyrighted property of—the author. Cover images (Sor María's portrait at age thirty-six, and embroidered altar cloth) are on display in and have been provided courtesy of the Convent of the Conception, Ágreda.

Book design and type composition by Melissa Tandysh
Composed in 10.5/14 Aldus, display type is Aldus Italic and Poetica Std

To S. Christopher, my light and heart

CONTENTS

LIST OF ILLUSTRATIONS

Mystifying aspects of María of Ágreda linger long after her simple cloistered life in seventeenth-century Spain. She lived and died without leaving her village. Yet the nun's legacy threads through many historical accounts of the American Southwest and Latin America. Her name still evokes wonder around campfires in Texas and New Mexico, and her writings are studied in universities worldwide for their influence on Spanish literature. Her prolific correspondence with King Felipe IV of Spain sheds valuable insights on the court life and politics of the era.

Her story, though woven in an age of miracles, is riddled with questions in today's age of science.

Did María of Ágreda, while praying in ecstasy, actually levitate before witnesses, as in the case of Teresa of Avila? Did she, in the quiet of her cloister, chronicle a spiritual union with God that guaranteed her place as a religious pioneer and seer for future generations? Did she, in effect—through spiritual if not physical means—convert Jumano Native Americans to Catholicism in colonial southwest America, as detailed in many historical treatises of the time? And, if so, how?

I first learned about María of Ágreda indirectly, through Fr. Solanus Casey, a saintly bearded monk who read the mystic's books on his knees for fifty years and gave copies of them to our family in 1952. Decades later, in 1997, high atop a bookcase that had not been touched in years, I spotted the four dusty volumes, each encased in worn, green, leathery binding with faded gold lettering that read *City of God*. Initially I thought of Saint Augustine, but upon opening them discovered that the title expanded to *Mystical City of God*, a translation of a seventeenth-century series by a cloistered Spanish abbess.

For six months each night after work, I immersed myself in the volumes, a set totaling twenty-seven hundred pages of archaic English translated over a ten-year period between 1902 and 1912 from an even more archaic baroque Spanish written not once but twice between 1637 and 1660. The set was based on the personal visions and private revelations of María of Ágreda and chronicled the life of Mary, mother of Jesus of Nazareth. Each time I was ready to set the huge tomes aside for a more contemporary diversion, some compelling account of Sor María's spiritual heartaches—or her archetypal portrayal of Mary—transcended the barriers of time and space and drew me back.

In doing so, I entered Sor María's world on her own terms, purposely skipping the brief historical references to her life and works in the opening article titled "Special Notice to the Reader." Not until much later, recalling her brief mention of being ordered to burn all her writings, did I emerge from the rarified milieu of her mystical writings to learn about other, more relative, aspects of her life, and what others said and wrote about her.

Historical accounts emerged of her friendship with the unpredictable king and her mystical appearances in the American Southwest. Literary scholars, I learned, studied her writing for its plentiful examples of baroque Spanish. Historians read her correspondence with the king for its unique window into seventeenth-century court life. Theologians scrutinized *Mystical City of God*—her devout portrayal of the life of Jesus' mother, Mary—for its dogmatic consistency, or lack thereof. And many overly deferential devotees absorbed her mystical treatises almost literally, to the exacerbation of scholars, historians, and theologians.

How could I reconcile all this, I wondered, with the writings of the sincere, self-effacing woman who had dedicated her life to the quiet transcendence of the spiritual path? Was she diabolical, as the Spanish Inquisition attempted to declare in her day—or delusional, as psychiatrists today might conjecture?

Ironically, despite her rich spiritual legacy, Sor María did not seem to be a frequent subject of religious studies in the United States, unlike in Spain, where many analyses of her symbolic "Mariology"—a term used to describe the study of Mary—were published in the hopes of furthering her cause for sainthood. Yet I discovered valuable scholarly materials about her, published in the United States and England, mainly through programs of Spanish literature, colonial history, and women's studies. The scholars' questions were many, and their conclusions were fertile and provocative. What were the freedoms of religious women in times past, I now wondered. How had Jewish mystics in Spain impacted their Christian counterparts? What acceptable venues existed for those talented women who today might be religious leaders and authors of note? Were they manipulated by their male ecclesiastical superiors? And, as a result, what rightfully could be their legitimate legacy today?

Attracted by Sor María's long-standing devotion to quiet prayer—the inevitable transcendent source of her mystical experiences—and inspired by the work of the late Mary Giles, founding editor of *Studia Mystica,* and Clark Colahan, author of *The Visions of Sor María de Agreda,* I decided to study Sor María more thoroughly from the inside out. In that she was still a relatively obscure figure, however, the body of material available by and about her in English was not very satisfying to this exploration. Ultimately I was compelled to visit her convent in Ágreda, Spain. I left there with photographs, taped interviews with her conventual successors, and a wealth of materials in Spanish that would take a long time to absorb. As I investigated, more of Sor María's autobiographical testimony emerged, from her childhood through the grueling interrogation by the Spanish Inquisition later in her life.

Throughout, my questions remained: What really happened in her life, and how did it square with her writings about the mystical process and her own experiences?

Could she have been a liar, delusional? Could there be a disconnect between her considerable accomplishments and those activities less comprehensible? How possible was it that there might be, however mystical or miraculous, some truth to the more phenomenal aspects of her life? How did María of Ágreda's experiences stand up against other such examples throughout the millennia among the major wisdom traditions? Her experiences strained credulity. Yet so many aspects of Sor María's life inspired me and could potentially inspire many others. I reengaged in my inquiry as I had begun—reading and listening to her, seeking consistencies as well as inconsistencies, but deciding to allow her to explain herself.

The result was an empathetic yet reportorial approach, as I worked to present Sor María's story as accurately as possible, but from her perspective as a spiritual aspirant, as recorded in historical documents and especially those of her own testimony. This represents a concerted effort on my part to search out Sor María's voice and help her to speak it—albeit in absentia so long after the fact—in a format and context accessible to a contemporary audience. My goal in doing this is to portray a highly accomplished and unusual woman whose story will prove thought provoking and inspiring to a wide audience today. The fact that she lived her life as a Catholic did not especially motivate me, although no doubt this allowed me to understand her more easily because of my own background.

This work, therefore, is not a scholarly treatise on the life of this extraordinary woman. Nor does it presume to render doctrinal definitions about the spiritual matters of which María of Ágreda wrote. Instead, it attempts to reconstruct through systematic research enough of a spiritual and historical backdrop to set the stage for the abbess to speak for herself—from autobiographical material and correspondence not yet available in English, from the convent's abundant archives in Ágreda, Spain, and from personal interviews with her conventual successors. This I have seasoned amply with the testimony of her contemporaries as well as modern day scholars.

In doing so, I worked to portray María of Ágreda's life and times in a way that is both objective and accessible, while attempting to contribute a comprehensible context for her unusual mystical experiences. Beyond that, and most meaningful to me personally, I hope that the universal aspects of María of Ágreda's all-too-human struggles and heartwarming triumphs will touch and inspire the reader directly.

—Marilyn H. Fedewa

CHAPTER 1

Who Is
María of Ágreda?

AT FIRST GLANCE, MARÍA OF ÁGREDA'S LIFE EVOKES THE heights and depths of a spiritual rollercoaster ride, plummeting down and scaling the landscape of her soul during her sixty-three years on earth. The abbess's writing, however, documents her hard-won spiritual lessons with examples akin to breaking the barrier of running the "four-minute mile" in spiritual terms. In the process, she marks precious milestones across the centuries for seekers the world over who long for peace and enlightenment.

This prominent seventeenth-century religious and political figure lived in—and never left—northeast Spain. Yet María of Ágreda is paradoxically regarded today in pockets of the American Southwest as a key historical phenomenon. Her writings, reverently packed in ornate travel boxes, accompanied noted colonial missionaries such as Junípero Serra and Antonio Margil as they evangelized California and Texas, founding missions and city centers, some in her memory.

More challenging to the imagination, however, is the fact that Jumano Native Americans in Texas and New Mexico called María of Ágreda the "Lady in Blue" who personally taught them Christianity, while nuns in her charge vowed their abbess had never left the convent. For this, and her many accomplishments, she is now feted in perpetuity in art collections

FIGURE 1. Map of Spain and Portugal. Map by author.

across the globe, as exemplified in a grand eighteenth-century portrait of her in Mexico's National Museum of Viceroyalty, one emblazoned with a scroll citing her missionary work in New Mexico at age twenty-one.

While many religious traditions describe the mystical phenomenon of bilocation, or appearing in two places at the same time, few have such elaborate documentation of the events. Fewer still provide a tangible human context for such unusual spiritual experiences. In María of Ágreda's case, historical records abound because the Jumanos' detailed testimony is recounted in seminal histories of the Southwest. Too, mission officials located and interviewed her in Spain, whereupon she shared with them her struggle to interpret the phenomenon.

Official reports, quoted by colonial historians through the centuries, cited the "blessed sister" as "handsome of face, very fair in color, with a slight rosy tinge and large black eyes," whereas the twenty-nine-year-old nun described herself as "under the command of obedience" and "beside myself with anxiety" at the unwanted attention.[1] Despite the sensationalism that resulted, in the interstices of a rigorous prayer schedule and her responsibilities as abbess, she embarked on the signature work of her life, an eight-volume series entitled *Mystical City of God*.

Rumors of the work-in-progress spread through the monks who copied and therefore read early versions in preparation for scrutiny by ecclesiastical censors. Soon María of Ágreda surged in popular esteem as a saintly woman sought out by commoners and nobility alike. She earned the attention and respect of her peers as well as that of then ruler of Spain, King Felipe IV, so much so that he sought her out on his way to battle at the Spanish frontier.

His treasury was depleted, the king told the mystic. The country was at war with France. The nation's human resources had been siphoned off in the colonization of the New World. The Spanish fleet of ships perilously sailed through hostile seas off the coast of Africa, trying to return to Spain with precious cargoes of silver to replenish his coffers.[2]

Before long, King Felipe IV of Spain considered María of Ágreda both his spiritual and political adviser, documented in six hundred confidential letters during their twenty-two-year-long correspondence. The cloistered abbess advised him in detail on his prayer life and on matters of governance. Many times her advice reflected the simple common sense offered from one friend to another. Other times, she dove straight to the spiritual heart of her mystical life: "Dilate all your heart and soul to receive divine love," she frequently exhorted him over the years in various iterations of the central theme of her life.[3]

When Felipe IV struggled with the decadence and ineffectiveness of his court officials, and the manipulations of his prime minister, María of Ágreda advised him in detail on how to sort out the chaff, while at the same time applying principles of fairness. And she didn't take just the easy assignments.

Like many advisers to those in high positions, María of Ágreda dreaded the consequences of advising the king about his love life. Yet she courageously set aside her fear and told him to be faithful in marriage despite the common knowledge of his frequent infidelities. When she couldn't appeal to him spiritually, she switched to pragmatism. He would increase his chances of having an heir, she wrote to him curtly, if he was faithful to his wife.[4]

In seventeenth-century Spain, this self-educated cloistered mystic— a Catholic nun likely of Jewish descent—faced challenges most people never have to worry about: the Spanish Inquisition, the demands of advising a beleaguered king, and the laborious task of writing and rewriting her books by hand. She also manifested unusual spiritual gifts that baffle the understanding of many.

Accounts of her early life quote witnesses who said they saw her levitate, like Saint Teresa of Avila, while in prayerful ecstasy.[5] Community members testified that she saw into their hearts and futures, and cured their illnesses. They also described the fervent missionary zeal she had harbored since girlhood, although she never physically left Ágreda.[6] As a result of this unfulfilled desire, her spirit seemed to her to reach out beyond the confines of her body, while she was reported by others as being seen in two places at once—like Saint Padre Pio, who also "bilocated."[7]

When castigated by superiors for what they considered her showy ecstasies, she clung to her passionate spirituality and relentlessly applied her intellect to understand the nature of her ecstatic visions. "A spiritualized condition can conquer the resistance of gravity . . . and penetrate matter," she wrote in later life, describing Mary's mystical gifts and no doubt thinking of her own experience of being in another country across the sea.[8] She also described in detail the Jumano Native Americans of Texas and New Mexico, including the weather and landmarks of their territory, their customs and lifestyle, and the Franciscan missionaries who worked among them. Thus, an unusual American legacy spread, as the story of the Lady in Blue was recorded in many historical treatises on both sides of the ocean.

At the same time, these phenomena ignited the suspicion of the Spanish Inquisition, which posited demonic possession as their cause and secretly surveilled her activities for years. When María of Ágreda was mistakenly implicated in a plot against the king, the Inquisition made a surprise appearance in Ágreda and interrogated her for eleven grueling days, under threat of excommunication. She was ultimately exonerated of any wrongdoing, heresy, or demonic possession, although sensationalism proved a periodic millstone throughout her life.

Over the years, María of Ágreda wrote fourteen books, the most prominent of which is *Mystical City of God*, a biography of Mary, mother of Jesus. In it, she threads references from the Bible's canonical Gospels, as well as insights from classical Christian and Jewish narratives and apocryphal texts about Mary that were popular at the time.

Mystical City of God also engages its readers in rich accounts of María of Ágreda's own visions—deemed by the Catholic Church as inspiring private revelations that are not required matters of faith—and her mystical immersion in the world of the spirit and deep prayer. In her writing, she shares many enlightening passages on the nature of her visions and supernatural phenomena. Miraculously, the book survived the decades-long scrutiny of the Spanish Inquisition and inexplicable orders to burn it. Through this printing, it has appeared in hundreds of editions and dozens of languages worldwide.

While María of Ágreda's legacy has yet to equal that of her countrywoman, Teresa of Avila, many modern-day Spaniards have come to value her contributions more in recent years.

In 1995 Spain's Radio Televisión Española (RTVE) named María of Ágreda as one of the nine most influential women in Spanish history. In 2002 twelve thousand people flocked to Ágreda to view the glass-encased crypt housing her incorrupt body, in honor of the four hundredth anniversary of her birth. The following year, US film director Mel Gibson read *Mystical City of God*, among other works, in advance of making his 2004 blockbuster film, *The Passion of the Christ*.[9]

In 2006 María of Ágreda was included in *Grolier Scholastic*'s new biography series on one thousand influential Hispanic Americans past and present, alongside political activist Cesar Chavez and father of California missions Junípero Serra. Scholarly treatises continue to emerge in the twenty-first century, exploring the nature of her life and its place in history. The iconography on her alone comprises hundreds of images exhibited worldwide—in oil paintings, woodcuts, engravings, statuary, and architectural insets.

In honor of the "heroic exercise of virtue" throughout her life, María of Ágreda was designated a "venerable" of the Catholic Church seven years after her death. Theologians in the seventeenth and eighteenth centuries described *Mystical City of God* as unparalleled, guided by a supernatural hand, a work with "a knowledge of the most sublime truths [that] inflame the heart with divine love."[10] Yet beatification—the next step toward sainthood—has yet to become a reality for her, in part because a faulty translation of her book relegated it to the church's dreaded Index of Forbidden Books. For centuries, it bounced on and off this blacklist, depending on each pope's disposition and the skill of her backers. Mystified connoisseurs of her work labor to understand this seeming contradiction.

The "wow" factor alone is certainly reason enough to read the extraordinary story of María of Ágreda's life. Yet if the reader considers her experiences to be out of reach, full of unattainable spiritual heights, it is a mistake. As in the lives of many great seers, writers, and statesmen, each pinnacle likely harbors its own precipice and nearby abyss. Indeed, because many of these achievers did not have mentors of greater wisdom or experience than they, often they endured many more cycles of trial and error than most people. That is one reason why they provide us with so many opportunities to learn from them.

Such is certainly the case with María of Ágreda. Despite her long, glittering résumé, she struggled throughout her life with anxiety, depression, and inertia. She fought her inner demons, failed sometimes, and picked herself up again, as we all can do.

Although María of Ágreda's tradition was Catholic, and she lived in the paternalistic church-state of Inquisition-era Spain, her experience was universal. Many of her insights call to mind the timeless truths offered by highly evolved seers of many religious and wisdom traditions. Her portrayal of Mary as the Divine Mother evokes touching images of Mary as the spiritual mother of all of creation.[11] Her description of Mary's spiritual prowess, and of Mary's invitation to María and all of humankind to follow in her footsteps, calls us to claim the birthright of our unlimited potential.

This is her journey.

PART ONE

A LITTLE GIRL
WITH BIG EYES

1602

CHAPTER 2

"Suddenly my perception expanded"

AS A CHILD, MARÍA CORONEL AWOKE MANY MORNINGS before dawn to the sound of her father in prayer, dragging a one-hundred-pound cross along the floor. She saw her mother draped in a dark Franciscan robe, holding a human skull before her face, and heard Señora Coronel's intoned contemplation of death and the everlasting life of the soul.[1] With such a stark introduction to the life of the spirit, María Coronel nevertheless made her own way through the wondrous mystical realms about which she so prolifically wrote later in life.

At the time of her birth in Ágreda in 1602, the religious and historical landscapes of seventeenth-century Spain stood out like the peaks of the Pyrenees Mountains that both weld and divide the Iberian Peninsula and the European mainland. The paint had been dry for only sixty-one years on Michelangelo's masterful depiction of the *Last Judgment* over the altar of the Sistine Chapel. Shakespeare (1564–1616) had just completed *Hamlet* and was about to embark upon *All's Well That Ends Well*. Galileo (1564–1642) braved imminent arrest by the church for his revolutionary evidence on a sun-centered universe. And Martin Luther (1483–1546) had long since nailed his Protestant manifesto on the Wittenberg church door.

In Spain, Cervantes (1547–1616) had rocked the literary world with his groundbreaking novel *Don Quixote de la Mancha*. The Spanish Inquisition

FIGURE 2. Ágreda, Spain, taken from Moncayo Mountain, overlooking Convent of the Conception (left), village (beyond the poplars), and surrounding foothills. Photo by author.

since 1480 had tenaciously excised convicted and suspected blasphemers and heretics. Christopher Columbus had journeyed to the New World four times at the royal mandate of Catholic monarchs Ferdinand and Isabel. The Spanish Armada had suffered its ignominious defeat in the English Channel in 1588, ending Spanish naval supremacy and considerably raising the bar for colonization efforts in America.

England had impressed its rule on the east coast of the New World, France in the Great Lakes and northeast regions, and Spain in Mexico, Florida, and the Southwest. Colonization efforts in America were replete with new hopes for religious freedom, new zeal for evangelical missions, and new balance sheets reflecting the riches of souls and goods in the vast unexplored land.

Meanwhile, Teresa of Avila (1515–82), just forty-five miles west of Madrid, had explored the realms of the spirit, levitated in ecstatic prayer,[2] traveled the Spanish countryside founding convents, and written *Interior Castle*, a multilayered exploration of the interior spiritual landscape.

The printing press, invented by Gutenberg 152 years earlier than Sor María's birth, afforded books to the masses, although romance adventure novels were more commonly available in Spain than Bibles in the vernacular. There, the Christian Bible initially became accessible in Latin to nuns and priests as excerpted by ecclesiastical scholars into liturgical prayer books called "breviaries," such as the one in María of Ágreda's possession.[3] Authors such as she and Teresa of Avila still wrote with a feathered quill pen and relied on the kindness of monastic scribes for multiple copies of their work.

To the northeast of Avila, less than the distance east from Madrid to the Mediterranean Sea, lay the frontier village of Ágreda, nestled in the foothills of the Moncayo mountain range in the Soria region of northeastern Spain. There the noble Coronel and Arana families gravitated and invested their considerable talents. There, on the Road of the Knights, stood the Coronel ancestral home where María Coronel was born.

If the walls of the stately home on the Road of the Knights could

FIGURE 3. The Coronel ancestral home, first site of Ágreda's Convent of the Conception, founded in 1618. Photo by author.

speak, they would tell of the two Coronel brothers' families residing there in 1602.[4] The walls would tell how their very structure was rent in two by a mother's dream, thirteen years later, forecasting the building's transformation into a convent for all the women of the family and the simultaneous exodus of all the men to join monasteries. They would tell of a cross-barred window studded with spearheads, which had been cut into the wall between the second-story parlor and the adjacent sitting room, and how the cloistered women within spoke with visitors through this ominous grille.

Most of all, the walls would tell the story of the early years of the building's most extraordinary occupant, María Coronel—later known as Sor María de Jesús de Ágreda—mystic, author, adviser to the king.

Today the street has been renamed Augustine Road, and the site of María of Ágreda's introduction into mysticism has been divided into two private residences, numbers 9 and 11, now nestled between other buildings built onto either side.[5] Considered a mansion in seventeenth-century Spain, to modern eyes it looks like a sturdy three-story stone relic, in a village little changed by time. The grille that was installed by María of Ágreda's mother, and which features two-inch spikes jutting from each intersection, was later moved in 1632 to the new convent facilities built on the edge of town near the convent of the Franciscan friars of Saint Julian.

Long before these events, however, a child was born.

Eleven babies would earn Catalina Coronel the right to speak with authority about the birthing process. According to her, María's birth was trouble-free, a new experience for the seasoned matron. But that was not all that was unusual about her first surviving daughter. As recounted by Bishop José Ximénez Samaniego, María's first biographer, Señora Coronel described the moment when she brought her baby daughter to church to offer her to God.

"It was a joy and consolation so extraordinary," Samaniego wrote, quoting Catalina, "that never before or after had she experienced a similar feeling."[6]

The wide-eyed source of this joy—María Coronel y Arana—was born on April 2, 1602, the third child and first surviving daughter of Francisco Coronel and Catalina Arana, in the frontier village of Ágreda in northeast Spain. Her mother Catalina, described by many as vibrant and magnanimous, was thirty-nine years old. Her father Francisco, approaching

FIGURE 4. Side entrance to Coronel home on Augustine Road (formerly Road of the Knights). Photo by author.

thirty-eight, was described as passionate and impulsive, although steadied by virtue.[7] Each wore the mantle of pious nobility of meager means, a canopy sheltering both sides of little María's ancestral family tree.

"My parents brought me up carefully," she wrote, "in a loving environment that nurtured my spiritual life."[8]

The child's maternal grandfather, Don Francisco de Arana, was a native of Ágreda. His ancient ancestors hailed from Basque country, not too far from the Bay of Biscay, near present-day Bilbao in northernmost Spain. María's maternal grandmother, María of Orobio, descended from a long line of Ágredan gentility, one of whom attained the title of Marqués de Paredes later in the seventeenth century.[9]

On her father's side, the Coronels enjoyed an equally noble lineage. "Divine providence favored my father with noble, gentlemanly and rich parents," María wrote of her paternal grandparents, Medel Coronel and María la Mura, "although his parents died at an early age, leaving him and his [younger] brother in shock at the catastrophe, to manage the estate as best they could."[10]

Several generations of her father Francisco Coronel's heritage are heralded in a handsomely decorated certificate of *hidalguía*, or "nobility," executed in 1532 by María's great-grandfather of the same name, Francisco Coronel of Añavieja, about six kilometers from Ágreda. The certificate lists her great, great–paternal grandfather, Diego Coronel (married to María Ruiz de Pulgares), and Diego's father, Rodrigo Coronel (married to María López).[11]

A witness to the certificate of nobility told how Diego Coronel's fingers had been severed during his wartime service in 1476, the stumps providing a lifelong reminder of his loyalty to the Crown.[12] "Diego Coronel served on horseback with weapons at Toro," seventy-three-year-old Juan Pérez testified, "when our Catholic rulers were at war with the king of Portugal." "After the battle," Pérez said, "he returned without his horse. What's more, in the fight he had lost four fingers on one hand."[13]

While there is no further mention of more ancient Coronel forebears in María of Ágreda's autobiographical material or in her convent's archives, a great deal of information has come to light in more recent years, to supplement the Coronel family background.

New research surfacing in the twentieth century links the Coronel family to a Jewish financier, Abraham Senior, who supported Christopher Columbus's initial voyage to America and served as Isabel and Ferdinand's chief tax collector. Soon, however, Inquisitor General Torquemada's Edict of Expulsion mandated the eviction of Jews from Spain. In lieu of leaving his homeland, Abraham Senior followed an accepted venue for Jews who wished to remain in Spain and adopted the all-but-extinct noble Coronel surname. Later in 1492, he was baptized as Fernandez Pérez Coronel, and many in his extended family followed suit.[14] As such, they joined the ranks of conversos, a term describing Jewish people who converted to Christianity.

Whether María of Ágreda's ancestor Rodrigo Coronel is Abraham Senior's son, or relative, is unknown. Convent historians indicate that María of Ágreda's paternal family is from another branch of Coronels, while contemporary scholars assert that they are virtually certain that every Coronel dates back to Abraham Senior because the name that he assumed with royal approbation had been recorded as extinct dating back to 1353.[15]

Understandably, many conversos publicly adopted Christianity as a survival mechanism, while maintaining Judaic practices in secrecy. Hence early conversos were under a great deal of surveillance and often lived in fear of reprisal through the Inquisition. Over the generations, however, many converso families adopted Christianity as their own, practicing it devoutly. And, much as the status of converso often provoked prejudice, comfort was found in the fact that even the sainted Teresa of Avila's ancestors numbered among them.[16]

Even beyond specific genealogies, however, Spain itself had long been steeped in the rich influence of its Jewish mystics. As the Kabbalah traversed over the Pyrenees from Provence to Spain, the intellectual commerce between Christians and Jews in Spain was widespread from the thirteenth through the sixteenth centuries. The author of the Zohar resided in Avila as he penned the Kabbalah's *Book of Radiance*.[17] The collections in Teresa of Avila's and María of Ágreda's libraries included many works by sixteenth-century Dominican theologian, the Venerable Luis of Granada, whose writings were likely influenced by the Christian Kabbalah.[18] Among the country's intellectuals, and within their folk traditions, Jewish and Christian thinkers often cross-fertilized each other, sometimes in formal treatises and more often in pervasive folk wisdom that is difficult to trace.[19]

Whatever the Ágreda Coronels' origin, María Coronel's immediate family certainly heartily embraced Christianity in the charitable atmosphere of Ágreda, a village long known for its equitable approach to diversity. Described as the "Village of the Three Cultures," signs leading into the village today proudly display the half moon of the Islamic Moors, the Christian cross, and the Jewish Star of David.

There, María's parents resolutely undertook their Christian responsibilities to raise their children and partake of community life. Her father was no doubt influenced by his own parents who had enrolled themselves and all six of their children as lay members of the Third Order of Saint Francis,[20] a noted catalyst among Franciscan mystics and ascetics. Many of María's early memories of her parents reflect the rigorous devotional practices of this order.

"My father rose at three in the morning," María recounted fondly in her autobiography. "While the rest of the family slept, he practiced the Exercise of the Cross, carrying a large cross on his back and praying with great fervor and tender sighs."[21] This same iron cross is on display in the convent museum today and weighs over one hundred pounds.

Her mother, whom she described as having a "grand and constant spirit," practiced her own spiritual exercises in the evening, after the day's work was done.[22] "She exemplified Mary's meditative prayer and often spent three or four hours at a time in the evening practicing various spiritual devotions," María wrote. In one such devotion, Catalina stretched out in bed with a Franciscan habit as a shroud and a skull over her face, in contemplation of the body's death and the everlasting life of the soul.[23]

Her parents' stark devotional practices made a lasting impression on María, no doubt influencing her own self-imposed austerities in later years. In this rarefied environment, the dark-haired, quick-witted child was perpetually curious and had been encouraged to be so. "Since my mother held me in her arms," she wrote, "she taught me to observe everything."[24] That María opened her wide brown eyes to the intensity of her parents' spiritual exercises, as well as the world around her, determined to understand them, was only natural. One day, her nonstop curiosity was rewarded with an enlightening surprise.

"My watchfulness grew into understanding," she wrote, recalling four intense insights that she described in terms of light. "This light filled me with the knowledge that God was the creator of the universe, and the cause of all effects." In the second and third insights, she reported understanding how "divine potency" imprints the human heart, then saw the three persons within one God, and their unity of essence. In the fourth, she saw the havoc that sin wreaks on human nature.[25]

"Suddenly my perception expanded," she wrote in adult words of her childhood experience, "even as I saw myself as nothing, the least of his creatures." "I saw the extremes of good and evil, of light and darkness, of grace and sin," she reported. "God etched this awareness into my heart with a divine force," she wrote. "His light enthralled me," she wrote, "and sweetly imprisoned me in holy love."[26]

According to "witnesses worthy of belief" whom Bishop Samaniego interviewed during María's lifetime, these occurrences did indeed happen. He considered María's initial experience as a "supernatural vision," after which she reasoned her way to the essence of Christian salvation.[27] While of course the child's upbringing—and the dramatic devotions of her parents—would have influenced her experience, she nevertheless demonstrated a rare depth of understanding for such a small child.

The senior Coronels were amazed at their pretty little daughter. As parents, they had labored to give her a spiritual foundation and vocabulary, and they proudly laid claim to their child prodigy. María, wrapped in the wonder of God's love, hardly noticed.

Yet her joy was bittersweet. For at the same time that María experienced God's love, she was anxious and worried that she might offend Him. If she lost Him, she knew that she herself would be lost, and she saw through to "the very center of her nothingness."[28] Despite this heart-rending insight, she reports herself as a happy and precocious child who for several years was "sweetly chained to [God's] holy love."[29]

As María grew, more people began to notice her. When she was just four years old, she drew the attention of Bishop Don Diego de Yepes of Tarazona. For a time, Yepes had served as King Felipe II's confessor. He was also a relative of Saint John of the Cross. His reputation was further enhanced by the fact that in 1606 he had just completed the biography of Teresa of Avila,[30] having served as Teresa's confessor for the last year of her life.

Yepes was so impressed with María's spiritual understanding at age four that he confirmed her, a sacrament usually reserved for children aged seven or older—when they reached the age of reason. He advised María's proud parents to take particular care with her education, encouraging them to set aside a special area in their home for her to pray and study by herself. Soon Catalina Coronel allocated space in their already crowded

FIGURE 5. Sor María's oratory window on third floor of her family home. Photo by author.

home, to establish a private oratory for little María.[31] There she tutored her in matters of religion and encouraged her daughter's inner sight.

While other children were playing matador or skip-rope,[32] María gravitated to her oratory, furnished by her mother with inspiring statues such as the Virgin of the Choir, the scourged Christ, Saint Michael the Archangel, and Saint Francis. A priest from the nearby Convent of the Friars of Saint Julian, Padre Juan de Torrecilla, was a frequent visitor. As Catalina's confessor, and subsequently María's, he not only held their trust, but also shared his considerable stores of knowledge with the inquisitive child.

Before too long, however, this idyllic phase ended. For many mystics who tasted the ecstasy of God's loving presence, often the utter desolation of his absence was not far behind.

Inexplicably, María's worst fear came to pass. She found herself alone. Despite her best efforts, as she reported about this period later in life, "her heavenly Spouse concealed himself and deprived her of the consolation of his assistance."[33] Over the years she grew more adept at describing her sense of the presence of God and the "interior knowing" that accompanied most of her visions, as well as the process through which she gained the inner spiritual light and quiet so integral to her equanimity.[34] At this time, however, she was barely six years old, and severely depressed.

María blamed herself, as is common with many children, in the face of incomprehensible adversity. The antics of her four-year-old sister, Jeronima, failed to amuse her. The friendship of her cousins failed to console her. Catalina's insistence on her return to normalcy failed to affect her. She cried frequently and kept to herself, praying for forgiveness and begging for the return of the deepest happiness she had ever known—the smile of God in her soul.

The mother who had previously hung on her every word now—out of sheer frustration—scolded and punished her for her obstinacy. The father who had cherished her sweet nature now disciplined her severely, in the hopes of reversing what he interpreted as laziness. Her parents were cold toward her, and their rapidly decreasing opinion of her added to her own of herself, only making things worse.

"I felt abandoned by my father and mother," she later told Ximénez Samaniego, even while praising her parents' virtues.[35]

She tried harder to please the senior Coronels, but she did so out of such misery that they were even more repelled. At age six, she received her First Communion, and for a brief time that year, she attended the only school for girls in Ágreda. Soon, however, she developed a frail constitution and frequently became ill, an affliction that she interpreted as righteous punishment for her sins. Her parents withdrew her from the school, and she received no other formal education in her lifetime.

On a pivotal outing when she was seven years old, María saw a religious play following the procession of Corpus Christi in Ágreda, an event that her father had helped to organize. *The New World as Discovered by Christopher Columbus*, by the playwright Lope de Vega, portrayed the saga of Columbus's travels and those he encountered upon arrival in the New World.[36] This depiction of faraway natives who did not know her Lord had a profound influence on the little girl. Although she was still infirm, the imagery caught fire in her lively imagination and deeply influenced her spiritual aspirations. María longed to be a missionary.[37]

The seven-year-old's yearning to travel abroad seemed ludicrous to parents barely coping with her ill health and disposition at home, not to mention the rarity of such travel for women. But they were receptive to her growing desire to become a nun, after hearing her declare at age eight her intention of lifelong chastity and at twelve her inclination to the religious life, no doubt greatly inspired by Pope Paul V's beatification that year of Teresa of Avila.[38]

María's malaise, however, endured for several years. Her parents, though compassionate and solicitous, considered her a burden. Catalina continued to tutor her daughter in matters of religion, but except for those few hours each week, María kept to herself, added penances to her solitary prayers, and meditated on what she felt she knew best— suffering. Later in life, she credited this period with the emergence of her "interior reflection."

"From the age of nine or ten," she wrote in 1650, "[my parents had] their children pray in constant devotions and had us engage in mental prayer, for which they withdrew into their bedrooms and indicated another [my oratory] for me to do the same. Ever since [then] . . . it seems the Lord filled my inner life with light."[39]

At age thirteen, María's already fragile health took a drastic turn for the worse, and she fell gravely ill. The previous year the Coronels had reserved a place for her at the nearby Convent of Saint Ann in Tarazona, in anticipation of helping her to fulfill her ardent desire to become a nun.

At this time, however, they gave up hope—not only for her life as a nun, but for her life at all.

After six months with no sign of recovery, María received Extreme Unction, the sacrament reserved at the time for individuals on the verge of death. Then her grieving parents arranged for her burial and awaited the inevitable.[40]

During her illness, María contemplated images of the passion of Christ. She thought about why he suffered. She remembered that she had been taught that he died for her redemption, and that of all humanity. Then she identified with his suffering because of her own.[41]

"This lesson . . . eroded the hardness of my heart," she wrote. "I became happy with my pain. . . . The doctors were amazed."[42]

As María embraced her pain, she recovered and found a captivating radiance in its place. "The Lord filled my inner life with light," she wrote, "and it was like placing a little girl at the start of an exceedingly straight road and path and saying to me, 'Here you are to walk without deviating or turning aside.' . . . Ever since, I found that when I focused my attention within, I would enter a state of exceedingly quiet prayer."[43]

María's mystical life had begun. With it, her strength and optimism returned. After her recovery, the inner light gradually found its way into her outer life. And while she was no longer the exuberant child she had once been, she rebounded back to health as a vital adolescent.

In contrast to her former solitude, María now befriended many girls in the village. She met them frequently at local festivals, and tried, although apparently ineptly, to engage in a social life.[44] Although she was certainly an attractive girl, no one had difficulty noticing the differences between her and the other teens of Ágreda. Too, the contrasts between her awkward attempts to socialize and the growing peace she experienced in prayer all contributed to her renewed withdrawal to her oratory, as she continued to explore the realm of the spirit.[45]

On the heels of María's recovery, her mother had an experience of such impact that it was to change María's life, and the life of the entire family, forever.

CHAPTER 3

"Everyone spilled copious tears"

THOUGH NOT ACCELERATED BY TODAY'S ROUND-THE-CLOCK techno-frenzy and demands, life in the seventeenth century was—in its own way—every bit as busy then as it is now. Without any of today's modern conveniences, Catalina Coronel had managed the smooth running of the household, the care and education of the children, and attended church daily. Francisco had managed the family's finances and the upkeep of their home.

The family's wealth, however, was mainly depleted by the late sixteenth century. To minimize expenses, Francisco Coronel and his family lived in the ancestral home, together with his brother Medel, and Medel's wife María, who was also Catalina Coronel's sister. Catalina bore eleven children, only four of whom lived. Her sister María bore seven surviving children, and by the time María of Ágreda was a little girl, her aunt and uncle had to move out because the house was overflowing with family members and domestics.

As a nobleman, albeit of modest means, Francisco Coronel had given generously of his time and expertise in support of civic affairs. He often spent his days out and about, helping to run the community. Over the years, he held many municipal titles and appointments. He managed the small village's funds and supervised many of its religious festivals held throughout the year. He also served as attorney for two companies of foot soldiers and assisted the state attorney on occasion. And he served on the city council as one of two church representatives from Our Lady of Magaña.[1]

In 1615 Catalina and Francisco were each in their early fifties.[2] Based on life expectancies then, they did not expect to live much more than another ten to fifteen years. It was time, they thought, to slow down and enjoy the fruits of their labors.[3] They had cared well for their family and home, managed their dwindling monetary resources with diligence, and been active members of the community.

At this pivotal juncture, Catalina had a vision that would forever change all of their lives. María remembered the day well.

"My mother had been praying," she wrote, although later sources characterized Catalina's experience as a dream. "She heard the voice of the Almighty, and he told her to give up her husband, her children and her property, and to convert our home into a convent. He told her to enter the convent herself, and to take her two daughters with her, and that her husband should join the Order of St. Francis with their two sons."[4]

Catalina knew immediately that her husband would not take to the idea.

Although a religious man, Francisco Coronel enjoyed married life. After all, he had prayed in 1585 before Ágreda's famed statue of Our Lady of Miracles for a virtuous spouse of good blood.[5] His brother Medel had stood beside him, similarly praying. Their impassioned pleas mirrored the partiality of the times for nobility, and possibly a pervasive anti-Semitic conditioning against marrying a Jew or converso, even among conversos themselves.

"God answered immediately," María wrote, "because my mother was drawn to the same statue, to make her own request for a Christian husband of laudable demeanor and good family." Her mother's sister was with her, María added, praying for the same thing. Soon, two sisters married two brothers, in what the Coronel family joyfully considered its own miracle.[6]

There is little wonder that Catalina fretted about her experience in 1615. She worried that although her family strove to follow God's will, they wouldn't be able to grasp her vision of it. She feared that she wouldn't be believed and that no one else would apply for admittance to the new convent. She included all these worries in her prayers.

"Nothing will be wanting," the Lord replied in her heart. "Obey."[7]

In her worry, the frantic woman ran out of the house to find her confessor, Padre Juan de Torrecilla. As she raced to Saint Julian's, she almost bumped into Torrecilla. Before she could tell him what had happened, he amazed her with his words.

"I have seen what you saw," he told her. "The same revelation has come to me. . . . You must sacrifice all of your family to the Eternal Father." Today, a crucifix on the roof tiles of an outbuilding of the present-day convent marks the place of their meeting, as Catalina rushed along the lane to see her confessor. Her destination—the Convent of the Friars of Saint Julian—just yards away, is now a cemetery.

"My mother and he debated about how to reconcile the will of the Lord with the will of her husband," María wrote good-humoredly.[8]

Francisco Coronel fumed. He would not have it. He was fifty years old and afflicted with stomach troubles. Now he could not sleep night or day.[9] He went to see his brother, Medel, of whom he was very fond. With great sadness, he shared with Medel the story of the vision and the divide it had caused in his household. Medel sided with his brother.

Catalina was disconsolate. She prayed for the Lord to placate and convince her husband, to no immediate avail. "Yet as with any perfect gift from the Father of light," María wrote, "he extended his divine right hand to help us overcome these tremendous trials." Help soon arrived, she added, in the person of Padre Pedro Otalora, a local Augustinian priest, who gave Catalina many helpful ideas about the practicalities of founding a convent.[10]

Catalina lobbied all who would listen, starting with her two daughters—María, aged thirteen, and Jeronima, who was not yet ten years old. Despite Catalina's pressure, the immediate and extended family thought the concept outlandish and fought over it for two years. Neighbors heard many of their boisterous arguments and took sides themselves. The entire community weighed in, with verdicts ranging from insane to inspired.[11]

In the end, Catalina's desire to found a convent, supported by her daughters and the pragmatic ideas of Padre Otalora, won the day. As a result, María's geographic expectations shrank even further. Saint Ann's Convent in Tarazona, while not the New World, was at least sixteen kilometers from Ágreda. Now—it seemed—she would not even get past her own front door.

FIGURE 6. Commemorative cross, marking location in 1615 where Catalina Coronel discussed with Padre Torrecilla the prospect of converting her home into a convent. Erected in 1632, during new facility's construction. Photo by author.

While Catalina and the reluctant Francisco busied themselves with the considerable logistics of founding a convent in their home, María continued to follow her interior path. She read voraciously, in her mother's breviary, and in any of her father's and Padre Torrecilla's books they would loan to her.

Spanish scholars today cite many cosmographies available in María's time. Among them are Isidoro de Sevilla's *Etymologies* and *On the Nature of Things*; Peter (Apianus) Bienewitz's *The Book of Cosmography, A Description of the World and All of Its Parts, Illustrated with Clear and Attractive Art Work*; Pedro de Medina's *Cosmographical Summa*; and others.[12]

María's retentive appetite for knowledge, coupled with her awe of creation and her fervent spiritual devotion, finally combusted with her impossible dream to journey to America as a missionary. At age fifteen, she couldn't hold it in any longer, and out it poured, in writing of her own. She called it "Face of the Earth and Map of the Spheres," part of a larger manuscript attributed to her by most recognized scholars of Spanish literature, but not officially recognized by Rome.[13] Much of it was summarized or quoted from her reading and augmented with her own rhapsodic insights.

"One cannot comprehend or grasp this wonder," María penned at her astonishment at the sheer size of the earth in the staunch presence of Moncayo Mountain. "[Yet] it does me good . . . to share what I have learned and experienced [with] my brothers."[14]

She may have heard the trill of birdsong on the balcony and looked up to see the blue Castilian sky welcome a winged flight to the foothills. Certainly, however, her heart flamed at the thought of the Creator of such wonders. "Oh deepest wisdom and divine painter! Who is not amazed and inspired to see the variety of creatures You created."[15]

In many of these places, María wrote to her brothers, Francisco and José, she saw people of an entirely different geographic orientation, whose feet, she wrote with incredulity, "are directly opposite to ours. Our nadir is their zenith, and our zenith is their nadir."[16] But she thought it important to caution her brothers, each two years into their Franciscan novitiates in Burgos.[17] "We should not judge on the basis of our own situation who is right side up. The truth . . . is that we are all right side up. There is a great diversity in human appearance and a variety of social customs," she wrote, citing examples of different people, ranging from the provinces of Asia to the colonies of New Spain.[18]

Yet whatever the variances among people around the world, María concluded and then penned for her brothers, "By the diversity of their outer appearance one cannot know their inner qualities."[19] "Oh, immortal and immense God," she wrote, filled with awe at the underlying unity throughout all of creation, "in your image and likeness You created them, my King, as You did the other creatures. They have souls like mine and five senses. The infinite price in your most holy blood that I cost, they cost, too, and are worth the same."[20]

"How I wish I could, even at the cost of my lifeblood," she agonized over her thwarted desires to go to the New World, "spread the holy gospel . . . from west to east and from north to south! Oh! How I wish I could . . . show the light to everyone who is without it so they might know the Father of all light, and so, too, that those who already have it might appreciate their good fortune and realize that by so doing they walk in light and not in darkness."[21]

"But," María wrote, perhaps silently bemoaning her station as a girl, "even if it should be too insignificant to be of any benefit to the travelers here below in their exile, still it would calm my burning desire, for like a wounded deer I long to go to the waters. . . . Should I not deserve it, may my desire kill me"—pausing here, perhaps, to indulge her tears—"and I be a martyr for it and for the defense of the faith that I so value and love beyond all saying."[22]

Meanwhile, Catalina's dream of founding a convent in the Coronel home occurred at a pivotal time in the history of her country's religious life. Convents and monasteries proliferated in sixteenth-century Spain, facilitated by two serendipitous factors: extraordinary religious passion and economic prosperity. By the early seventeenth century, however, the economy was weak and—all too often—needy men and women professed religious vows in order to obtain free room and board and to avoid military service and taxation. Impoverished nobility were not immune either, turning over expensive-to-maintain estates to the church.[23]

At the time of Catalina's vision, there were well over nine thousand monasteries in Spain for men and about half that many convents for women. The fulfillment of Catalina's desire was further complicated by the fact that her neighbor across the road—also with the help of Padre Otalora—had just signed a will in 1612 with provisions to make her home a convent for Augustinian nuns at her death. To make matters worse, the Council of Castile was about to embark on a study that would result in the reduction of the number of religious houses and a freeze on the formation of new ones.[24] As if all that were not enough, Catalina knew that she would need a great deal of "divine compassion to marshal six wills into a united desire," María wrote, "because if anyone of the family had an inclination to resist, the new convent would be an impossibility."

She was not deterred. "Instead, my mother was cheered that her children steadfastly pursued their vocations," María recalled. "My brothers had already studied with the Franciscans [at Saint Julian's], and would continue in their profession [at Burgos]. My younger sister had had fervent religious desires since the age of nine. As for me, I had already decided to join the Carmelite convent, so my mother inferred that I could just as well profess in our home."[25]

That left Francisco senior, who considered the permanent abandonment of his marriage bed a momentous decision. "My parents prayed continuously about it," María wrote, "even deciding to live in [sexual] continence" while they decided.

Almost five years passed before her father relented. Then when Francisco Coronel again consulted his brother Medel, he learned that Medel and his entire family now considered entering the religious life. Soon thereafter, Francisco and Catalina again stood under the statue of Our Lady of Miracles. This time, for an entirely different purpose.

"My parents remembered they had prayed to the Blessed Virgin for the miracle of finding each other," María wrote. "They went back to the church, to present to Her their sacrifice of one another, in her service. Monks and prelates accompanied them. Everyone spilled copious tears of joy."[26]

CHAPTER 4

"I found myself much troubled, sorrowful and discouraged"

NOBLE STATURE NOTWITHSTANDING, FRANCISCO CORONEL knew that founding a convent would take more money than he had. "Not counting the value of the house and all of its furnishings," María wrote, "my parents had barely seven thousand gold ducats. Whereas to convert our home to a convent and run it [in perpetuity] would take at least nine or ten thousand ducats."[1]

Though Francisco had reluctantly joined the quest, once he committed to it he was formidable. He approached the town authorities and even his friends to make up the difference. As a result, the gentry contributed two thousand ducats, the village of Ágreda gave another thousand, and the surrounding towns gave yet another thousand.[2]

With this modest endowment of almost eleven thousand ducats, the Coronels forged ahead with their plans. Francisco invited the padre provincial from Burgos to his home and signed the deed over to the church.

Reconstruction plans notwithstanding, Francisco Coronel maintained his sense of conviviality and still found time to participate in the community's religious festivals, as evidenced in provincial archives of the period. Records for 1617 show him producing, with others, four comedies for the two festival days of Corpus Christi and Our Lady of Miracles. "One for each morning and each afternoon," was written in the record. "The opening comedy featured a heavenly theme, and the other three reflected more worldly humor."[3]

At the same time, Catalina worked on the design of the new convent. Alterations to their home began in August 1618 under her and her husband's supervision. María's oratory was converted into a chapel, and many of the family bedrooms were redesigned into smaller sleeping cells to accommodate up to fifteen women. Smaller homes nearby were acquired, and a new wing was built onto the southwest side of the house, today comprising 13 Augustine Road.[4] The infamous speared grille was built into the wall between the second-floor parlor and the adjacent sitting room.

The specifications for the grille's size and sharply protruding spikes were gleaned not—as one might initially assume—from Catalina's somewhat draconian practices by today's standards, but from the requirements laid out in the charter of the nuns of the Conception as founded by Beatriz de Silva in 1489. While forceful intrusions on women in convents had long since subsided by María's era, the protective symbolism remained, as exemplified by the fearsome spikes of the grille. It was one of many modifications to the home, although full compliance to the charter would not be achieved until a new facility was built some years later.

"The success of the conversion exceeded my parents' desires," María wrote. "With far less resources, they had accomplished what others would have needed a million ducats to do. Valuing the needs of the spirit above those of personal convenience, they lacked for nothing. Thus we appreciated the wisdom of the ages, that . . . the poor may possess riches far beyond those of wealthier means."[5] These spiritual riches infused the principles of faith guiding the new convent and the rule of its constitution.

The Immaculate Conception of Mary, according to María of Ágreda, "surpassed all others in the order of nature and grace."[6] In later years, María wrote in detail—much to the consternation of straitlaced seventeenth- and eighteenth-century theologians at France's famed Sorbonne University—how two humans, uncommonly pure in spirit, could physically produce what some today would describe as an enlightened being. In writing this, years after the convent's founding, she was nevertheless ahead of her time, in that the doctrine of Mary's Immaculate Conception—not to be confused with Jesus' conception—was not pronounced as dogma until Pope Pius did so over two centuries later, in 1854.

To be sure, the doctrine of Mary's freedom from original sin had gained popular and church support dating back to AD 850, but there was much debate about its definition. John Duns Scotus (1265/66–1308) had written convincingly on the issue of Mary's sinlessness in the thirteenth century. By 1476 Pope Sixtus IV allowed the liturgical celebration of the Mass and Office of the Feast of the Immaculate Conception. Then the renowned Portuguese beauty, Beatriz de Silva, founded the Conceptionist order in 1489.

Yet the topic was not without controversy, in Spain and worldwide. "It is contrary to our need for Christ's redemption," argued some. "It is an important sign of God's presence within us," said others.

According to present-day Mariologists, seventeenth-century Spaniards hotly engaged in pro and con discussions on the concept of the Immaculate Conception. "Maculists" and "Immaculists" churned out over twelve thousand pamphlets on every aspect of the issue surrounding Mary's sinlessness from the instant her parents conceived her. It was an issue that María of Ágreda would take up with gusto and devotion later in her life, influencing not only the King of Spain on the doctrine, but also the pope of her later years who would make the most definitive statement on the doctrine until Pope Pius IX's edict in 1854.[7] It was also an issue that some today think may have provided the initial impulse to condemn her work, despite the fact that her position was in concert with the church's ultimate decision on the dogma.

Suffice it to say that the Coronel family founded their convent under the order of the Franciscan Conceptionists with a great deal of awareness and conviction. Thus on December 8, 1618, the feast day of the Immaculate Conception of Mary, the first Mass was said in the new convent of the same name, Purísima Concepción.

Soon after that first Mass, it was time for the most contentious step in the convent's founding—Francisco Coronel had to leave his ancestral home. His sons had already left to join the Franciscan order in Burgos, shortly after Catalina's striking vision over two years earlier. Now, at the age of fifty-four, Señor Coronel would venture forth from the walls within which he had been born, bequeathing them to the monastic nuns in order to himself become a religious novice in a distant city.

Amid many tears, Catalina knelt down for his affectionate blessing, and then he left.[8] With his brother Medel at his side, as well as three other men from Ágreda, Francisco entered the Franciscan convent of San Antonio de Nalda, in Burgos, as the lay brother Francisco of the Holy

Sacrament. He chose the name in solidarity with his wife, who would soon be called Sister Catalina of the Holy Sacrament. The official dedication took place over a year later.

On January 13, 1620, a lengthy procession spiraled past Saint John the Baptist Church, through Ágreda's central plaza, along two miles of its narrow, winding streets. Many nobles and prelates started at Saint John's, with the vicar general of Burgos, Rev. Fr. Antonio de Trijo, and the bishop of Tarazona, Padre Antonio de Villalacre, also a provincial minister. Hundreds of spirited villagers joined along the way, until reaching the new Convent of the Conception on the Road of the Knights.[9]

There Franciscan officials from Burgos formally dedicated the convent as a Conceptionist foundation of Poor Clare cloistered nuns within the Franciscan order.[10] Three Conceptionist nuns from the Convent of San Luis in Burgos were appointed as temporary administrators until the new facility could produce its own.[11] Long after María's lifetime, the Conceptionists would split off from the Poor Clares, as her own convent has done. Some of these "new" Conceptionists remained affiliated with the Franciscans, as did Purísima Concepción, and others did not.[12]

Catalina and María donned the veils of nuns on that day as novices, along with five other women of Ágreda. María took the name "Sor María de Jesús," Spanish for "Sister Mary of Jesus." Like Teresa of Avila, the name of her birthplace—Ágreda—was often added onto her name at the end, making it "Sor María de Jesús de Ágreda." In her mature years, after she was elected abbess of her convent, the title of "Madre" was often added before her name, and she was called "Madre María" or "Madre Sor María."

In deference to the mother of Jesus, who is also called "Mother Mary"—sometimes translated to "Madre María"—and to respectfully distinguish between the Spanish nun and the Blessed Mother, this biography maintains the Spanish "María" for its subject throughout and "Mary" when referring to the mother of Jesus. In this way, a balance is achieved between the Spanish origins of Sor María and the English-speaking readership of this book.

The young novice, therefore, humbly embraced the religious name of "Sor María."

Her younger sister, Jeronima, though eager to join, had to wait two more years before taking her preliminary vows because of her age, but she was allowed to reside with her mother and sister until that time.

Including the three nuns from Burgos, and three additional women who would join soon thereafter, the new convent's enrollment, at fourteen, had almost reached its full capacity of fifteen within the first few months.[13]

For Sor María, the street and building exterior were still the same and provided the familiar home environment where she had grown up, albeit with modifications. The other women, however, had at least left their homes to join the new convent.

Now Sor María would not get past the front door. Literally.

Cloistered convents are, after all, cut off from the world. Although Sor María had led a relatively sheltered life until this time, now her physical world would shrink even further. A housekeeper, in the employ of the convent, shopped at the market for supplies and delivered messages to and from outsiders. Doctors visited on-site, and family visitors hunched up to the small speared grille to speak with their loved ones in the adjacent room.

Added to this was the complete dedication to prayer, contemplation, service to the poor (feeding them in the visitors' room, with foods grown in the tiny convent garden and served by the housekeeper), and the many simple tasks of self-sufficient subsistence.

Despite the new restrictions, it was an atmosphere in which one could easily imagine the newly veiled Sor María de Jesús thriving. This was not to be, however, at least for several years. The nuns from Burgos, well intentioned though they were, did not run a very tight ship and provided little spiritual guidance to those in their charge. In turn, the young novice Sor María—diligently following her own inner light unaided by a spiritual director of equal or greater experience—was bound to make waves, and indeed she did.

When left to her own devices, eighteen-year-old Sor María gravitated to a life of extreme austerity and penance, aided by her lifelong conditioning to extended periods of prayer and solitude and the example of her parents. Spiritual ecstasies and trances were the frequent result, and she was given a private cell, in order not to disturb the others.

In her zeal, however—not unlike Saint Francis and others—she overdid it during these early years. Somehow she procured an abrasive garment of mail weighing over twenty pounds,[14] a hair shirt, and a girdle of spiked rings to conceal under her robes. She also had chains and fetters,[15] as well as a crucifix with spikes, to press into her heart while praying and a board to sleep on, to inflict pain and discomfort.

With the best of intentions, she fasted frequently and often made prayer vigils throughout the night. The other nuns thought her exclusionary and proud, and the supervising nuns from Burgos watched on with disapproval.

Catalina, who had wanted a stricter administration from the beginning, was conflicted. She was unhappy that her daughter was even more troublesome than she had been as a child, yet she hoped for a remedy in the form of more disciplined "discalced" or "reformed" administrators from the Conceptionist convent of the Knights of Grace (Caballeros de Gracia) in Madrid, from whom the convent had received its charter regulations.

Like many others at the time, the Madrid Conceptionists had reformed their practices, adopting many more austerities than other "convents of convenience" of the day, where widows and other women retreated or retired, more for security and solitude than a religious life in itself. The reformed convents came to be called discalced because one of their more noticeable practices involved going barefoot, or wearing minimal sandals of straw or wood—*discalced* being the word for "without shoes." For the time being, however, the well-heeled Conceptionist nuns from Burgos held the reins of power.

In these early days of her novitiate, Sor María's rarified spiritual experiences increased, and she sought the advice of her brother, now Padre Francisco Coronel.

"My dear brother," she wrote to him, "since God has led you to a spiritual life, too, perhaps you will advise me." Communion consoled her with an extremely delectable flavor, she told him. She felt ecstatic when deep in prayer, "quite changed," until finally she "felt no bodily sensations and was completely wrapped inwardly."

"This was my first rapture," she told him, "it was so unusual and new, I was frightened."[16]

Then one day in 1620, in the throes of ecstasy after receiving Communion, unaware of any outer stimuli, Sor María levitated while in deep prayer. There were witnesses.[17]

Soon Sor María became an overnight phenomenon, although she did not know it. No one told her that she had been seen levitating. At the same time, the other nuns took to watching her during her private prayer sessions. Some even cut a hole in her cell door, to observe her unawares. Frequently they brought in curious outsiders to watch and to try to move her, by fanning or blowing through the hole.

"Whenever she was rapt in ecstasy," Ximénez Samaniego wrote, "her body was raised a little distance above the earth where it remained motionless. . . . Many religious and seculars . . . tried the experiment on her body, which, by a slight motion of air, could be moved as easily as if it had been a feather."[18]

Early in 1623, Sor María found out about these violations of privacy and dignity through a beggar she happened to meet by chance at the convent door.[19] She was mortified. "If I had been accused of some crime and condemned to public disgrace," Sor María lamented to the Burgos abbess, "it would not cause me as much grief as I experienced when I learned that others had seen me in ecstasy."[20] The nuns from Burgos were not sympathetic.

Sor María locked herself in the lower choir and drank syrup in order to break her fast and disqualify herself from receiving Communion—all in order to also avoid the ecstatic trances and the external manifestations that came with them.[21] Yet for someone who gravitated as naturally as she did to meditative states of prayer and contemplation of the divine, it was an impossible task. She was not successful. As she engaged in heartfelt prayer, her soul seemed drawn into a divine vortex. The levitations—and the accompanying notoriety—continued, although even these would soon be eclipsed by an even more extraordinary phenomenon.

Sor María sought Padre Torrecilla's advice. The priest realized the problem could not be solved at the local level and asked for help from the provincial office. Soon Padre Antonio de Villalacre arrived to question Sor María.

Sor María poured out her heart about what had come to be called her *exterioridades*, or external manifestations of an unusual nature. Villalacre thought her actions well meant though extreme. Yet she had carefully omitted any mention to him, or to Torrecilla, of the type of temptations she was warding off, as a result of impure sexual thoughts. In the seventeenth century, these were not elements comfortably discussed among religious women, and they were certainly not issues that a beautiful young virginal nun under vows of chastity would to reveal to a man. Not until her later years was she was able to more benignly address the struggles during what she termed her three "bad years." Then she looked back upon such "occasions of sin" as natural developments in a young woman's life and took care to advise the nuns under her care on how to handle them with equanimity rather than inflicting pain that would only foul their tempers. Much of her pragmatic advice is recorded in *Ladder to Perfection*.[22]

Nevertheless, Villalacre was convinced that the levitation, and other manifestations, were divine favors resulting from her pious, albeit overly rigorous, devotions. He made specific recommendations for more privacy for Sor María and a new, more experienced confessor. He also suggested that she lessen her extreme practices of mortification.[23]

The Burgos abbess did not implement Villalacre's recommendations, nor did the other nuns cease their gossip and secret exhibitions of Sor María in the midst of the permissive, loosely run cloister. Things went from bad to worse.

Finally, in the spring of 1623 the Burgos nuns called for an ecclesiastical examination of their unruly novice. Fortunately for Sor María, the two priests sent from the provincial office in Burgos included Padre Antonio Villalacre and his brother, Padre Juan Villalacre. They had known María's family for many years, and Padre Antonio had officiated when Francisco Coronel had deeded his home to the church and again at the convent's dedication ceremony.

The two priests listened patiently to the administrators' complaints and then interviewed Sor María privately for several hours. When she had responded to all their questions satisfactorily, they excused her, and she raced gleefully to the chapel for Communion for the first time in a long time. She fell into an immediate ecstasy. The priests, however, resorted to one more test, to determine if there was any of the Devil's handiwork in her astonishing experiences.

With no prior hint of what they were about to do, the priests called to Sor María mentally, in what might at best today be termed an unreasonable test. In their thoughts, they instructed her to return to the *locutorio*, a convent term for the parlor and the adjacent room connected by the speared grille cut into the wall, through which they had conversed. The priests reasoned that if she were in league with the Devil, she would not respond. If, however, she were an obedient nun, she would hear their call in the depths of her spirit and answer it out of complete adherence to her vow of obedience to her superiors.

We do not know—during what was the height of the Spanish Inquisition—what her punishment would have been if she had failed the test. For Sor María—demonstrating the first of many instances throughout her life of a highly refined interpersonal spiritual attunement with others—immediately returned, as instructed.[24]

At the Villalacres' recommendation, the nuns from Burgos were sent back to the Convent of San Luis, and María's mother, Sor Catalina of the Holy Sacrament, was named temporary president. In the meantime, the provincials decided on new administration, until such time that the convent could generate its own abbess from within. Sor Catalina's wish was finally granted when the provincials commissioned two nuns from the discalced Caballeros de Gracia in Madrid, the Conceptionist convent known for its strict reformed discipline and procedures. On November 3, 1623, three stalwart knights of grace arrived from Madrid.[25]

Before the two priests left, however, they had ordered Sor María to pray that her exterioridades would end, and to do so without telling anyone. Soon enough the levitations ceased, and the other nuns, most pointedly Sor María's mother, perceived the change as a sudden fall from grace. They openly disdained her apparently diminished sanctity. It was a humiliation Padre Antonio said she must endure in silence.[26]

The priests also insisted that Sor María modify her severe austerities, as well as her dietary deprivations. She mainly agreed but successfully bargained her way to vegetarianism, omitting meat, eggs, and cheese for the duration of her life.[27] She also pushed the envelope, in looking to the discalced nuns for approved methods of physical atonement, as shown in a letter to the reverend mother of the Caballeros de Gracia dated August 20, 1623.

"For a long time," she wrote to Madre Sor Ana de San Antonio, "I have been wanting to wear a coarse cloth habit like yours, Reverend Mother. We can't get the right material here. Could one be sent for me, please? A big one, because I am tall, and let it be rough so that I can be like your nuns."[28]

Soon Sor María received her new coarse habit and thrived under the watchful tutelage of the interim abbess, Madre María de Cristo. Her rich interior experiences were balanced by the plainness of day-to-day life in the now reformed convent. Despite the derision of the other nuns who did not understand the mysterious absence of her showy ecstasies, Sor María took care to treat them with good-natured respect. She accepted new assignments and excelled in them and eventually assumed the duties of mistress of the novices.[29] Over time, the other nuns responded to Sor

María's kindness, and the convent settled down under the loving but firm guidance of the nuns of Gracia.

One day during prayers, Ximénez Samaniego reports, the other nuns saw a "great luminous globe" hover over Sor María's head. They knelt in awe, and each later reported to Madre María de Cristo a feeling of great supernatural joy at the sight.[30] On hearing of it, Sor Catalina must have spurted vindicated prayers of thanksgiving, as she carefully spread word of the perceived return to grace of her curious offspring.

When in March 1627 the "Gracia mothers" were recalled to Madrid, Sor María embraced her departing superior and friend, Madre María de Cristo, and the two agreed to stay in touch. Their correspondence over the next few years, and Sor María's with the other Madrid nuns, provides rich detail about Sor María's generous spirit and the imminent expansion of the Ágreda convent.

Throughout this time, there is ample evidence of Sor María's kind-hearted nature and her growth in authority and tact, qualities she carried with grace throughout her life, and which readily inspired the love and regard of others in return. A kind word was never wanting from her mouth or pen. She kept track of the other nuns' health and always offered her prayers.

To Sor Francisca in Madrid she sent a pot of honey, noting the other nun's comparison of the Virgin's sweetness to honey. To Conceptionist friends in Madrid who took exception to her generosity, she sent bacon and dried fruit, writing, "We know we are poor and that Ágreda isn't a grand place like Madrid; but you really mustn't tell us not to send you a bit of bacon on that account." With others she opined about the convent's early days, writing, "All the troubles we went through were well worth while, since they brought such a blessing to us in the end."[31]

With the exodus of the Gracia mothers, Sor Catalina was the most likely candidate to manage the convent, but she had been ill. Instead, at the urging of Sor María's peers, the padre provincial appointed Sor María as president of the convent, two weeks before her twenty-fifth birthday.[32] Instead of feeling honored at the time, Sor María was taken aback by the gravity of the responsibilities and concerned that her nature and experience were more inwardly directed than would be beneficial to the responsibilities of the position. Yet she dutifully filled the position, counting on the fact that she was far too young to be named as the convent's abbess without a papal dispensation, the average age being forty.

To her surprise, a year later a document arrived in Ágreda from Pope Urban VIII. In it, he granted the dispensation for Sor María's age, effectively opening the way for her to become abbess. On May 28 of that year, in an enthusiastic referendum on her leadership, the nuns officially elected her as abbess, a post she would hold throughout her life, except for a three-year sabbatical in her early fifties.[33]

"In the eighth year after the foundation of this convent, in the twenty-fifth of my life," Sor María humbly wrote after the election, "obedience imposed upon me the office which I unworthily hold at the present day, namely to be the abbess of this convent." "I found myself much troubled, sorrowful and discouraged," she continued, "because neither my age nor my inclinations were such as are requisite for governing and commanding, but they were rather such as befitted one who should be governed and obey."[34]

In her distress, Sor María turned to prayer. "I fled in this affliction to our Queen and Lady as to my only refuge in all troubles," Sor María wrote. The answer to her prayer was not long in coming, and the nature of her prayerful experience foreshadows the various types of visions that Sor María would have throughout her life. For in prayer, Sor María found that "the Most High animates the intellect by certain subtlety and light, thus adapting it for the exalted knowledge."[35] In this way, "our most amiable Mother and lady revealed Herself still more fully to her slave," Sor María wrote, "withdrawing the veil from the hidden sacraments and magnificent mysteries which are contained, though unknown to mortals, in her most holy life."[36] This vision deepened Sor María's abiding devotion to Mary. Yet the young nun was still concerned about her new responsibilities.

"My daughter," the spirit of the Heavenly Queen replied, "do not be disturbed in thy heart. . . . I will be thy Mother and Superior. . . . Obey me, and I will favor thee and will continue to be attentive to thy affliction."[37]

Sor María wrote that she was immediately soothed with a "blessed and supernatural light," and the "knowledge of eternal life," but that the consolation of the Blessed Mother came at a price. "She added the command that I write the history of her life according as her Majesty herself should dictate and inspire me."[38]

With the press of all her new responsibilities, it was not a call Sor María felt immediately able to answer, although she wrote that it "was continually present to my mind for the space of ten years, until I attempted the first writing."[39] Little did she know in 1627, however, how this calling would infuse her life with purpose, danger, and intrigue for many years to come.

Fortuitously, another benefactor surfaced—an ecclesiastical one—when Padre Provincial Andrés de la Torre visited Ágreda that year. He had come previously from time to time, after learning about Sor María from the Villalacre priests. So impressed was he that when his term was up in Burgos, he returned to Ágreda, moved into Saint Julian's, and devoted himself to serving as Sor María's spiritual director, a position he filled until his death twenty years later.[40] At long last, she would have the benefit of seasoned spiritual counsel.

Padre de la Torre proved an apt mentor for Sor María. Enrollment in the convent burgeoned. And Sor María—now Madre Sor María—flowered in her new role as abbess. She excelled in her administrative duties and soon envisioned a much larger convent facility. Padre de la Torre was additionally qualified in architectural design, a talent he put to good use in designing the expanded convent with Sor María.

As the Villalacre priests had recommended, Sor María tried to put the exterioridades behind her. She was successful, in the main. Word had already leaked far beyond the convent walls, however, of other experiences she had had that were far more unusual than those of levitating while in prayer. For during that same period, something even more extraordinary had been happening to Sor María, as her fervent missionary zeal continued to erupt. And while these additional exterioridades had mainly receded, according to the priests' instructions, news of them had not.

As a result, Sor María was about to become known all the way across the globe, even as far as the New World where she had so ardently longed to preach.

PART TWO

AMERICA'S MYSTICAL LADY IN BLUE

1620

CHAPTER 5

"The finest persons
of any people we saw"

BY HER NINETEENTH YEAR, THE EVENTS IN SOR MARÍA'S
life had already stretched the limits of credulity for even most of her religious contemporaries—reaching the age of reason by age four, suffering
the "dark night of the soul" before age ten, levitating in the sight of other
nuns at age eighteen. How then can modern readers accept or interpret
these phenomena? Is a leap of faith the only way? Certainly Christ's life
was replete with miracles, and he even counseled his followers, "You will
do greater things than I" (John 14:12).

Yet most phenomena, if scrutinized closely, reveal a continuum, a
path from point A to point B that perhaps is not immediately apparent.
Rock can become sand, over eons. Coal can transform to diamond, under
extreme heat. Mozart did compose music at age five.

In Sor María's time, a hologram or wireless PC would have seemed a
miracle, or the work of the Devil. Yet today the underlying technology,
even if it is not clear to nontechies, is at least intelligible to technicians
and engineers. As Sor María writes in *Mystical City of God*, miracles
might be "performed . . . by the addition of a new quality" that is often
natural, yet one that has been divinely influenced for a new effect.[1]
So, if an astronaut can experience weightlessness in outer space when
competing weight and gravitational forces are neutralized, why not

a saintly person unencumbered by earthly concerns, in the delicate uplift of prayer?

With this hairline crack in the Great Wall of understandable incredulity, and in anticipation of further exposition, we reenter Sor María's life to consider in her own words, and through historians' accounts, yet another extraordinary phenomenon, that of bilocation, or appearing in two different places at the same time.

Sor María considered herself the least of God's creatures, and yet she felt blessed many times over by his generosity. Her heart expanded in gratitude, and then it seemed to break, when she envisioned the myriad of souls populating the world with whom she wanted to share Christ's love. These feelings frequently surfaced in trances after receiving Communion.

"In this state of mind," she reported years later to Padre Pedro Manero, general director of the Franciscans,

> the Lord would let me know occasionally that He wanted me to work on behalf of his creatures and . . . [those] most disposed to convert, the ones toward whom his compassion was then most inclined, were the New Mexicans and the inhabitants of other remote kingdoms [Texas] in that part of the world.
>
> No sooner had the Most High revealed to me his will in this matter than my intense feelings of love for God and my neighbor were renewed, and I called out from the innermost part of my being on behalf of those souls.[2]

Inexplicably, in Texas, New Mexico, and Arizona, many Native Americans claimed to have heard her cry. One man in particular, the Jumano Indian chief named Capitán Tuerto, responded most notably.

He was a fierce-looking, easily identifiable gentleman with one eye, hence his name Tuerto, the Spanish word for "one-eyed." Whether his disfigurement was the result of a perilous encounter with a mountain lion, or one of the formidable Apache vaqueros, is not recorded in colonial texts. However, his regard for the supernatural woman he identified as the Lady in Blue is on record in many historical documents written during and about the era.

She had, he claimed, appeared to him and his people many times to tell them about her Lord, the Christian God. He and his people understood

FIGURE 7. Saint Augustine Church, Isleta Pueblo, New Mexico, site of original San Antonio Mission where Jumano Native Americans identified Lady in Blue to missionaries in 1629. Photo by Jeanne Kendall.

her, and she them, although they spoke to each other in different languages. The Jumanos reported themselves as reverberating deeply to her teaching, with hopes not only for baptism in the Christian faith, but the establishment of a mission in their territory.[3]

According to Capitán Tuerto and his people, the Lady in Blue made frequent journeys to see them from 1620 to 1623. She appeared to materialize out of thin air, but they did not question her methods. Instead they enjoyed her company and revered her teaching. However, after three years the Lady in Blue told them a time would come when she could no longer visit them and instructed them to seek baptism from the missionary fathers.

In 1629 Capitán Tuerto led a delegation to the San Antonio Mission in Isleta, renamed in 1716 for Saint Augustine. It was the sixth such annual delegation, and its purpose each year was the same—to request baptism, as instructed by the Lady in Blue. Until the delegation in 1629, their requests for baptism and a mission had fallen on deaf ears.

During the same period that Capitán Tuerto and his people interacted with the Lady in Blue, later identified as Sor María of Ágreda, she reported to her superiors her impressions of experiencing another land during her spiritual ecstasies. She described what and whom she saw to her confessors, trying to make some sense of it all. Yet it was difficult to explain her experiences even to herself, much less to others. When the nuns in Sor María's convent in Spain reported her continual physical presence there, the priests began to suspect a miracle.

At the end of her trances, Sor María remembered countless details of areas and people she had visited. The arid mountain air was not unlike her own countryside bordering the rolling ranges of the Moncayos. The sun shone brilliantly there as it did over Spain. The azure sky enveloped the people of the river valley, just as it did the nuns of the Convent of the Conception.

Yet many things about the experiences were dramatically different, and Sor María knew she was in a new land—unaccountably so, for she also knew she had not left the convent. Somehow, it seems, her abiding desire had come true—to preach about her Lord to the natives of the New World. Had she traveled overseas spiritually, she wondered, despite her vows as a cloistered nun? If so, how could she explain the realistic nature of her visions: the smell of the earth in her nostrils, the heat of the land beneath her feet, the voices of the natives in her ears?

Inspired by the expansion of her heart, and the ardent curiosity of the native people she saw greeting her on a faraway hillside, she set aside her misgivings, surrendered to the mystery, and humbly answered the call to the missionary work before her. The Jumanos in turn were indeed disposed to receive Sor María's teaching, she reported to inquisitors years later. The natives were full of questions for her, and she responded effusively, with a contagious love and joy.

"I told them God was the creator of the whole universe and its conservator," she testified. "I described Him as [three] persons who were one in essence—the Father, Son and Holy Spirit; and that the Son took human form to redeem us."[4]

When the Jumanos pressed for further initiation into Christianity, however, Sor María would not help them. Not only could she as a nun not baptize them, for that was the prerogative of the priesthood, she had also—in the "real world" in Ágreda—promised to pray for the removal of her exterioridades. That meant she would not be returning, and she told them so. They must be baptized, she told them, "preparing them

FIGURE 8. Sor María's original blue cape, habit, veil, and walking stick. On display in convent museum. Photo by author.

first that the sign of baptism was the holy cross on which Christ died, crucified, for our salvation."[5]

As reported by many historians of the time, the Jumanos of the seventeenth-century American Southwest called her the Lady in Blue for the sky blue cape prescribed by the Conceptionist charter and worn over their cream- and brown-colored robes. She is said to have visited them over five hundred times, most frequently from 1620 to 1623, walking among them through the land, and conversing with them in their own tongue. Yet as attested by those in Ágreda, she never left the cloistered convent.

Early records of the Jumanos cite several main locales, at least four of which come into play in the story of the Lady in Blue.[6] Depending on the explorer's language of origin, these Native Americans are called Jumanos, Humanas, Choumans, Rayados, Xumanas, and other variations.[7] And while scholars believe that over time they were absorbed into the Wichita, the Apache, and the Tejas,[8] preliminary efforts surfaced in Texas in the late twentieth and early twenty-first centuries to resuscitate their tribal identity.[9]

The first mention of Jumanos appears in the exploration records of Álvar Núñez Cabeza de Vaca, referencing his journey in 1535, in southwestern Texas near present-day Presidio, to an area known as La Junta de los Ríos, where the Rio Grande and Rio Conchos meet.

"They [gave] us many blankets of skin," he wrote, "and they had nothing they did not bestow. They have the finest persons of any people we saw."[10]

In 1582 the Jumanos are again mentioned, this time by Antonio de Espejo, in a region of present-day New Mexico that is east of the Rio Grande.[11] These Jumanos recalled visitors from years earlier, clearly describing to Espejo the features of Cabeza de Vaca and three of his distinctive-looking companions. Yet another mention came in 1598, when Juan de Oñate, colonizer of New Mexico and founder of many of its first settlements, journeyed to the "salinas of the Pecos . . . and to the pueblos of the Xumanes," or "Las Humanas."[12]

Many early Spanish settlers tended to confuse different Native American groups because of some common features that crossed tribal boundaries, such as striated facial tattoos, which the Jumanos and others did employ. This erroneously obscured the Jumanos' tribal identity, as contemporary research details sixteenth- and seventeenth-century

Jumanos as a distinct tribe of nomads residing in these and other locations, with periodic trafficking among them.

Skilled communicators and inveterate traders, the Jumanos made annual trade journeys among their people in the northern Texas canyons, the plains, and those in the Las Humanas pueblos of New Mexico. In the early seventeenth century, their offerings included salt, obsidian, and buffalo hides, as well as timely news from the Caddo, the Wichita, and many Texan peoples. As such, the Jumanos played an important role in the exchange of commodities and information among many tribes and colonists.[13]

One of the major Jumano encampments was in a fertile area between the South Canadian River and the North Fork of the Red River. Careful distillation of colonial explorers' records pinpoints this location in present-day northwest Texas, north of Palo Duro Canyon and east of Amarillo, a prominent Native American trading center.[14] This conceivably coincides with the area identified by Sor María as one of the last places she visited, a location she described to her confessors as four hundred leagues north and northwest of Mexico City.[15]

Two additional locations are celebrated yet today in West Texas for the history of the Jumanos and the Lady in Blue. One bears evidence of one of the tribe's encampments along the Concho River near today's Sterling City, San Angelo, and Paint Rock, Texas.[16] The other anchors Jumano history as the first historical mention of their tribe in the area of La Junta de los Ríos. There the Jumanos hunted buffalo in the southwesterly plains northeast of the Rio Grande and journeyed across Texas to the east, to the Salinas pueblos of New Mexico, southeast of Albuquerque. Wherever they went, they brought with them goods and news.

The trip from present-day Amarillo west to Albuquerque is about a five-hour drive along Interstate 40. From San Angelo, Texas, it is even longer and less direct. In July's merciless heat along the arid terrain, modern travelers would make this trip in air-conditioned cars, perhaps sipping a chilled Coke purchased at a rest stop. In the early seventeenth century, just a few decades before the Indians assimilated horseback riding from the Spanish,[17] Jumanos made this journey on foot, with teams of dogs pulling laden stretchers of goods to trade at the pueblos.[18]

Spanish colonials measured the distance from Santa Fe to the first reaches of the Jumano encampment in southwest Texas at 112-plus leagues, or over 336 miles.[19] The Jumanos measured the distance in sunrises and

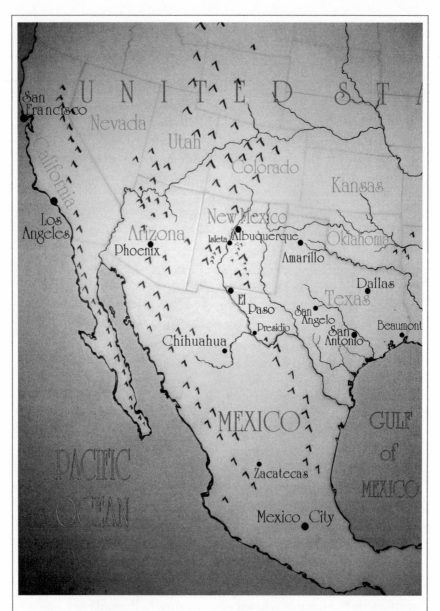

FIGURE 9. Map of southwestern United States and Mexico, with present-day city locations and (shaded) state lines and names, as references to key locations in the history of the Lady in Blue. Map by author.

FIGURE 10. Southwestern plains terrain across which Jumano Native Americans traversed on trading missions and annual migrations. Photo by Jeanne Kendall.

sunsets, a few weeks' trek, depending on their loads. In 1623 their journeys took on a new meaning.

According to their own accounts, a beautiful Lady in Blue had since 1620 visited the Jumanos of Texas and other neighboring tribes, to share with them the teachings of her Savior. They revered her and looked forward to her visits. Then after three years, she told them that she would no longer visit them and emphasized that they must request baptism and further teaching from the priests at the mission.

Compelled by her insistence, in 1623 they added another leg to their annual summer trade mission and visited Saint Anthony's in Isleta, just outside Albuquerque—a two- to three-day journey from the pueblo trading centers. For six successive years, to no avail, they went to Isleta to request that the sacrament of baptism be brought to their people many days' journey to the east. The missionaries, understaffed and inundated with more than fourteen thousand locally converted Native American souls to tend to, paid them little attention.[20] They were turned away.

During the same time in Spain, beginning in 1620, Sor María had begun to report unusual experiences to her confessors. Among these experiences were visions of another place and climate and different people than those in Ágreda. She felt compelled by God to preach to them about Christ, and in doing so, she said they understood her, and she them, without any language barriers. Her descriptions of the people's customs and countryside were so rich in details that after hearing about this time after time, the confessors decided to report it to their superiors.[21]

Her confessors' superiors, sensing unrest in her cloistered convent, ordered her to pray to God for the cessation of these and other exterioridades. She obeyed and reported in later years that in the process she also informed the Jumanos that she would no longer be able to visit them. In response to their protestations, she told how she insisted that they go to Isleta for further instruction in Christianity.

CHAPTER 6

"It is difficult to interpret . . . spiritual processes, in terms of matter"

COMMUNICATIONS IN THE SEVENTEENTH CENTURY, BECAUSE more leisurely than today, left much to be desired in terms of timeliness. Whether hand-carried or shipped in courier bags transported by caravans, messages and letters addressed domestically often took weeks or months to deliver, and those addressed overseas took many more months aboard ships. "Letters crossing in the mail" held an entirely different meaning than today's physical correspondence. Electronic messaging and phones were not available to speed up the process or for midcourse corrections. These factors, coupled with the time needed to process new information and mobilize a response, meant that if there were a misstep anywhere along the way, these cycles could take years in their completion. Such was the case with the reports about the Lady in Blue cycling between Ágreda, Madrid, Mexico City, and New Mexico.

Not until 1622 did the Franciscan minister general meet with Sor María during a visit to Ágreda and learn about her extraordinary supernatural experiences of another land that had begun in 1620.[1] He was clearly fascinated with her detailed accounts of the New World, as well as with her sincerity and spiritual acumen. With the minister general's encouragement, Padre Sebastián Marcilla—a confessor of Sor María's in tandem with Padre Torrecilla—wrote to Archbishop of Mexico Don Francisco de Manzo y Zúñiga.[2]

Marcilla did so in 1626, at which time he informed Manzo of Sor María's visions of preaching to the Native Americans and her unquestioned devotion to God. Then he included many of the specific details of her experience:

> It is very probable that in the course of the discovery of New Mexico and the conversion of those souls, there will soon be found a kingdom . . . more than four hundred leagues from the city of Mexico to the west or between the west and north, which it is understood is between New Mexico and la Quivira. . . . It will be of assistance to obtain information concerning three other kingdoms, one called Chillescas, the other that of the Jumanos, and the third that of Carbucos. . . . These being discovered, an effort shall be made to ascertain whether or not in them . . . there is any knowledge of our holy faith, and in what manner our Lord has manifested it.[3]

Archbishop Manzo, like others, had followed the stories of the explorations of the Southwest since Coronado's expedition in the early 1540s. Of the three Native American groups Marcilla mentioned, he was familiar only with the Jumanos. He also knew that many explorers had searched for a legendary place Coronado had called Quivira, in pursuit of the untold riches to be found there.[4] As Manzo had heard it reported, Quivira's distance from Mexico City was said to be four hundred leagues or more to the north. This now appeared to approximate one of the locations identified for Padre Marcilla by the Spanish nun.[5]

Manzo was keen to investigate this. In 1628 he appointed Padre Esteban de Perea to head the New Mexico mission work, a post Perea had held previously from 1617 to 1621, but which most recently had been filled by Padre Alonso de Benavides.[6] Archbishop Manzo prepared a letter of inquiry to Benavides, dated May 18, 1628.[7]

In it, Manzo ordered Benavides and the missionaries to inquire among the natives from Texas (which Sor María had pronounced as "Tixtlas") to see if they showed previous knowledge of the faith and if so, to research these claims. He must ask them, Manzo wrote, how they acquired their information and then notify him of the results, for the "great spiritual and temporal advancement to the glory and service of our Lord."[8] Perea would hand-carry this letter to Benavides in New Mexico, in the supply caravan of 1628–29.[9]

At the same time, thirty missionaries arrived in Mexico City from Spain. They accompanied Perea on the caravan from Mexico City to help the sixteen surviving priests and three lay brothers working out of Isleta with Benavides.[10] One of the priests was Padre Cristobal Quirós, whose name will appear again later. Upon arrival, Perea would take over as head of the New Mexico missions and present the letter to Benavides about the nun.

Throughout the journey, the new missionaries were awash with speculation about the mysterious apparitions in the New World of which they, too, had heard from the discussions about Manzo's letter. By that time they may also have heard of the bilocations through Franciscan officials in Spain.

The caravan, including priests, military escort, and thirty-six oxcarts of provisions, left Mexico City on September 4, 1628, and arrived at Isleta on June 3, 1629, three years after Marcilla had penned his letter.[11] The Jumanos arrived soon thereafter—again.

Padre Alonso de Benavides was familiar with the Jumanos from the plains to the east. Each year, for the previous six years, they had presented themselves at Saint Anthony's in Isleta, requesting baptism and the establishment of a mission at their encampment many days' journey away. They had even asked for a specific missionary, one who had worked with their pueblo brothers at Las Humanas.[12] "I didn't have enough clerics, and so I continued to put off the Humanas . . . until God should send me more workers," Benavides reported later to his superiors.[13]

On July 22, 1629, a band of fifty Jumanos arrived at the mission to again make their request.[14] Although Benavides had not yet left, Perea—as the new custodian—received them this time. Informed by the archbishop's inquiry, he was now very intent on knowing what had prompted their repeated attempts.

Why had they come? Perea asked them, in a combination of Spanish and sign language.[15]

For the water of baptism, the Jumanos replied similarly.

At whose instruction? Perea wanted to know.

A woman wearing the habit urged us to come, they said.

FIGURE 11. Garden outside Saint Augustine Church, Isleta Pueblo, New Mexico. Photo by Jeanne Kendall.

Trembling with excitement, no doubt, Perea immediately sent for Benavides, and the two continued to engage the Jumanos. The one-eyed Capitán Tuerto led the Jumano delegation. With him were eleven other Indian captains, representing neighboring tribes and allies.[16]

"We called them [in]to the convent," Benavides wrote later. "Gazing at a portrait of Mother Luisa . . . they said, 'A woman in similar garb wanders among us . . . preaching.'"[17] The priests pointed to the same picture of the elderly nun wearing the blue cape of the Conceptionist nuns of Saint Clare, asking if that was the woman.

"The clothes are the same, but not the face," they replied, describing their Lady in Blue as "not old like this, but young" "and beautiful."[18]

Why hadn't they told them before? the priests asked.

"Because you did not ask us, and we thought she was around here, too," they replied.[19]

"Immediately we decided to send . . . priests," Benavides wrote. "With these same Indians as guides, they departed on that apostolic mission. After traveling more than one hundred leagues . . . toward the east, they reached the Xumana nation, who came out to receive them in procession, carrying a large cross and garlands of flowers. They learned from the Indians that the same nun had instructed them as to how they should come out in procession to receive them, and she had helped them to decorate the cross," although the priests did not see her themselves.[20]

Conservative estimates gauge the procession of eager Jumanos at about two thousand, while Benavides points to ten thousand, with the neighboring tribes in attendance from the area surrounding Palo Duro Canyon.[21] While this area was later abandoned by the Jumanos, perhaps due to conflicts with the Apaches, the tribe remained constant in their desire for a mission.[22] Three years later they led another missionary party two hundred leagues south of Isleta, along the La Junta de los Ríos area, and then easterly.[23]

"The missionaries from New Mexico came all the way down to San Angelo to the confluence of the three Concho rivers," said historian Marion Habig (1901–92), who spent several years physically traversing Texas missions and their environs. A protégée of Henry Bolton, noted historian of the West and Southwest at the University of California, Habig gave an interview in 1982 with the University of Texas' Institute of Texan Cultures and later published his findings in 1990.[24]

"It is difficult to interpret . . . spiritual processes, in terms of matter"   57

Compelled by the potential of such a miraculous event, Benavides left Isleta in the autumn of 1629 and arrived in Mexico City in March of 1630. There he reported his findings to Archbishop Manzo and was soon dispatched to Madrid "to inform his Majesty . . . and our father general" of the "notable and unusual things that were happening in their holy custodia."[25]

He arrived in Madrid in August of 1630 and proceeded to write a thorough report on mission activities for his Franciscan superiors as well as the king. To this day, his documentation provides historians with many valuable population statistics and classifications within New Mexico at the time,[26] although many scholars suggest that his numbers were inflated.

In writing his report, Benavides also devoted a chapter to the incident of the Lady in Blue, an account destined to be cited, researched, and recounted by historians and devotees alike from colonial days to the present. In doing so, Benavides speculated that the Lady in Blue was the Conceptionist nun Mother Luisa de Carrión, who in addition to transporting herself from Mexico seemed now to also have the power to make herself appear young and beautiful.[27]

The report created an immediate sensation. Extracts were quoted, and it was translated into Latin, German, French, and Dutch.[28] The first printing of four hundred copies was soon devoured, and another set was printed.[29] The Jumano Indians had come a long way, from being ignored for six years at the Isleta mission to being celebrated in a country far across the sea.

Dating his report August 1, 1630, Benavides submitted it to the commissary general of the Indies, Padre Juan de Santander, who then added a preface for the benefit of the king. The 111-page document covered the activities of the fifty friars then serving over sixty thousand Christianized natives in the impoverished Pueblo region of the New World. One by one, Benavides described the Native American tribes residing in ninety pueblos and divided into twenty-five mission districts, making sure to point out that the numbers of missionaries were few, and they had not yet discovered all the native populations.

"The Humana nation," he added, had "a conversion . . . so miraculous, that it deserves to have its story told."[30]

Benavides recounted the arrival of the Jumanos at the Isleta mission and their renewed request for missionaries and baptism because of the Lady in Blue. Then he told how he and Perea soon sent two priests, Padres Juan de Salas and Diego Lopez, escorted by three soldiers, to follow the Jumanos to their encampment.[31]

Before the priests arrived there, however, as reported to them later by the Jumanos who awaited them, the springs from which their people drank had dried up, and the buffalo had disappeared. The Jumanos said the "enemy of souls, the devil" then told them that the priests would not come and that they should leave.[32] A saintly spirit, however—the same woman dressed in blue—advised them differently. Benavides wrote:

> At daybreak the saint spoke to each one of them individually. She told them that they should not go, that the clerics they had been searching for were drawing near. Conferring among themselves, they decided to send twelve very reliable captains to see if it were so. On the third day out, they ran into the priests. . . .
>
> The padre showed them the portrait of Mother Luisa de Carrión, about which they said that their lady was dressed like that, but was younger and more beautiful. . . . And always when Indians from those tribes came to see us again, they looked at the portrait and talked among themselves, saying, "The clothes are the same, but not the face."
>
> . . . [Then] having assembled more than ten thousand souls . . . with a great shout, they all raised their arms, got up on their feet, and asked for holy baptism. . . . It seemed to the padres a great harvest of souls, with few laborers to complete it.[33]

The priests agreed to the Jumanos' request and began their sacramental benedictions at once, in an area speculated by some scholars to be within present-day San Angelo's city limits, near what is now known as South College Hills.[34] "Before they left . . . the primary captain [said] . . . 'Father . . . you can achieve a great deal with God, and with this holy cross. We have a lot of sick people: heal us before you go.'"[35]

"They had to bring people in all afternoon, all night," Benavides reported, "and all the next morning until ten o'clock. There was one cleric on one side and one on the other, making the sign of the cross, [and] saying [prayers]. . . . They instantly got up, cured of all their infirmities—blind people, lame people, people afflicted with dropsy—everyone cured of his afflictions."[36]

As a result of this event in 1629, and the second missionary trek to the same tribal group, the Jumanos—inspired by their Lady in Blue—may be credited with spurring the first mission activity in the state of Texas, previously relegated to the period between 1682 and 1793.

"One of the missionaries stayed there . . . for six months," Habig declared. "Established in 1632, that was the first mission in Texas," he said. "That's where San Angelo is . . . and the Indians there were the Jumanos."[37] A historic monument alongside the Concho commemorates the priests' work with the Jumanos in this location in 1632 and their mission, though it was an operational facility for only six months.[38]

Meanwhile, in late August of 1630, Benavides reviewed his report—entitled the *Memorial of 1630*—with the minister general of the Franciscan order, Padre Bernardino de Sienna. Sienna reassured Benavides that the Jumanos' Lady in Blue was Sor María de Jesús, telling him what he knew about her bilocations to America from her own accounts eight years earlier when he had visited Ágreda.

Benavides now realized that in assuming the Lady in Blue was Mother Luisa de Carrión, he may have targeted the wrong nun, although Mother Luisa's appearances were legendary in another area, to the Moqui people north and west of Albuquerque, New Mexico, and the Hopis in Arizona.[39]

Sienna vouched for Sor María's integrity and sincerity. He gave Benavides special permission to visit the cloistered nun personally in Ágreda and at the same time instructed her to answer all of Benavides's questions to the priest's complete satisfaction.[40] For as both priests realized—because of Benavides's firsthand knowledge of New Mexico—he was perhaps the only person who might verify or repudiate her claims.[41]

In early spring of 1631, a traveling friar delivered a letter to the convent. It was from the office of the minister general and indicated that Benavides would soon visit Ágreda to investigate the matter of the Lady in Blue. Sor María's spiritual director, Padre Andrés de la Torre, understood that Benavides served as an official of the Spanish Inquisition in New Mexico, but he was quick to remind Sor María that Benavides was not necessarily visiting in that capacity.

Sor María reflected about the Jumanos and her unusual relationship with them. Clearly she felt powerfully connected to them. Yet, her experiences of them were private and so interwoven with the fabric of her silent prayer that it was difficult to face the possibility that her accounts might rise to confront her in the flesh and blood of an investigator. Now an official sought her out—from the New World previously confined to the mystery of her spiritual visions.

Years later Sor María was able to explain in exquisite detail—in *Mystical City of God* and to the stern interrogators of the Spanish Inquisition—how all this took place and how it fit in with her other visions of Christ, the Blessed Mother, and the angels that served them. In these early years, however, she struggled.

"It is difficult to interpret such elevated intellectual . . . and . . . spiritual processes, in terms of matter," she wrote.[42] Her terms foreshadowed what some neuroscientists or medical interns today might describe as a vital area of study—a case in point being the present-day Alpert Medical School's scholarly "Concentration in Contemplative Studies" at Brown University, in which medical students probe the effects of contemplative practices on cognitive and physiological functions.[43]

In Sor María's era, however, words did not exist to explain the phenomena she experienced, other than those used to describe the mystical realm. And in those early years of her life, she did not yet have the spiritual depth of experience to explain how the events could have taken place. In this void, she desperately sought spiritual guidance about what had happened to her.

In the early 1620s, Sor María consulted her confessor, Padre Juan de Torrecilla. She had confided in him since she was a child and hoped to gain some perspective and insight from him. Unfortunately, those who were superior to her in rank were not necessarily more experienced than she in the esoteric realms of the spirit. Even with the best of motivations, all too often their awe at the sensational nature of her experience overrode her pressing need for guidance.

Padre Torrecilla was "more kindly than cautious," she wrote many years later. Dazzled at the time by Sor María's report, Torrecilla began to "talk publicly about all this."[44] He also told others in his order and discussed the matter with another of Sor María's spiritual counselors, Padre Sebastián Marcilla. And that is what started the cavalcade of letters between Ágreda, Madrid, and the New World.

CHAPTER 7

"My confessors . . . [were] extremely fond of these sensational topics"

IF THE FAMED ENGLISH WRITER C. S. LEWIS HAD LIVED in Benavides's time, the friar might have shifted uncomfortably at an insight frequently attributed to Lewis: "The two hardest things in the world to find are a good cup of coffee and a pure intention."

As Benavides well knew, Spain's motivations in colonizing the New World were multifaceted. Religion, wealth, and power were all at the top of the list. Additionally, Spain was not the only country interested in the rich potential of America. England, France, the Netherlands, and Portugal also set sail for the New World and also set their caps for a significant piece of the pie.

Nevertheless, Spanish royalty consistently emphasized from the beginning that "preaching the holy gospel . . . is the principal purpose for which we order new discoveries and settlements to be made."[1] Such efforts cost dearly. Since the days of Ponce de León's expeditions in the early 1500s, Spanish monarchs often financed these expensive enterprises privately.

To do so, the Crown engaged adventuresome individuals termed *adelantados*, translated as "governor-generals." These entrepreneurs, with their own and other backers' money, colonized various territories in America, in return for titles of nobility and property, as well as varying percentages of valuable commodities. By royal decree, and at the expense of the Crown, two missionaries accompanied all exploration parties in order to accomplish the important work of converting souls.[2]

Then in 1598–99, many New Mexico Native Americans were unforgivably ill-treated by adelantado and founding governor of New Mexico Juan de Oñate. The Crown prosecuted him, banished him from New Mexico, and, as it confronted other problems in Florida, seriously considered withdrawal from both areas. The Franciscans, whose apocalyptic zeal had drawn them into New Mexico since 1573, were eager to remain. Ultimately, the Crown took over the financing of New Mexico colonization, and the Franciscans absorbed the work previously done by secular colonists.[3]

Thus, Benavides pointedly directed his 1630 report to the sensibilities of both the Franciscan order as well as twenty-five-year-old King Felipe IV, who had inherited Spain's progressively weakened economy since the fall of the Armada in the days of his grandfather. Benavides balanced the spiritual content of his report with Native American demographics, population statistics, geographic guides, and descriptions of verdant crops, exotic wildlife, as well as mines full of gold, minerals, and gems. He also included anecdotes that he knew would be popular of miraculous cures and baptisms by the thousands. He knew that if he was to garner more human and financial resources, he must motivate both the Franciscan order as well as the Crown.

These same mixed motives would have accompanied Benavides to Ágreda. In addition, it was well known at the time that Benavides hoped for the establishment of a new bishopric in New Mexico, which he himself would fill. If Sor María's experiences were bona fide, he well could have reasoned, they would indicate a miraculous sign from God in support of the New Mexico missions.

On April 30, 1631, Benavides arrived in Ágreda. With him he brought Padre Marcilla, Sor María's former confessor and now the presiding provincial in Burgos. Together with Padre Andrés de la Torre, they would—for two weeks—examine Sor María's accounts of her experiences. Benavides was immediately taken with her and described her later in detail:

> Mother María de Jesús, Abbess now of the convent of the Immaculate Conception, is about twenty-nine years of age . . .

handsome of face, very fair in color, with a slight rosy tinge and large black eyes. The style of her habit, as well as that of all the nuns of that convent . . . is the same as ours; that is of brown (pardo) sackcloth, very coarse, worn next to the body. . . . Over this brown habit is worn a white one of coarse sackcloth with a scapular of the same [material] and the cord of our Father Saint Francis. . . . They wear no shoes or sandals other than boards tied to the feet. The cloak is of blue cloth, coarse, with a black veil.[4]

Benavides may have been charmed by Sor María's appearance, but one should note that under normal circumstances, he never would have seen her face. In those days, cloistered nuns were protected from the sight of strangers by a veil drawn completely over their faces. Benavides's task at hand allowed him an exception, in order to compare her actual features with the Jumanos' descriptions. Too, the Inquisition was still in full swing in Spain, and Benavides was an officer of the Inquisition in the New World. Sor María, on the other hand, as a nun under vows of obedience, was obligated to fully satisfy his inquiries based on an order of the Franciscan minister general. Sor María was clearly intimidated.

Does this mean that Benavides "led the witness"? Probably.

Does it mean that some exaggeration of the truth occurred? Yes.

Does it mean that the bilocations were fabricated? Not according to Sor María.

"I can assure you beyond any doubt," Sor María wrote to a superior years later, "that the case did in fact happen. . . . [Yet] I was about twenty [when this first happened] and inexperienced . . . [and] whether or not I really and truly went in my body is something about which I cannot be certain,"[5] suggesting instead that her experiences may have been spiritual rather than physical. Today, this type of phenomenon is often understood as psychic in nature—anathema to the present-day nuns of Ágreda because it evokes a paranormal skill set often disassociated from the grace of God.

Regardless, however, of any debate about the origin of such phenomena, the sensationalism surrounding them inevitably invaded the privacy and quiet of the Ágreda cloister without sensitivity to the vows of those within. Ironically, the invasion began from within. Sor María had considered her discussions with her confessors to be confidential. Yet

Padre Torrecilla—in his enthusiasm about her special gifts—could not help talking about the marvels he had heard from her. To Sor María's consternation, the other nuns not only knew about her experiences, they spoke of the phenomena openly.

"As the story was transmitted through so many friars and nuns," Sor María wrote, "it was unavoidable that . . . it would be adulterated, especially on a subject where imprudent religious enthusiasts feel one is doing something grand by adding on more . . . than has really occurred."[6]

During Benavides's visit, as their discussions ensued, he compiled a notebook of Sor María's experiences. At the end of the two weeks he had her sign this, as well as compose a letter of her own, encouraging the missionaries in New Mexico. "Under the command of obedience," Sor María wrote, "I have signed it with my own name,"[7] "when the truth is that I went along with it passively, not actively, and that I was horribly pained that the report was put together. I was trembling, beside myself with anxiety and never realized what I was signing."[8]

Later, however, Sor María felt more comfortable in revealing which things were recounted accurately and which were not. For example, at Benavides's prompting, Sor María said that the bilocations occurred from 1620 through 1631, whereas later she reported that they had mainly ceased by 1623, when she had prayed for the cessation of the exterioridades. Additionally, Benavides claims that she transported a monstrance and some rosaries from the convent in Ágreda to New Mexico.

"On one occasion, I gave the Indians some rosaries," she admitted later, "[but] my confessors . . . [who were] extremely fond of these sensational topics . . . one day ordered me to take a monstrance containing communion wafers that the missionaries might say Mass. . . . But for my part, I was afraid to do something like that and touch the monstrance in which our Lord had been; [so] I returned it to its place. . . . Then in the confusion, the nuns lost track of the monstrance and must have thought I took it with me."[9]

Too, Benavides reported that Sor María said she was transported by angels, with Saint Francis and Saint Michael on either side of her. "That was a remark of mine in conversation," she wrote. "I said they were my wings, calling them that metaphorically and reflecting that just as wings help birds to fly, [the saints and angels] help us fly to God."[10]

After all is said and done, however, Sor María's primary claim of bilocation remains consistent with much of Benavides's knowledge of the missionaries and Native Americans of New Mexico and beyond. Both Benavides's report as well as the testimony of the Jumanos corroborate Sor María's detailed information about individual priests, Native Americans, and specific events. And, while there are cogent alternative rationales for the Jumanos' motivations in standing by their accounts of the Lady in Blue and lobbying repeatedly for the establishment of a mission, Sor María insisted that it had in fact happened, and did so with a remarkable array of details.

"She is well acquainted with Captain Tuerto," Benavides wrote, "and gave me all the peculiar marks of his features. . . . She also . . . gave me the exact description of [Father Cristobal Quirós] . . . saying that he is old but that he did not show any signs of gray hairs, that he was longfaced and ruddy."[11]

More importantly, throughout the recounting of Sor María's experiences, what also remains, across the years and among different audiences, is her unerring dedication to her spiritual path and her missionary zeal to share it with those far and near. To the missionaries of New Mexico, she truthfully wrote that she envied them their missionary opportunities.

"I confess that if I could purchase it with my blood, or my life, or cruel martyrdom, I would do it," she wrote, in words consistent with her adolescent zeal in "Face of the Earth and Map of the Spheres." "[For I] envy your Reverences this task . . . [and] offer all my heart and soul to help with prayers . . . those who are the custodians of souls and who are occupied in the work of Conversion."[12]

Nevertheless, in her typical selfless fashion, she showered them with her well wishes and prayers and encouraged them with all her might to continue in their work. She described the Jumanos as "capable and worthy" people who like all God's creatures were created to serve and worship the Lord.[13]

In the process, she identified the warlike Apaches, through whose territory the plains Jumanos must pass each time they journeyed between the plains of Texas and Las Humanas pueblo.[14] She also reiterated in later years that "I saw each one of the kingdoms clearly and knew their names," stating that she was able to distinguish the various locations, climates, and customs of the New World areas from those of her own more familiar terrain.[15] "Their foods were primitive, and for light they used wooden torches. I would address them and explain all the articles of faith, exhorting them and teaching the catechism. They were receptive to all

FIGURE 12. Detail of altar cloth embroidered by Sor María, portraying her impressions of New World wildlife. On display in—and image courtesy of—Convent of the Conception, Ágreda.

of this and sort of bowed, acclaiming the great good they were receiving and making entreaties [for baptism]."[16] "The region[s] of Quivira and the Jumanas," she said, "are the last to which I have been carried."[17]

At the end of the investigation, Benavides wrote about it to the friars in New Mexico.

> I do not know how to make you understand the impulses and the great uplift to my soul . . . when this blessed Mother told me that she had accompanied me at the Baptism of the Pizos Indians and that she recognized me as being the same person whom she saw there. She also assisted Father Christobal Quirós in several baptisms and . . . told how one time the Father was standing baptizing in his church when a number of Indians gathered around the door; that she was there and pushed them in with her own hands and arranged them in their places . . . and that they laughed when . . . she pushed them so that they would push the others. . . . She

also told me what . . . happened to our Fathers and Brothers, Fray Juan de Salas and Fray Diego Lopez, in their journeying among the *Jumanas,* and that she took care of them and directed them all the time, so that they went to call them, just as in fact they did.[18]

By the next year, Padre José Ximénez Samaniego had begun Sor María's biography, a labor of love that would extend into his later years as bishop of Plasencia, even after her death. At the time, and over the decades, Ximénez Samaniego interviewed Sor María and scrutinized all the testimonies, including Benavides's meetings and correspondence with and about Sor María.

The bishopric in New Mexico would not materialize for Benavides, but he was awarded one in India. En route, in 1635–36, he died at sea. Ximénez Samaniego, however, had likely consulted him before then. Later, Ximénez Samaniego reported that Sor María's answers regarding the bilocations "were so exact, that a person who had been there for many years and had traveled over that entire country could not have answered with more truth and sincerity."[19]

CHAPTER 8

"An engineer came to remove the rocks with gunpowder"

AFTER SOR MARÍA SUCCEEDED IN HER PRAYERS TO REDUCE the exterioridades, she devoted herself to the communal life of the cloister. The schedule was rigorous, calling for the nuns to retire at nine in the evening, then rise at two for prayers before dawn. When the other nuns went back to rest from four to six in the morning, Sor María was frequently unable to sleep.

She filled the time with private devotions, then rejoined the others when they rose for choir and Mass. This was followed by chores until Angelus prayers at noon and lunch, and an afternoon filled with acts of charity, administrative duties, and confessions. Choir resumed at five in the evening, followed by dinner at six, prayers at seven, and sleep at nine.

Sor María frequently practiced additional devotions from eleven at night to two in the morning, as reported in detail by Ximénez Samaniego. These included thirty minutes kneeling with her father's iron cross on her shoulders; thirty minutes kneeling with arms cruciform and hands pressed on iron nails; thirty minutes lying on the iron cross and meditating on the seven last words of Christ; followed by a ninety-minute meditation on the fruits of Christ's passion.[1]

While the exterioridades were mainly gone, Sor María's deep levels of prayerful meditation still spilled over into ecstasies that begged for expression. As she had in her teen years, Sor María turned to writing to express the inexpressible. Sometimes she wrote in the wee hours, and sometimes in the afternoons, other duties and schedule permitting.

While she did not yet feel ready to embark on the biography of Mary, during this period she produced *Spiritual Garden for the Life of the Soul* (in 1621), *Ladder to Perfection* (in 1627), *Laws of the Spouse* (in 1634), and *Litany to Our Lady* (in 1630), the latter of which—years later—would prove to be a matter of contention with the Inquisition.[2]

A few years before Benavides arrived in Ágreda, Sor María had another brush with death. The year was 1626, and her father had just passed away during the previous year. Her mother had been ill, but at this time the daughter again appeared likely to precede her mother in death.

Whether caused by the intense and often brutal austerities that Sor María imposed on herself or other medical reasons—or a combination of the two—her constitution weakened to the point of paralysis. The doctors could offer no cure, and Sor María resigned herself to the infirmity with as much cheerfulness as she could muster. To receive Communion, two nuns carried her in a chair to the convent chapel.

As she worsened, death seemed around the corner.

At the same time, a great drought plagued the land. Ximénez Samaniego reports that the townspeople asked the friars and nuns of Ágreda to pray for rain in the presence of a long-cherished statue of the Madonna of the Martyrs. It had been brought to Ágreda in times past by Christians fleeing from Zaragoza in the face of persecution. Those pursued were ultimately martyred for their faith. Then in 1626, as the religious community fervently prayed, Ximénez Samaniego reports that rain drenched the land.[3]

Inspired by the people's devotion, the paralyzed Sor María requested to have the statue brought to her cell. After praying before it, Sor María "arose from her bed perfectly cured," Ximénez Samaniego wrote. Glowing with health that same night, she sewed a cape for the statue out of a precious cloth of rich white gauze from a family heirloom chest she kept in her room. To this day, the cloth sheaths the statue in its place of honor in Ágreda's cemetery, in memory of the fallen martyrs as well as the cured abbess.[4]

Sor María's health, however, came at a price. With a conviction that reverberated throughout her entire being, she felt a profound calling to write the story of Mary's life. She prayed fervently to the saints and the princes of light, the angels, for guidance, years later recording her doubts and fears about her ability to complete "such an arduous task" in the introduction of *Mystical City of God*.[5] She does not mention at that time whether her prayer and its response was in the form of the interior knowing that she distinguished in later years from actual corporeal visions. Yet the response was nonetheless clear.

"Her guardian angel revealed to her," Ximénez Samaniego wrote, "that . . . God miraculously kept her alive . . . [to] make known to the world the glorious and extraordinary prerogatives of his most august Mother."[6]

Sor María was conflicted. As she began to absorb her new duties as abbess in the following year, she had little time or psychological space to write the biography of Mary. Out of necessity, she sank herself into her administrative work as abbess and the direction and guidance of the nuns now in her care. The biography, however, was continuously on her mind as she embarked upon her new responsibilities.

Despite the young abbess's initial misgivings about the suitability of her temperament for the position, Madre Sor María set aside her reluctance and surrendered in obedience to what she perceived as the will of God as administered through her superiors. She embraced her new duties with a gusto that echoes loud and clear centuries after her death. For even before taking the reins, she had evaluated the physical facilities of her ancestral-home-turned-convent, noted the cramped quarters and bustling neighborhood, and visualized a new convent altogether.

At her initiative, the village of Ágreda had deeded land to the convent for this purpose as early as 1624, and a cornerstone was ceremoniously set.[7] No one, however—even Sor María herself—had envisioned the speed with which she would embark upon the expansion once becoming abbess. At her behest, Padre Juan Villalacre attended a bidding auction at which some of the country's most noted master builders and craftsmen from throughout Biscay, Castile, Aragón, and Navarra came to scout new jobs. Bids for the new Ágreda convent ranged from nine thousand to fourteen thousand ducats. Two local (Sorian) stonemasons and master craftsmen, Juan de la Llama and Pedro Pérez, were awarded the six-year contract at one thousand ducats per year, with an additional eighteen hundred ducats to be awarded throughout, according to progress and needs.[8]

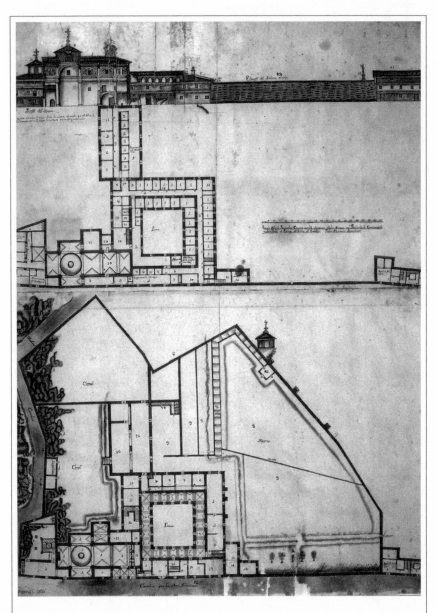

FIGURE 13. Architectural plan, new Conceptionist Convent in Ágreda. Cornerstone set in 1624, construction complete in 1633. On display in— and image courtesy of—Convent of the Conception, Ágreda.

Before Sor María's first year as abbess was out, the plans were drawn for the larger facility just outside the village, providing for a more spacious, self-sufficient, and serene atmosphere for the contemplative life of the cloister.[9] Soon Ágreda would echo with explosive detonations and excavations, expensive work in light of the fact that the funds from the original convent's founding were largely depleted.

"We ourselves had not twenty reales on the day we embarked upon the expansion plans," Sor María noted in convent archives, citing a sum of money worth less then than three months' common wages.[10] As a result, the Franciscan provincials guaranteed the finances, though no doubt hoping that private funds would be raised to cover the considerable costs.[11]

Was this egotistical folly for an uneducated, cloistered nun without financial resources, much less one whose talents obviously lay more in the architecture of the spirit than that of the earth? Is the story of the construction to be left to the local Ágreda legend of the two angels who purportedly served without pay as the principal master craftsmen? Are we to imagine Sor María intuiting complex engineering plans and herself supernaturally excavating boulders and laying brick?

While her life to date might lead one down that esoteric path, and while there are certainly noteworthy events connected to the construction of the new convent, in fact Sor María's approach in this case shows the development of an entirely new strain of talents. And during this seven-year-long proving ground, observers of her life may find the seeds of authority, delegation, wisdom, and diplomacy that emerge so naturally by the time, years later, she is called upon to advise the King of Spain.

"Everyone marveled at how a poor nun, destitute of human means, undertook and completed in so few years the construction of such a grand convent and church, including the entire plant, furnishings and adornments," wrote Sor María's confessor in later years.[12]

From their first meeting, Sor María recognized in Padre Andrés de la Torre a wise and heartfelt spiritual guide. Even while completing his term as provincial, he visited her several times between 1625 and 1627, in anticipation of his duties as her spiritual counselor. During these visits Sor María's eyes widened to the fact that her new confessor was also a skilled architectural designer of monasteries.[13] Thus even before he had relocated to the nearby Saint Julian's, he set his hand beside Padre Villalacre's to help design the new convent.

Several years earlier, the charter of the Conceptionist order had specified the requirements for the physical facilities of the renovated Coronel family home, such as the nuns' diminutive sleeping cells and the intimidating speared grille through which they conversed with visitors. The nuns' schedule was spelled out, too, as well as their attire—the signature sky blue cape worn over the white robes. Due to lack of space, however, the original facility had difficulty meeting the requisite self-sufficiency conditions for its occupants, in terms of cookery, gardening, and livestock. Too, the increasing number of applicants signaled the need for a larger complex. "The original convent was very cramped," another nun wrote, "and it was difficult for the nuns to guard their silence and engage in prayer and contemplation."[14]

Benefactors soon emerged. Many leading families and wealthy individuals of the community and surrounding areas believed in the spiritual vision of the remarkable young abbess. After the first gift of one hundred reals, Sor María knew the work of building the new convent would never falter for lack of funds, despite the doubling of expenses over the course of its completion.[15]

Sor María and Padre de la Torre envisioned that the new facility would more completely fulfill the Conceptionist charter's very specific requirements for the cloistered living quarters, grounds, and gardens. It also provided for a new—attached—church, which would allow the nuns to attend Mass with the townspeople while remaining hidden from view. In a manner defined by the charter, the back of the church would attach to the new convent at the point of the convent's first-floor choir. The two would be separated by a huge floor-to-ceiling "window," specified by Pope Julius in 1511 in the Conceptionist charter as "networks of iron behind a curtain of black linen" to separate and obscure the nuns from the community members who attended Mass in the church. The center of the large grille would feature a small window through which would fit a host and chalice for the nuns to receive Communion.[16]

The site for the new convent was nestled between the outer edge of the village and the Franciscan friars' convent of Saint Julian. Significantly, the site was long heralded in local lore as the place where the Christian fugitives from Zaragoza were martyred.[17] A portion of the land sat atop what locals referred to as "the Rock," an imposing hillock of flint that would not easily lend itself to change.[18] Few could imagine ahead of time the elegant baroque masterpiece that would emerge from this glacially entrenched obstacle.

In evaluating the parcel of land, Sor María carefully thought through the layout and placement of her new complex. The convent and its gardens and outbuildings would be built on the portion of the property farthest from the town, in the southeast segment of the parcel. In addition to its proximity to Saint Julian's, wherein resided the nuns' confessors as well as visiting clergy, this area—at the base of the Moncayo slopes—also faced an expanse of open land ideal for livestock and gardening. The new church, according to Padre de la Torre's plan, would fit along a slender segment of the parcel nearest to the village, inviting easy access to the townspeople without increasing foot traffic past the cloister.

According to this layout, the house and gardens were destined to replace the imposing mass of flint that stood temporarily in their stead. The result was an admirably adapted irregular facility snugly conforming to the existing road, the walls of Saint Julian's, and the extent of excavation possible upon the Rock.

In the first phase of construction, many townspeople and nearby laborers stepped forward to help, as attested in the list of names recorded in the convent's construction logs. Initially they directed their attention to the acquisition of voluminous materials and tools, such as pickaxes and spades, beams for rafters, lime, and slabs of stone for walls and floors. The nearby countryside of Soria and the rocky Moncayo mountain range proved a fertile foraging ground for the teams of carpenters and stonemasons who scoured the hills for the necessary raw materials. Before long, however, it was time to attend to the Rock. Pedro de Sabogal, an engineer, was called in for his demolition skills with gunpowder.[19]

"Our house is proceeding very well," Sor María wrote to Madre María de Cristo about the explosions resounding throughout the little village. "An engineer came to remove the rocks with gunpowder. It is amazing to see—he removes more than five hundred 100-pound measures in a day."[20]

The bombastic charges—administered in twenty-five hundred individual blasts—seemed a small price to pay for the stately cloister to come.[21] While attending to their daily rituals in Sor María's ancestral home, the nuns blessed each explosion and envisioned their future quietude. Soon Sor María's itemized logbook of expenses detailed the shape of their new grounds in the form of the outer walls. On November 17,

1629, she listed 929½ reals paid to the stonemasons for their work in constructing 169 sections of garden walls enclosing the grounds of the future cloister.

"Next will come the cells," she wrote to Madre María de Cristo in Madrid, "and the building will be very ample."[22] Indeed, by November of the following year, 1630, Sor María told her friend that the residential building was almost complete. As her correspondent knew, its interior walls—according to the Conceptionist charter—must be built thirty-two feet high, with one-and-one-half-foot buttresses and cornices that ran their length around the house.

"It is very pretty," Sor María wrote excitedly to Madre María de Cristo. "Even the two cellars are admirable. The vaulted ceilings are in place [in the refectory] and to increase the natural light they have finished the walls with [white] plaster and plasterboard paper. It lacks only illumination and the final brickwork inside and in the [prayer] garden, before we can begin on the church."[23]

"We could move in now," Sor María wrote upon completion of the house in April 1631—just one week before the arrival of Padre Benavides. "But I will not do so. I have told the Padres that the church will soon be complete, and that then we will go to her. Until then, we will admire the workmanship and remain quiet."[24] Later that same year, Sor María's mother died, gratified to have seen a great deal of the construction come to fruition.

"They are just finishing the lavatory and laundry," Sor María wrote in October 1632, "with water drawn from the river. And they also have found a small spring in the orchard" for drinking water and cooking. The plumbing, though ingenious for its day, presented two of perhaps the only imperfections in an otherwise exemplary plan. The first was an excess of moisture in the convent building, which Sor María repaired almost as soon as she and the nuns occupied their new house. In addition, trenches and drainage pits were dug to draw the water away from the building. The second was a lack of fresh, on-site water, requiring the nuns to trudge through the back orchard to draw and carry water in pitchers over three and a half kilometers back to their new home. This problem was eventually fixed, but not until 1650 with the financial backing of one of the convent's principal benefactors, Don Francisco Antonio Echarri of Tarazona.[25]

"When I visited Ágreda," Señor Echarri wrote then, "and saw the nuns exhausted and in such need of water, I arranged that same day to

FIGURE 14. Interior convent courtyard accesses contemplative prayer garden, as well as vegetable gardens and livestock shelters on property perimeter. Photo by Pedro Antonio Calavia Calvo.

remedy this. The cost was 24,000 reales, and I gave it to the abbess in wheat." With his help, Sor María engaged local engineers who took three months to dig and install aqueducts and underground tunnels along the two-mile distance from the Somera spring to the convent. "Finally, on December 7, 1650, the entire community assembled outside the cloister as the nuns joyfully intoned their gratitude by singing the hymn of the Conception," Señor Echarri wrote about the incident years later. "Then the water flowed to the convent and it has not stopped since."[26]

Despite the irregularity of the parcel of land deeded to the convent, architects and scholars through today have praised the form and function of the monastic facility and its church. They note the cruciform shape of the church, patterned after Vignola's Gesù of Rome, the perfect square of the

FIGURE 15. Convent of the Conception, on the outskirts of Ágreda, offers three arched public entrances (far left) to its church and reception area. Photo by Pedro Antonio Calavia Calvo.

cloister embracing its central courtyard, and the ample external corrals and gardens. Latter-day seventeenth-century architects considered the facility as a model convent and cited many other Conceptionist convents influenced by the Ágreda design and construction.

Along the exterior as viewed from the street, visitors first see the long garden walls and sturdy eight-feet-tall stone parapets punctuated with brick pillars every ten to twelve feet and topped with iron spears. These walls run the length of the church—which is situated parallel to the street lengthwise—and along the visitor's entrance to the convent. Then the walls angle inward to enclose the rest of the building and grounds. Above the walls, the church's dual bell tower looms above its vaulted nave and apse, as well as the second story of the cloister.

Clearly Sor María designed the convent to protect the austere and contemplative life of its nuns. Yet, she also foresaw the facility's commerce, over time, with the outside world. Indeed, some of her contemporaries said that Sor María had an uncanny ability to see into the future, as well as to cure the sick through her knowledge of medicines and to forecast the time of people's deaths despite medical opinions to the contrary.[27] Not surprising, then, is that during the course of construction, Sor María very pragmatically envisioned visitors' and workers' ingress and egress to the convent and its grounds.

A narrow entry between the street wall and the church allows access by carriage or foot to the church's three iron-gated entrances, semicircular arches fanned with brickwork set in lime and sand. Farther along this path is a matching arched doorway opening to the convent's vestibule for visitors. Beyond that is a gated access to the convent's granaries and stores.

Despite the cloistered nature of the convent, Sor María envisioned many visitors arriving along the access path to the church and convent, for which she specified measurements and construction materials. While this may have been excessive for the farmers' carts engaged in the collection and distribution of grain at the time, just ten years after the completion of the entire complex, the royal messengers of King Felipe IV would many times traverse this corridor.

At the fourth door—then and now—visitors are greeted by a lay housekeeper who ushers them into one of two visiting rooms featuring an inset grille in the wall through which they converse with the nuns in the adjacent room beyond the wall. If something is to pass between them, it is set on a tray in another opening in the wall and passed from one to the other by a manual turnstile. One of these visiting rooms features a dining table, at which the nuns feed the poor, with food passed by them to the housekeeper through the turnstile.

Beyond the visiting rooms, or locutorios, are the nuns' offices, archives, library, chapel, and dining hall as well as access to all the functional areas such as the coal bunker, corral, gardens, and henhouses. The dining hall is an austere yet impressive room with vaulted ceilings, massive weight-bearing beams, windows beginning at a height of four feet, and a baroque pulpit for spiritual readings during meals. Other areas include the kitchen, bakery, larder, workroom, laundry room, as well as a separate house for the housekeeper and a hospice for the sick. Many interior areas feature polished brickwork flooring, cast in stone wherever possible, for its long-term durability.[28]

The second story consists of the nuns' sleeping cells—small individual square rooms—each furnished with a humble sleeping cot, a small table and stool, and white walls decorated solely with a crucifix. The sparsely spaced windows along the first and second story of the convent are all encased, according to the Conceptionist charter, by iron grilles.

"It is one of the most unique, accommodating, tidy and well-adorned monasteries that it is possible to desire for the needs of Discalced Religious," wrote Ximénez Samaniego, describing the beautiful church, extensive choirs, the isolated platforms for prayer, and all the necessary office and visiting rooms.[29]

The atmosphere in which Sor María attended to the final phases of construction could not have been more upended. Gunpowder blasts punctuated her days, while the Lady in Blue's notoriety in the wake of Padre Benavides's visit spread throughout the cloister, the village, and beyond. Nevertheless, she studiously attended to her spiritual and administrative duties as abbess, as the beautiful new church emerged under her supervision.

One day during early evening prayers—before the nuns had formally moved into the new convent—Sor María startled the other women by instructing them to immediately send for the construction foreman, a monk assigned to the position by Padre de la Torre. In turn, Sor María hurried to the small locutorio to await him.

A wall that had just gone up, she anxiously told him, had been weakened, perhaps by the blasting, and might collapse at any time, injuring the workers. He must tear it down immediately, she said, and replace it. The amazed monk checked the wall and found her assessment to be accurate. Later, Padre de la Torre asked Sor María how she knew this, not having been on-site. Her guardian angel, she told him, had transported her to the corrupt wall, at which she soon saw the danger.[30]

This, and another remarkable event during the same period further added to the lively stories of her bilocations to America and caused her in later years to clarify her perceptions of angels and the nature of her visions.

Ágreda's governor of arms, a nobleman who periodically visited the convent, recounted the other event. According to him, Sor María's compassion was stirred by the case of a notorious Moor, imprisoned in a castle in Pamplona. She prayed for the Moor, telling nuns and visitors alike that he was a creature made in the image and likeness of God. When the governor had occasion to visit the Moor in Pamplona, the prisoner told him he had been catechized by a nun who visibly came to the castle to pray with him and teach him. Further, he said, she had inspired him to seek baptism in the Church of Our Lady of Miracles in Ágreda and to take the Christian name of Francis.[31]

The governor arranged for the Moor's baptism in Ágreda. Many local and church dignitaries attended, after which a group took the newly baptized man to the original Convent of the Conception, as the new one was still under construction. Just as they approached the open doorway, three nuns walked by—unawares—with their veils lifted.

"Is this the one who converted you?" he was asked.[32]

"No," he said of the first nun, "but her attire is similar."

"No," he said of the second, but when the third nun passed, he exclaimed, "It's her! It's her!"

At the behest of her superiors, the experiment was repeated and recorded—this time with all the nuns of the community.

"Not her," he repeated time after time, until Sor María appeared.

"Look, look," he exclaimed, "this is the one." Then he addressed her personally. "Tell me," he asked, "how could you remain here in the convent, and also come to Pamplona to convert me while I was locked up in the castle?" According to the account, Sor María did not respond.

"Gentlemen," the amazed Moor cried out, "this is the nun who appeared to me in Pamplona and converted me."

The parish baptismal records were later amended to reflect his claim, crediting his conversion to Sor María's appearances and teaching.

Meanwhile, under the hands of the two primary craftsmen, Pedro Pérez and Juan de la Llama, the convent church grew in a structure and ornamentation reminiscent of Renaissance temples, most notably Vignola's Gesù of Rome. Housed in a cruciform shape, the interior headboard is rectangular and straight, following the lines of Madrid's Basilica of Saint Lawrence at El Escorial. It was a similarity noticed by many, including— ten years later—by King Felipe IV whose grandfather had masterminded the construction of El Escorial.

The richly laden altar rises for two stories upon tiers of golden pillars. At the highest peak rises the crucified Savior in the embrace of the Holy Spirit and surrounded by angels and saints. Yet in the center of the altarpiece, above the tabernacle, blue as the strips of sea and sky etched into the ceilings, with rays of gold bursting from behind, stands the statue of the Heavenly Queen in radiant, azure peace. The vaulted

FIGURE 16. Main altar and vaulted ceiling of convent church. Altar features Mary in its center, set beneath her son, the crucified Christ. Photo courtesy of Convent of the Conception, Ágreda.

FIGURE 17. Communion grille connects convent interior and monastic nuns of Ágreda with congregants attending Mass in convent church. Photo by author.

ceilings—ovals bursting atop porticos spiraling heavenward—are etched with raised circles, ovals, and diamonds pulling the spirit upward in a geometric motif.

At the rear of the church, the lower choir is situated behind the floor-to-ceiling grille, and an upper choir abuts a grand and resonant organ. The ornamentally carved wooden choir stalls especially delighted Sor María, who had selected the master carpenter with Padre de la Torre.

Finally, with the installation of the stained glass windows, Pedro Pérez and Juan de la Llama had but to complete the altar steps before the seven-year-long effort was complete. Years of notations in the book of construction expenses detailed the many stonemasons and artisans who participated in the project. When expenses doubled, so, too, did the alms forthcoming from the gentry as well as those less fortunate.

"The whole clergy, nobility and commoners gave their assistance," wrote an elderly Ágredan widow to her granddaughter about the inspiring collective efforts of all involved. Donations and labor poured in when needed, from rich and poor, men and women alike, even the sick and disabled. The full cost amounted to 22,213 ducats and 19 maravedis, much of it contributed as the construction occurred, with some obligations left over that the convent absorbed as debt and paid over time.[33]

Yet when the time came to tally the figures and mete out final payments, which would have increased that figure, Pedro Pérez and Juan de la Llama were nowhere to be found, having quietly left without collecting their pay. The intrigue left in their wake led many people to conclude that these dedicated workers—who had been with the project since the beginning—were angels.[34] Aside from the lore of the construction's completion by supernatural means, the new convent was certainly blessed by the "miraculous" generosity of many.

Indeed, the entire town shared in the joy of the convent's completion. A holiday spirit permeated Ágreda on July 10, 1633. People gathered for the procession beginning at the original convent on the Road of the Knights and proceeded to the new convent's church on the edge of town. At a solemn High Mass, the bishop of Tarazona presided over a packed congregation of locals and visitors, lay and ecclesiastics alike. Later, the townspeople continued in a fiesta, while the nuns happily relocated to their new home.[35]

There in the spacious new convent in the shadow of Moncayo Mountain, Sor María continued to experience increasing urgency to chronicle the life of Mary. After experiencing repeated apparitions and revelations from the Virgin—which would continue throughout the abbess's life—Sor María answered the powerful calling. Encompassing almost twenty-seven hundred pages in the original, *Mystical City of God* would inspire many over the centuries, despite endangering Sor María during her own lifetime and perhaps costing her the mantle of sainthood, at least as of this writing in the early twenty-first century.

PART THREE

BIOGRAPHER OF THE
HEAVENLY QUEEN

1635

CHAPTER 9

"A knowledge of light, holy, sweet and pure"

AT TIMES, SOR MARÍA'S POWERFUL SPIRITUAL DYNAMISM
seemed endless. Her energy manifested itself in the courage and leadership needed to oversee the design and construction of the new convent
and church and the organization of the spiritual exercises and well-
being of those in her charge. That completed, she reflexively retreated
inward, and as she did so, the call to chronicle the life of Mary persisted
and increased.

Clearly, Sor María realized that it was one thing to revel in her inter-
nal life of prayer and extraordinary insights, and it was another altogether to write it down for all to read, including the ever-present eyes
of the Inquisition. Understandably, it was a call to which she did not feel
immediately able to respond. "I resisted this undertaking many years,"
she admitted, "not having the boldness to attempt the execution of something so far above all my powers."[1]

Too, the years in question were not quiet ones. News abounded in
Spain and beyond of the abbess's supernatural visits to the New World.
Benavides sought her out from America during the multiyear construction of the new convent. Franciscan officials, intrigued with her unusual
experiences, found new reason to visit Ágreda. Even the king heard
reports of Sor María's mystical visions.

In 1635 the Holy Office in Madrid opened an inquiry about Sor María's bilocation accounts, relegated to a category the Inquisition labeled as *lo maravilloso*, or "sensational marvels" potentially attributable to witchcraft. Officials in Logroño—between Burgos and Ágreda—were delegated by the Madrid office to determine whether "the nun at Ágreda . . . goes into [ecstatic] trances in public, whether she hands out crosses and [rosary] beads [to the Indians, and if so] what sort of divine grace she says they confer."[2]

Fortunately, Padre de la Torre was one of the four people assigned to give statements about her. As an Inquisition examiner in his own right, and Sor María's confessor, his testimony held great weight. Protectively, he and the Logroño examiners decided to minimize the possibility of Sor María's physical bilocations as the Lady in Blue, as well as her ecstatic levitation. In doing so, rather than exploring the possibility of a miraculous phenomenon, they maintained a low profile with the intention of getting the inquiry dropped for lack of substance. Their strategy was effective, and no charges were made.[3] It was a warning, nevertheless, that sent shivers of well-founded dread through Sor María. Her file as the Lady in Blue was now on record, albeit minimally for the time, and would menacingly resurface in 1650. While the Inquisition's incidence of executions had lessened over time, excommunication—an agonizing threat to someone as dedicated to the church as Sor María—was still a risk.

"In this tribulation I cried to the Lord with all my heart," she wrote during this period, at the onset of her work on Mary's biography, "if it be his will that I should be freed from this danger and burden."[4]

Obscurity, however, was not a luxury accorded to Sor María. As the number of visitors to the cloister increased, accounts of her spiritual experiences inspired the religious aspirations of well-to-do noblemen and noblewomen from throughout Spain. Inevitably, her list of correspondents grew to include high-level politicians, such as Don Fernando de Borja, viceroy of Aragón and Valencia, and his influential son, both of whom befriended her throughout their lives.[5] And equally natural was that many noblewomen applied for admittance to the Ágreda cloister, further increasing enrollment in the new convent as well as the responsibilities of its renowned abbess. These included widows, mothers, nieces, and confidantes of important dukes, members of the court, military officers, and church officials, as well as rich and titled women in their own right.[6]

The call to write the life of the Virgin, however, did not subside. Sor María discussed it numerous times with Padre de la Torre, albeit not without her own version of shy manipulation. "Frequently [I] tried to prevent my superiors from being moved by any accounts of my interior experiences, disguising, as much as I could, many things, and in tears begging the Lord . . . [that] the very thought of allowing me to engage in this enterprise would fade from their minds."[7] In retrospect, this could well have been a premonition of the many heartaches she would endure after writing the book and being ordered to burn it more than once.

At the time, however, it became not only an issue of being true to herself and to her devotion to Mary, but also to her very vows of obedience as a nun. "[Even the] encouragement of the holy angels," Sor María wrote, "would not have been urgent enough to rouse my will to an enterprise so arduous and foreign, if to them had not been added the motive of obedience to my superiors, who are set to govern my soul and teach me the way of truth."[8]

She prayed for guidance and asked the Divine Mother for help in understanding and surrendering to God's will. She struggled to understand the nature of her visions, and she worried about the return of the exterioridades and, by implication, her safety from misunderstanding. She also relied upon the counsel of Padre de la Torre, who encouraged her to embark upon the task. Not to do so, she realized, could seriously undermine her integrity and her vows as a nun.

"If I remain silent," she finally concluded, "woe is me."[9]

As Sor María surrendered to this new path, she reported Mary's growing presence in her life, sometimes through an interior knowing filled with light and clarity, and sometimes in the sweetest of words spoken in her heart. In this way, the unusual tree of Sor María's soul, when pruned at one site, sent the sap to nourish sprouts in other mystical ways. Once pledged to her new mission, the words poured freely from her heart to her feather quill pen to the sheets of manuscript paper on her desk. So much so that in the first twenty days of her endeavor, she completed Book 1, comprising 326 pages (in later printed form), of the eight-book tome that would become known as *Mystical City of God*.[10]

All of her efforts would not proceed so swiftly, however. The first writing of *Mystical City of God*—begun in 1637—would take eight years to complete, and it would encompass close to twenty-seven

FIGURE 18. Sor María's writing desk and quill with which she wrote *Mystical City of God*. On display in—and image courtesy of—Convent of the Conception, Ágreda.

hundred pages.[11] Yet despite the lengthy project before her, the value of the delay in embarking on the book was not lost on Sor María.

"I believe this was not without the special providence of his Majesty," she wrote, "for in the course of those [earlier] years I would not have been able to preserve the tranquility of spirit, which is necessary for retaining the proper light and information. For not in all states of mind can the soul engage in that exalted activity which is necessary to [under-stand] such exquisite and delicate influences."[12]

Nonetheless, at a very young age, Sor María had been gifted with spiritual insights far beyond her years, and the grace that she felt during these insights buoyed her with a rarefied bliss. Yet, true to her nature, she never took pride in her experiences, always crediting the Lord's infinite generosity. It is a tact we can easily envision her taking with the Jumanos, preaching humility and virtue.

This invaluable understanding about the nature of her visions provides much of the content of the opening chapters of *Mystical City of God*. "Lest I suffer shipwreck in that sea of marvels," she wrote, "the most exalted Lord caused me to feel a virtue . . . strong, sweet, efficacious and gentle; an enlightenment which illumined the intellect . . . tranquilizing, directing, governing and attracting the whole range of interior and exterior senses. . . . [And] the more intellectual the light, so much the more . . . substantial and certain is the knowledge attained."[13]

Unable to maintain this state indefinitely, however, Sor María periodically plunged to the reality of her impoverished humanity. Each time, she interpreted these setbacks as her fault, and they so devastated her that they changed her approach to life. The fear and dread that she experienced in anticipation of the seeming periodic loss of God's friendship became a primary motivating force in her life, to the extent that she grew to consider it her good fortune.

"Ever since I have had the use of reason, I was conscious of especially one blessing, which in my estimation is the greatest of all those bestowed upon me by God's liberality," she wrote. "Namely, a great and penetrating fear, lest I should lose Him. . . . On account of this dread . . . I have in these latter times begun to send up earnest and heartfelt prayers . . . that I may be guided and led along the secure paths hidden from the eyes of men."[14]

The subtle atmosphere of the cloister certainly provided a fertile ground in which to grow the seeds of Sor María's uncommon spiritual gifts. From matin prayers before dawn with her nuns through the soft devotional hymns at evening choir followed by Mass and Communion, she planted herself ever more deeply on the spiritual path. Privately, as she had since her childhood, she also practiced many contemplative devotions and spiritual exercises throughout the day and night. All this served to refine her spiritual understanding and enhance her spiritual sight. She realized that explaining this process to her readers early in the text would be important, so that they might understand the nature of her visions.

"It seemed to me proper to preface this history with an explanatory chapter, describing and explaining," she wrote, "the manner in which the Lord manifested to me these wonders."[15]

In response to her repeated prayers, Sor María reported that the Lord spoke to her soul, promising a refined state of mind and a path of light revealing hidden spiritual treasures. For her part, Sor María was to walk in that path of light and to preserve it by leading a perfect life of virtue. She surrendered wholeheartedly, and the results were immediate.

"I felt a change within me," she wrote, "and a highly spiritualized state of mind. To my understanding was given a new light, which illuminated it and infused into it a knowledge of all things in God. . . . It is a knowledge of light, holy, sweet and pure, subtle, penetrating, sure and agile, causing love of good and hatred of evil."[16]

FIGURE 19. Interior convent hallway leading to Sor María's writing room. Courtesy of Convent of the Conception, Ágreda.

Sor María directed this knowledge and light toward her subject matter, the life of the mother of God. The kaleidoscopic images in her heart and soul blended into a series of unified visions that were crystalline in their clarity and as real to her as the desk at which she sat to write her series of books. Putting these experiences into words, however, was another matter. Like other mystics, she found herself trying to express the inexpressible—citing "a breath of the power of God" and "an emanation of a most subtle light."[17] At times, she felt that to portray her experiences accurately was almost impossible.

With her characteristic empathy for others, Sor María set aside mystical hyperbole to bestow on the reader very specific descriptions of what she "saw" in her visions. Interestingly, descriptions of her rarefied experiences adhere very closely to those of her mystical predecessors, such as Saint John of the Cross and Saint Teresa of Avila.

Simply put, and following in the footsteps of Saint Augustine, Sor María divides her visionary experience into three basic categories.[18] "Corporeal vision" describes the state in which she saw spiritual beings and events with her physical eyes. "Imaginative vision" describes the state in which she saw images in her mind's eye, a state mirrored in many seers' experiences during contemplative prayer. Finally, Sor María describes "intellectual vision," a state in which her mind "saw" or was led to understand many complex spiritual truths.[19]

In this area of intellectual vision, or interior knowing, Sor María's refined intellect and understanding excelled, and this is where she found her greatest surety and comfort. Just as an artist's eye is cultured over time to distinguish among hundreds of shades of blue or seemingly infinite ways of portraying the same concept, Sor María navigated the complex interior realm of the soul with greater and greater understanding over time. Occasionally, however, Sor María reports seeing Mary or angels physically. These events were challenging to explain because in the case of angels—as she testified to the Inquisition years later—seeing a spiritual being with physical eyes is impossible.

"The angels are an abstract species," she told the Inquisitors. "They are made of a spiritual substance. So God gives an intellectual understanding of them, endowing a certainty that the one communicating to me is an angel. . . . At other times, [even though] we cannot see a spirit with our physical sight, because it has no materiality, sometimes . . . the angels take on more of an aerial body, which *is* possible to see."[20] By way of example, Sor María wrote, "I saw on a certain day six angels whom the Almighty had appointed to assist and guide me. . . . His Majesty gave to my interior being a new light . . . by which I was made capable [of] . . . seeing and understanding [them]."[21]

In her own self-effacing way, Sor María describes the layers of understanding in her visions. What most people would interpret as the most impressive vision—that is, the corporeal—she describes as "inferior." Whereas the more spiritual or intellectual vision she describes as more exalted and taking place in the superior part of the soul.

"Thus, when I see and recognize the Queen and . . . the holy angels, [when] I see them in themselves, I descend to a lower grade of knowledge . . . [despite] feeling the divine effects, which each one excites in the soul."[22]

In contrast, regarding intellectual vision, she writes effusively, describing an unwavering and illuminated confidence in her interior knowing, which today many spiritual teachers might describe as an inner voice of certainty, albeit one all too seldom heeded. "The Most High animates the intellect by a certain subtlety and light, thus adapting it for the exalted knowledge . . . [which is] accompanied by certainty. Faith," she takes care to emphasize, "accompanies the vision and the Omnipotent gives to the soul power to appreciate the value of the knowledge and the light."[23]

Even with such clarification, however, inevitably over the lifetime of a mystic distinctions sometimes blur and human error occurs. "Often it happens," Sor María admits, "that the enlightenments pass through all these channels and conduits in succession: the Lord gives the intelligence or light, the most holy Virgin reveals it to me and the angels express it to me in words. . . . It also happens, that I receive only the understanding of things, and then I am left to find for myself the terms which befit that which I hold in the intelligence. In finding these terms I may err . . . for I am only an ignorant woman."[24] In this way, Sor María wends her way through esoteric spiritual terrain, hoping to have prepared the reader to use his or her own discernment in absorbing the material.

These distinctions, however, were lost on some of Sor María's critics, many of whom overscrupulously reverted to a passage in chapter 1 of the first book, which states that readers may consider it "not mere opinions or contemplations, but reliable truth." The 1912 English translation even punctuates the end of this paragraph with an animated "Thus speaks the Lord God Almighty!" as though the last sentence were God's dogmatic pronouncement.[25] In the original, however, that sentence was not a direct quote; it was a statement that—in the context of all her other clarifications—could just as well have meant "this is what I was led by God to believe."

Understandably, her critics might have been so shocked by the emphasis in this dramatic passage, original or translation notwithstanding, that they overlooked the qualifier earlier in the same paragraph, that Sor María engaged in her writing "as far as [her] shortcomings allow." In her all-too-human attempts to portray a divine message, Sor María many times emphasizes the potential for human error. Her innate humility emerges many times throughout the text, where she periodically refers to herself as a "mere terrestrial creature,"[26] a "lowly worm" or "vile wormlet of the earth and the least of his creatures,"[27] making allowances for error yet bravely forging forward.

To accommodate such visionaries, the Catholic Church has traditionally acknowledged the value of private revelations, while clearly distinguishing them from theological doctrine or public revelations as sanctioned in the Bible. Private revelations, according to this position, are offered to all for the inspiration that might be gleaned from individual discernment of the passages, without obligating the reader to any particular conclusion.

This pragmatic approach encourages the inspirational value of mystical writings, while allowing for human error that might be represented in common perceptions of specific historic eras. Thus Sor María's readers today can embrace her spiritual insights without feeling conflicted about inferring as infallible many of her outdated seventeenth-century conceptions of the physical universe or even her well-meaning estimates of specific ages and times in Mary's life, which enrich the flavor of the text. "Let those who thirst come to the living waters," Sor María wrote, inviting her readers to find their own truth in the story of Mary's life. "Let those that are seeking for the light, follow it to the end."[28]

Yet when Sor María finally set her feather quill pen to paper to chronicle the life of Mary, she had no notion about the format of the final product. She had no outline, no publisher lined up, no market analysis at her elbow ready to show to Padre de la Torre, and no public relations plan to launch once the book went to press. She had no idea about

FIGURE 20. *Mística Ciudad de Dios* original bound document, opened to cover page. Book set atop original correspondence between King Felipe IV of Spain and Sor María of Ágreda. Picture placed manually on opposing page by author. Photo by author.

the length of the book, how many times she would write it after being ordered to burn it, or what impact it would have on future generations.

She did, however, in contemplating her mission, grasp the scope of her calling to portray the life of Mary. This responsibility weighed heavily upon her, to chronicle the life of the Heavenly Queen from beginning to end. Mary's life, after all, bracketed the life of her son and the Savior of mankind, Jesus Christ. Mary's life would therefore embrace the life, passion, and death of her son and the redemption he offered to the world. Sor María was intimidated by this daunting task, and no doubt the Inquisition's role in evaluating it, but once she accepted her calling she wholeheartedly surrendered to it.

As Sor María plunged into the story of the life of Mary, she symbolically portrayed the mother of Jesus as the womb or mystical city of God that nurtured her son. The title page of the book, as published posthumously in Madrid in 1670, encompassed over one hundred words:

Mystical City of God
The Miracle of His Omnipotence and the Abyss of His Grace
The Divine History and Life of the Virgin Mother of God,
Our Queen and Our Lady, Most Holy Mary,
Expiatrix of the Fault of Eve and Mediatrix of Grace.

Manifested in these later ages by that Lady
to her handmaid Sister Mary of Jesus,
Superioress of the convent of the Immaculate Conception
of the town of Ágreda, of the province of Burgos in Spain,
under obedience to the regular observance of the seraphic father
    Saint Francis,
for new enlightenment of the world, for rejoicing of the Catholic
    Church,
and encouragement of men.[29]

CHAPTER 10

"A most beautiful . . . Queen, crowned with the stars"

SOR MARÍA'S SEMINAL VISION OF MARY IS OFTEN INFUSED
with meditative images from the book of Apocalypse as attributed to
Saint John the Evangelist. Frequently throughout the text of *Mystical
City of God*, out of deference to both her readers and spiritual adviser,
as well as to the watchful eye of the Inquisition, she took care to cite the
Biblical sources of her inspirations. As she opened Book 1, she described
a deep state of contemplative prayer, "an enlightenment which illumined
the intellect . . . tranquilizing the whole range of interior and exterior
senses."[1] In this state she described her vision of Mary, citing an oft-
quoted passage of the book of Apocalypse.

"Presently I saw a most precious veil covering a treasure," she wrote,
"and my heart burned with desire to . . . look upon the sacred mystery
which I understood was hidden beneath. . . . [Then] the veil fell entirely
and my interior eyes saw . . . a great and mysterious sign in heaven. I
saw a Woman, a most Beautiful Lady and Queen, crowned with the stars,
clothed with the sun, and the moon was at her feet" (Apocalypse 12:1).[2]

This dazzling image evolved into Sor María's representation of Mary,
and it was further infused with Saint John's imagery later in the book of
Apocalypse. John "saw a new heaven and a new earth . . . the holy city,
New Jerusalem, coming down out of heaven from God, made ready as a

bride adorned for her husband" in gold and countless jewels (Apocalypse 21:1–3, 18).[3]

In Sor María's heart, she equated this image with Mary. As the Mother of God, Sor María reasoned, Mary provided a dwelling for Christ in her womb, just as John described the city of Jerusalem as "the dwelling of God with men" (Apocalypse 21:3). Thus the New Jerusalem became to Sor María an enduring metaphor for Mary, and she began to refer to Mary as a "mystical" Jerusalem, coining the title phrase for her book, *Mystical City of God*.

Sor María wrote eloquently about Mary as the New Jerusalem, clarifying that "all her gifts, her greatness and virtues are the cause of new wonder to the saints. New also, because She came after all the ancient Fathers, Patriarchs and prophets, and in Her were renewed and accomplished all their clamors, their prophecies and promises. New, because she came without the contagion of guilt and under a new dispensation from the law of sin. New because she entered into the world triumphant over sin, the devil and the first deceit, thus being the greatest new event since its beginning."[4] Sor María additionally interpreted the moment of the New Jerusalem's coming down from heaven as an eternal moment depicting "the creation of Mary by the hand of the Almighty."[5]

This creation represented to Sor María the spiritual—or immaculate—conception of Mary, and it held great personal and religious meaning for Sor María's family. They had, after all, donated their ancestral home to the church and founded in it a cloistered monastic convent under Santa Beatriz de Silva's Order of the Immaculate Conception. Scant years later, Sor María had built an entirely new facility and an attached church, earning for herself the title of founder, alongside her parents. The beginning of the Blessed Mother's biography, therefore, would open not with Mary's early life, but rather with the very nature of Mary's earthly and spiritual conception.

The doctrine of Mary as the Immaculate Conception, while certainly popular in seventeenth-century Spain, would not be pronounced by the church officially as dogma until 1854, long after Sor María's death. Although this doctrine about Mary's sinlessness had gained popular support in the church since AD 850, the topic was not without controversy, in seventeenth-century Spain and worldwide.

"Only Christ was born without sin," argued some, "it is contrary to our need for Christ's redemption." "Yet," countered others, "the Immaculate Conception is an important sign of God's presence within us."

Discussions about the Immaculate Conception so animated seventeenth-century Spaniards that present-day Marian scholars still cite Sor María's era as having a pivotal impact upon the instatement of the doctrine. Then, "Maculists" and "Immaculists" churned out over twelve thousand pamphlets on every aspect of the issue surrounding Mary's sinlessness from the instant her parents conceived her, not to be confused with the virgin birth of Christ. For Sor María's part, she devoted over 260 pages of Book 1 of *Mystical City of God* to the period of time preceding Mary's birth.

A few years later, after King Felipe IV of Spain learned more about the extraordinary mystic in Ágreda, he obtained his own copy of her manuscript incrementally, as it was being written. In their correspondence, Sor María urged the king to approach two successive popes, Innocent X and Alexander VII, on behalf of the Immaculate Conception. The king did so, making it an affair of state. He formed a special council headed by a prestigious Spanish bishop whom he named as ambassador to the Holy See, and he sent continual emissaries to Rome to advocate for the doctrine.

To this day, Marian scholars credit Sor María of Ágreda and King Felipe IV with favorably influencing Pope Alexander VII on the doctrine. According to these scholars, Alexander VII's 1661 decree is considered the turning point in the evolution of the Immaculate Conception. Many consider it the definitive statement on the doctrine until it was fully established by Pope Pius IX in 1854.

Even now, the Spanish Plaza in Rome is a must-see each year in December. There, prominently displayed atop the center column, is a statue of Mary as the Immaculate Conception. Each December it is lavished with flowers, a celebrated reminder of Mary's loyal Spanish advocates, which every pope visits each year on the feast day of the Immaculate Conception.[6]

In 1637, however, the controversy still raged, and Sor María walked a fine line in portraying the conception of the Heavenly Queen. Little did she realize that her description, while deeply inspired, would provide such fodder for theologians for centuries to come and perhaps be a leading cause for the continual delays in naming her a saint.

"[Mary] was a new creature from the heaven of the divine mind," Sor María wrote, emblazoned with devotion for the Heavenly Mother.[7] And while descriptions of the physical and spiritual aspects of Mary's conception absorbed equal space in her text, the humble nun also ventured to describe the material manner of Mary's "first Conception . . . namely . . . that of the most pure body of Mary."[8] Of course, Sor María was not indiscreet in her descriptions, yet for a seventeenth-century female writer, also a cloistered woman of the cloth living according to the vows of poverty, chastity, and obedience, it was unquestionably a daring move.

"The conception happened according to the ordinary course of nature," she wrote, enraging theologians at the Sorbonne for decades to come, "[yet it] was nevertheless directed, supplemented and perfected by the action of divine grace, without disturbing the proper effect due to the law of nature."[9]

According to Sor María—no doubt informed by popular apocryphal gospels circulating at the time—Mary's parents, Anne and Joachim, were twenty-four and forty years of age, respectively, when they married. Yet twenty years passed, and the couple had no children. Anne, according to most accounts, was sterile, while Joachim supposedly was not. "The father was not naturally sterile," Sor María wrote, "yet on account of his age and moderation, his natural powers were in a measure suppressed and weakened."[10]

While careful to state that the couple was modest and brief in their physical coupling, Sor María gingerly asserted that it had taken place so that Mary's physical body was formed from the healthy and highly refined physiologies of her parents.[11] She did not introduce this subject lightly.

Refinement, Sor María knew, was a matter of degree. Just as polished marble is finer than common clay, just as the song of a nightingale is sweeter than the warble of a wren, just as a faceted diamond is more brilliant than crystal, so too humans—while all equal in the eyes of God—embody varying degrees of talent and refinement. The spiritual refinement of Mary's parents, Sor María knew, had a definite impact on the nature of their daughter's soul. In addition, Sor María clarified how the physical material of their union applied to the growing body and spirit of their child.

"The parents were so entirely governed by grace and withdrawn from concupiscence and . . . imperfections . . . which induce original sin," she wrote, "that [they] furnished a material exempt from imperfection . . . [and] free from sin . . . even if divine Providence had not previously arranged every particular of this event."[12] Presaging the mechanics of inherited genetics while always crediting God, Sor María continued, "The Most High . . . permit[ted] only what was strictly required according to nature, in order that the proper material might be furnished for the formation of the most perfect substance within the limits of a mere creature."[13]

This was miraculous in itself, Sor María acknowledged, because of Anne's sterility. "The faculties and the material were of the natural order," she wrote, "but the manner of moving them happened by the miraculous power of the Divinity."[14]

This insight led Sor María to further distinguish between the physical and spiritual aspects of Mary's conception. In this way, building upon the understanding of revered thirteenth-century doctor of theology Saint Thomas Aquinas, Sor María described the first stage of Mary's conception as physical and the all-important next stage as spiritual.

Mary's "first"—or physical—conception, Sor María wrote, though natural in every way, was "supplemented and perfected by the action of divine grace, without disturbing the proper effect due to the law of nature." In both the mother and the father, Sor María concluded, "nature and grace concurred."[15] "[Grace] absorbed, yet not confounded nature," she wrote, "exalting it and perfecting it in a miraculous manner. Thus grace was the origin of this Conception, while it called into its service the activity of nature in so far as was necessary for the birth of that ineffable Daughter from her natural parents."[16]

Mary's "second"—or spiritual—conception took place, according to Sor María, in an equally exceptional way, in that the Lord accelerated the physical maturation of the tiny embryo that was to be Mary. "The formation and growth of other human bodies," she wrote, echoing the common understanding of the day appropriated from Saint Thomas, who in turn drew it from Aristotle, "takes many days in order to organize and fit them for the reception of the rational soul. Thus for a manchild are required forty and for females eighty days, more or less, according to the natural heat and disposition of the mothers. In the formation of the virginal body of Mary, the Almighty accelerated the natural time to seven days. Then the Almighty wrought the second Conception by creating the soul of his Mother and infusing it into the body."[17]

In this devotional portrayal of Mary's conception, Sor María envisioned the blessing of the Holy Trinity upon the soul of Mary. The Trinity, she wrote, claimed Mary as "our true Daughter and Spouse and a Mother to the Only begotten of the Father," praising her gifts and grace even above "the brightest seraphim of heaven." And, Sor María continued, Mary was superior to Adam and Eve, "untouched by the darkness of original sin, and blessed with the most perfect use of the light of reason, corresponding to the gifts of grace, which She had received. In every aspect She enjoyed the light, the friendship and the love of the Creator."[18]

Throughout Sor María's endearing presentation of the stages of conception and their duration, her portrayal reflects the common scientific and theological understanding of her era—albeit now archaic—which in turn relied upon the church's "Doctor Angelicus," Saint Thomas Aquinas. Armed with this understanding, and the 1999 Vatican assurance that *Mystical City of God* contains no heresy or error of doctrine, such accounts provide the reader with ample occasion for individual discernment when presented with private revelations such as Sor María's.

In her small convent cell in Ágreda, Sor María confessed her awe of the Heavenly Queen's conception. She was filled with admiration and praise, and she struggled with what she perceived as her inability to express these marvels in mere words. The order of nature had been rearranged, she wrote. Grace had brought about "the formation of a new earth, and of a new heaven (Is. 65, 17) . . . where Divinity presides . . . and whither a thousand angels are delegated to form a guard over a tiny, animated body not larger than that of a little bee."[19]

In the aftermath of the posthumous publication of Sor María's manuscript, many accused her of blasphemously portraying Mary as divine, as standing on an equal footing with God himself. There are ample opportunities throughout her book to form this mistaken impression, should a reader be prone to do so.

"The impetuous floods of the Divinity met in this holy City of the sanctified soul of Mary," Sor María wrote in the work's first volume. There Sor María also described Mary's miraculous and supernatural virtue from the instant of conception, as well as Mary's infused knowledge of the order of all of creation. And Sor María quotes from a vision in which an angel spoke to John the Evangelist, saying that Mary's soul was favored with a "participation of the Divinity and its attributes and perfections." So much so, the angel said, that Mary might appear "as if illumined with the eternal splendor of God."[20]

Indeed, Sor María is consistent in her adulation of Mary throughout the eight books of *Mystical City of God*. Since the set is often written from Mary's point of view, they touchingly portray the loving presence of Mary throughout the painful passion and death of her son. In the volumes entitled *The Incarnation* and *The Transfixion*, Sor María describes Mary as the closest of possible participants in the redemption effected by her son. Sor María's descriptions of Christ's teaching as well as his suffering are replete with images of Mary's tremendous empathetic maternal love, her constant communion with Jesus spiritually, her sharing in his agony, and therefore her considerable role in the redemption offered to humanity.

"The resemblance between Christ and his most holy Mother is clearly manifest," wrote Sor María, describing the shared "sword of sorrow" that "pierced the heart of Son and Mother" in the Garden of Gethsemane, to the extent that Mary was to "concur and cooperate in the Redemption."[21]

So touching is Sor María's portrayal of Mary's maternal love that noted film icon Mel Gibson read *Mystical City of God*, among other references, in preparation for writing his film script for the runaway success *The Passion of the Christ*, released in 2004. Many film critics noted that Gibson's film portrays Christ's passion with a poignant treatment from Mary's point of view, frequently focusing on Mary's magnetically sorrowful eyes as they follow the repeated tortures endured by her son.

There are other notable similarities between Gibson's and Sor María's treatment of the passion. As in the film, *Mystical City of God* describes Mary meeting Jesus on the way to Calvary and Mary's wishing she could die in her son's place. It portrays the insidious presence of Satan throughout the proceedings, the cloths provided to Mary to wipe her son's blood,[22] and the gentle nun's pained descriptions of ceaseless blows battering the Savior and his shredded flesh. In doing so, Sor María provides countless images of Mary's unflinching strength, her motherly love for her son, and the unbreakable though often unspoken bond between them.

By the time the final volume entitled *The Coronation* was written, depicting Mary's life after the death of her son, Sor María describes Mary's ascension to the throne of God and the Trinity's invitation to her to become "absorbed in the abyss of our Divinity."[23] Since Mary's assumption into heaven was not made doctrine by the church until

1950,[24] almost one hundred years after the Immaculate Conception became dogma, once again Sor María demonstrated the visionary nature of her private revelations.

"She seemed another Christ by communication and privilege," Sor María wrote, reasoning that Mary had given Jesus the "form and existence of man."[25]

Despite this and similar accolades, Sor María never shied from clarifying that Mary was a "daughter of Adam and a mere creature" and that all the "splendors of Divinity contained within Her are only a participation" suitable to the woman who was to be his mother.[26] Even the invitation of the Holy Trinity, Sor María clarified, was extended to Mary only "as far as is possible to a mere creature."[27]

This concept of a "mere creature," however, and its potential, is an intrinsic part of the beauty and the inspiration of the biography as revealed to Sor María by Mary. Through Sor María's revelations, as imparted to her by Mary, the readers of *Mystical City of God*—as mere creatures themselves—are invited to participate intimately in not only the story of the redemption, but in its process of sanctity. As Sor María progresses in her text, and shares the revelations of Mary, what emerges clearly is that this is not meant to be a passive experience. By the express invitation of the Blessed Mother, Sor María is invited to engage on the path of spiritual perfection, as is the reader.

CHAPTER 11

"The wounds of love, body and soul"

EVEN A CURSORY READING OF *MYSTICAL CITY OF GOD* REVEALS countless effusive descriptions of Mary that are reminiscent of the soul-stirring litanies of the Blessed Virgin recited by the faithful over the centuries.

"Beloved Mother," Sor María called Mary in her maternal role, also "Mother of Grace," "Blessed Mother," "Sweetest Mother," "Holy Mother," "Mother of Piety," "Mother of God," "Mother of Wisdom," "Mother of the God of Love," "Virgin Mother of Christ," "Spouse and Mother of the Word."[1]

In evoking these loving images of Mary, Sor María shows the ever-widening embrace of the Blessed Mother's unbounded maternal love, to include not only her son but all of humanity. Sor María's devotion rose proportionately with these revelations, and her descriptions of Mary rose accordingly. She described Mary as the "Blessed Lady," the "Great Lady," the "Most Holy Mary," and the "Most Blessed Virgin."[2]

Then, as the story of Mary's life unfolded before the eyes of Sor María's soul, Mary's role expanded even further. After the death and resurrection of Christ, Mary's role in the church continued, alongside that of the apostles. So potent did Sor María perceive Mary at that time in the Blessed Mother's life that she described her as "Mistress and Queen of the

Church," even "the only strong Woman of the Church."[3] Later, Mary rose in Sor María's estimation to the stature of "Heavenly Queen," "Mistress of the World," "Powerful Queen," "Invincible Queen," "Great Queen of the Angels," "Queen of all creation," and "Mistress of the Universe."[4]

Loving hyperbole notwithstanding, one of the most essential and optimistic of Mary's roles as portrayed by Sor María is that of spiritual teacher. Essential because spiritual seekers most often benefit from guidance. Optimistic because Mary clearly stated—as did her son—that all people have the potential for spiritual perfection. "If thou and the rest of the souls are solicitous in imitating me," Mary told her, "the Most High will produce in thee the same effects as in myself."[5]

In this way, the entirety of Mary's life served as an uplifting example to Sor María and all of humankind. Portraying this example and modeling her life after it was Sor María's primary directive in writing the biography of Mary, which included the life of her son. Yet Mary counseled Sor María not to be content to "strive after the love of God and salvation of herself alone." Perfection, which Mary assured Sor María was entirely possible and expected, required that Sor María work on behalf of other souls, implying the publishing of her writing to help bring about the inspiration of others.[6]

Testimony abounds throughout the centuries that Sor María was successful in accomplishing these goals. A short eight years after her death, she was named a venerable of the church, in honor of her own "heroic life of virtue." Then, after countless prepublication reviews of the manuscript of *Mystical City of God,* the first Spanish edition was launched in Madrid in 1670. Since then, the hundreds of thousands of readers— worldwide—of the many reprints and editions of *Mystical City of God* in numerous languages have commented on the work's great impact on their spiritual lives.

"Venerable María of Ágreda is instrumental in a much deeper level of conversion in me," states one advocate in London. "She increased my faith in general, and my devotion to the Blessed Virgin Mary in particular."[7] "No other book, except the Bible," avows an aeronautics engineer in California, "has ever written down as much truth in one place for others to read. I hope for her sainthood."[8]

In the process of unveiling Mary's exemplary life, Sor María felt privileged to portray many of the sacramental and spiritual mysteries abounding in Mary's experiences and those of her son. Sor María

FIGURE 21. Frontispiece of first published edition in 1670 of *Mystical City of God* featuring Duns Scotus (lower left) and Sor María (lower right) with Mary (top center) poised over Jerusalem. In convent archives. Courtesy of Convent of the Conception, Ágreda.

accomplishes this through her rich and detailed descriptions of the main events in the life of Mary and Jesus, wonderfully augmenting those that are represented in the New Testament of the Bible. Thus the reader shares in the behind-the-scenes portraits painted by Sor María through Mary, from the presentation of Mary at the temple, Joseph's feelings at Mary's virgin pregnancy, and the Holy Family's flight to Egypt, all the way through Christ's public and private life and death and Mary's own assumption into heaven.

In addition, in Sor María's visions of Mary, she felt that she was given specific instructions about many areas related to her own spiritual path and the path of all Christians who aspired to union with God. These included pragmatic and inspiring guidelines on Sor María's religious life—her vows of poverty, chastity, and obedience—as well as considerable enlightened insight on the nature of divine love, the role of suffering, the path of virtue, the gifts of the Holy Spirit, the theological mysteries, and more.

When occasionally throughout *Mystical City of God* Sor María shared some of her own personal history, she recounted instructive dialogues she had with Mary. Frequently she expressed to Mary her fears and insecurities about her duties as abbess, as well as the challenge of chronicling the life of the Blessed Mother. She also asked Mary specific questions about matters of faith that troubled or confused her. To these Mary offered personal—though universally applicable—guidance to the young nun.

"Do not smother divine love in anxiety," Mary advised the often distraught nun, in practical terms that might well augment today's psychotherapy.[9] Ultimately, Sor María set aside her misgivings and mainly thrived in both the administration of the convent, as well as in writing the biography of Mary, but she was always happiest as a disciple studying at the feet of the Heavenly Queen.

In turn, "the Queen and Mother of Mercy promised," Sor María wrote, "[that] she would instruct me how to model my life after her own."[10] Indeed, before the end of Book 1 of *The Conception*, Mary began instructing her pupil regularly at the end of most chapters. These sections, often entitled "Instruction given by the Queen of Heaven," served as supplements to the actual story of Mary's life, and they provided countless guiding insights that Sor María was to share with spiritual aspirants throughout the world through her writing.

Throughout the text as well as the instruction sections, Mary's spirit mentored her pupil and the reader on many interrelated gifts of body and soul, even the mystical gifts of inner light and vision. The clarity of intuitive vision, Sor María learned, overflowed from the glory of a quiet and devout soul. By purifying the senses, Mary taught her, the body is "assimilated to the soul." And by repelling "all activity or passivity hurtful and destructive of the body . . . the body becomes glorious, clear, incorruptible, agile and subtle."[11]

Very apt to Sor María's own experiences, Mary taught her the importance of deep inner silence to the visionary process. "Revelations demand a very excellent predisposition," Mary told her. "God does not communicate them, except when the soul is in the state of quiet and peace."[12] In the process of attaining a peaceful quietness, Mary advised a retreat from the sensible world and a divestment of even the "odor" of sin, thus creating a state of purity and sanctification.[13] "In that most happy state," Mary instructed her, "[souls] cannot be imperfect or opposed to the will of God. [Rather, this gift] disposes the body to receive the light and at the same time to give it forth."[14]

Despite Sor María's heightened spiritual attainment, she always felt that she had a long way to go. Short of attaining the beatific vision of God—which she never claimed herself but attributed to Mary—Sor María reveled in her raptures, welcomed her intellectual visions, and always embraced the tasks before her with wholehearted fervor. Yet she frequently endured periods when she felt abandoned by the presence or light of God in her soul. And she was subject throughout her life to a cornucopia of illnesses and physical maladies that would have felled a weaker woman. During these periods, she focused on her administrative duties, cared for the nuns in her charge, and relentlessly applied herself to the manuscript of *Mystical City of God*. This was difficult to do, however, without experiencing self-doubt and discouragement and her own personal dark night of the soul.[15]

At times like this, she felt as though her faculties were disturbed and her writing impaired, a state about which authors have complained throughout the centuries. "I cannot find words," Sor María wrote, "to explain what I see and conceive."[16] In turn, Mary's spirit regularly reassured Sor María when doubts or lack of confidence assailed the nun. "I assure thee of His protection," Mary said, "and of the power of his divine arm to direct thee and guide all thy actions toward perfection."[17]

An apt pupil, Sor María generally took heart from this encouragement and made a special effort to stay open to the knowledge and understanding imparted through her visions. In them, Sor María was especially
receptive to Mary's language of the heart.

In that the heart is often called the seat of love, and many consider
the heart to be the seat of spirituality, it is no mystery that the language
of religious mystics is replete with the language of love. Expressing
the inexpressible, however, has long been the bane of author and artist alike. Describing love and its nature is perhaps at the pinnacle of
this challenge.

Romantic love is sometimes portrayed with an image of a man and
a woman gazing devotedly into each other's eyes. Unconditional love is
easily evoked by the image of a mother tenderly cradling her newborn.
Definitions and descriptions of love abound—love at first sight, puppy
love, unrequited love, love lost, love of country, love of neighbor, love-
lorn, love child, lovesick, love-torn, love bird.

Divine love, on the other hand, has traditionally been more difficult
to characterize. "The soul is itself no longer," Teresa of Avila wrote. "It is
always inebriated . . . as if a living love of God . . . made a new beginning
in it."[18] Saint John of the Cross, Teresa's contemporary, in describing the
"spiritual betrothal" of the soul to God and the "living flame of love,"
said that "in this state God and soul are united as the window is with the
light or the coal with the fire."[19]

Scant decades later, about 150 miles northeast of Avila, Sor María
caught and carried the torch of her spiritual forebears and blazed new
paths in the process. In *Mystical City of God* she described eruptions of
the "vast volcano of God's love," the "wounds of love, body and soul,"
and the "sweet and attractive pain of love . . . that the more it prevails
the more it is sought."[20]

As Sor María chronicled Mary's life through mystical visions and
private revelations from the Mother of Jesus, she devotedly portrayed
Mary's boundless love for her son. "Life of my soul and Soul of my life,
the Sustenance of all my joy of living," Mary serenaded her son in prayers
that were like "scarlet lace, with which She bound and secured his love."[21]

To effectively invite this love, in her personal instructions to Sor
María throughout *Mystical City of God*, Mary frequently encouraged
Sor María to "dilate her heart."[22] This proved to be timeless counsel on
many levels.

Modern-day medicine and technology abound with examples of the usefulness of dilation. In optometry, eyedrops dilate the pupil of the eye so that a doctor may examine its health. In photography, lens aperture adjustments on a camera allow for varying levels of light in a photograph. More pointedly, in cardiology the healthy dilation of blood vessels and arteries facilitates the essential flow of blood in and out of the heart. In Sor María's day, the concept of dilation was more metaphorical, yet no less meaningful.

The nature of the heart is, after all, very close to the nature of the soul. In sixteenth-century France, Saint Francis de Sales (1567–1622) wrote of the importance of listening "to hear God speak in the depths of the heart." In the twentieth century Pope John Paul II preached that "the heart in biblical culture, and also in a large part of other cultures, is that essential center of the personality in which man stands before God as the totality of body and soul."[23]

"Take notice then, my Daughter," Mary instructed Sor María, "that the example of these events of my life should serve thee for thy instruction and direction. Treasure up this example lovingly in thy bosom and allow it to dilate thy heart."[24] It was a lesson that Sor María embraced wholeheartedly and one that she often shared in later years with her spiritually recalcitrant friend, King Felipe IV of Spain. When she was just setting out to write *Mystical City of God*, however, she had not yet met the obdurate king and had only begun to assess her country and her king from the perspective of her new mission to reproduce her lessons from Mary for others.

Known for her *"energía bondadosa"*—kindhearted energy—Sor María was nevertheless very critical of herself and others when it came to matters of religion. And there was a great deal of cause for her concern.[25]

While Sor María labored in the sweet recesses of mystical prose, other convents in Spain did not enjoy the same tranquillity as the Ágreda cloister or its reformed sister convents. Some convents and monasteries ventured out to another end of the spectrum altogether, giving those nuns who remained pious great reason to maintain a low profile and hold close to the prayerful regimes of their orders. Charges of magic, witchcraft, sexual misconduct, and heresy proliferated against religious and laypeople alike, some of them justified.

The Convent of San Placido in Madrid gained nationwide notoriety early in the 1630s when its spiritual director was accused by the

Inquisition of demonic prophecy and convicted of heresy. The convent was temporarily disbanded and the nuns placed in other facilities. This debacle would have gone unnoticed in the saga of Sor María had it not soon reeled in her future friend and advisee, King Felipe IV. For the convent was founded by the marqués Gerónimo de Villanueva, a gentleman who served as the king's "prothonotary"—a position then equivalent to secretary of state.[26]

For years, the marqués had engaged in an illicit affair with the abbess at the Convent of San Placido, Doña Teresa de Silva. He had also earned the dubious distinction of procuring similar liaisons for the king. Yet by 1638, many of the infractions had been resolved and the formal case against the convent had abated. The abbess had reformed, and the disbursed nuns were recalled. Villanueva, however, had not reformed. Nor had the proclivities of his king changed. Tales soon proliferated about yet another steamy affair between the king and a beautiful young nun.

Historical accounts of the incident portray the king entering a San Placido convent cell ablaze with candlelight. The nun lay swathed in flowing robes on a cot surrounded by four large candles atop pillars. To the king's surprise, however, she did not respond to his greeting and upon further inspection appeared dead. Fearing foul play, he drew his knife just as the abbess Doña Teresa emerged from the shadows.

The king then surmised that the four tall candles had been placed around the cot to simulate the appearance of a funeral bier, and he accused the abbess of conspiring to foil his intentions by murdering the young nun. The abbess objected, arguing that the convent and she had reformed and that she regretted having taken part in the original arrangements for the liaison with Villanueva. Even while realizing the enormity of consequences about to befall her by angering the monarch, she held fast to the conviction that she was right in attempting to stem his passion.

Suddenly fearful for her life, the young nun bolted upright, and the ruse of her simulated death was exposed. After many angry words, the king departed, and the story of the thwarted event spread throughout Madrid and beyond, amended over time by the equally sordid accounts of the consummated affair that was said to have taken place a few days later with the same nun, under quieter circumstances.[27]

While Sor María had no occasion to refer to such debacles per se in *Mystical City of God*, neither did she shy from making her position clear on the pitfalls of vice.

CHAPTER 12

"Catholic kings are not successful in the government of their countries"

COLORFUL TALES LIKE THAT OF SAN PLACIDO ABOUNDED in the lives of royalty and most certainly throughout the early and mature years of Felipe IV, a man said to have equaled—if not actually inspired—the exploits of the legendary Don Juan in Tirso de Molina's seventeenth-century plays. For, at the age of thirty-three in 1638, having been married to Isabel of France for seventeen years, Felipe IV had long been notorious for his wandering eye and growing list of illegitimate offspring.

Even before Sor María and the king met, his decadent lifestyle and escapades were a great source of anguish to her. Like most of her countrymen and countrywomen, Sor María believed the king to be well meaning while perhaps weak in the implementation of moral standards and fiscal administration. She was not alone in her opinion that the morals and finances of the court and country stood in dire need of reform. Since religion and politics were inseparable in the everyday life of Spain at the time, it was only natural that the two topics would also erupt intertwined in the chronicle Sor María so earnestly poured out. Scribes at the nearby Convent of Saint Julian, who were engaged to make copies, read the sheets that they copied and were amazed at the force of Sor María's convictions as inspired by the Virgin Mary and directed against the king.

"And thou, Catholic prince and monarch of Spain . . . I direct this humble and earnest appeal! Cast thy crown, thy monarchy," she admonished him, "at the feet of this Queen and Mistress of heaven and earth."[1]

Spain, of course, was a Catholic country, with no separation of church and state. Her king served not only as monarch, but also as Defender of the Faith. As such, Felipe IV's interest in the welfare of the church was considerable. His efforts to colonize the New World were equally motivated by hopes to convert many of its natives, as well as to acquire its considerable natural resources to supplement his own depleted coffers and to increase Spain's power base amid constant rebellion and war. Yet his personal and professional record left much to be desired.

The Thirty Years' War among Catholic and Protestant European countries was still in full swing. Spain warred not only with France and Germany, but also sparred dangerously with the military power of Pope Urban VIII. Among Spain's dominions, unrest was constant in Portugal, and rebellion frequently flared up in Catalonia. Even the 1.5 million ducats arriving annually from the New World colonies were not enough to fund all the conflicts.[2]

Distracted by his midnight ventures as well as the manipulations of his devious prime minister, Felipe seemed little equipped to solve his country's growing dilemmas. He reported his empty treasury to the Cortes of Castile, assembled in Madrid, and the war with enemies in Italy, Germany, Flanders, and Brazil. Meanwhile, his prime minister— Gaspar de Guzmán, known as Count-Duke Olivares—neglected and offended potential noble backers from Castile to Catalonia.[3]

The country's and the monarch's difficulties, according to Sor María as inspired by Mary, were directly attributable to the failure of the leaders to lead spiritually exemplary lives. "If the Catholic kings are not successful in the government of their countries," she wrote, "in the preservation and the spread of the Catholic faith, in overcoming their enemies . . . all this happens, because they do not follow this guiding Star [Mary], which shows them the way."[4]

Sor María wrote vociferously against war and political intrigue in *Mystical City of God* and in her later correspondence with the king. She railed against the shortcomings of Catholic kings in Europe, and in her fatherland,[5] citing the grave offense to the Lord because of Catholic kings fighting among themselves. "If we in our days see the glory and happiness of Spain so much diminished," she wrote, "it is the fault of our negligence by which we oblige Her to withdraw her protection."[6]

While adamant, these lines do not imply disloyalty on Sor María's part. Quite the contrary, her intense Spanish patriotism is a quality readily apparent throughout every phase of her life, and it is inextricably tied to her passionate embrace of Catholicism. Peace among nations and missionary acquisitions, after all, meant material and spiritual success for her beloved Spain. This emerges clearly in the missionary zeal of her teenage writing in "Face of the Earth and Map of the Spheres," in her discourses with Padre Benavides, and in her letters to the missionaries of New Mexico.

In the absence of Spain's success, however, Sor María looked to the spiritual state of her country and king and found them sorely lacking. Impassioned by her mission to share the teachings of Mary as unveiled through her visions, Sor María did not hold back from expressing the need for reform. Several of these criticisms were written in 1637, in the first twenty days of her initial writing. These were copied and gossiped over by the scribes and presaged many similar and more pointed comments to come.

Ironically, Sor María still savored and hoped to protect her quiet life in the cloistered convent. As she embarked on the lengthy manuscript of *Mystical City of God*, however, her wish for obscurity clearly became one that would not be fulfilled either in her lifetime or beyond it.

The king originally learned about Sor María in the context of Benavides's memorials about the New World. Although not inconceivable, there is no evidence that he also heard mention of the Inquisition's inquiry about her in 1635. As the pages of *Mystical City of God* flew from Sor María's hands, however, news began to spread beyond Ágreda, at first among the Franciscans and then in a widening circle, of the marvelous mystic who was writing the incredible history of the life of the Virgin.

Meanwhile, Felipe IV's treasury and status continued to spiral downward. Since age eleven, as a young crown prince, Felipe had come under the thumb of a manipulative nobleman, Count-Duke Olivares, who acted in an honorary position as the crown prince's "principal chamberlain." Olivares used the position to great advantage, raising it from its potentially servile nature to that of *privado*, making himself a court favorite and royal confidante.

Since those early formative years, Olivares had insinuated his way into the prince's confidence, in the guise of mentoring the lad. Inevitably, the prince relied upon him increasingly, to the extent that when Felipe III died in 1621 and Felipe IV was crowned king at age sixteen, Olivares had amassed considerable power and soon rose to the position of prime minister. He used this position to speak for the king, act on his behalf without consultation, and maneuver the king further and further into isolation from his subjects.

If the young king had been stronger and more experienced, he and Spain would have fared better. Quick-witted and intelligent as he was, the sixteen-year-old was no match for the seasoned statesman, twenty years his senior, who always managed to stay several steps ahead of him.[7] In their first year in power together, war with the Netherlands besieged Spain. As a result, more taxes and armed forces were needed—more than they could reasonably expect to raise. Olivares embarked on an ill-conceived program to acquire both. In doing so, he unwisely strong-armed many loyalists, offending them and sparking a number of conflicts that plagued the kingdom for decades.

Everyone, including Sor María, knew of the king's and Spain's increasingly dire straits. What's more, Olivares was frequently cited as the cause. Yet, the prime minister's power base was so strong that for many years few would openly oppose him, and even fewer were likely to succeed in their efforts to do so. In the process, Spain's resources and stature seemed to sink even further.

During these years, the king learned of the partially completed—though voluminous and growing—manuscript of *Mystical City of God*. Inevitably, he read a copy, no doubt one belonging to a Franciscan official somewhere in the upper links of the chain of Sor María's supervision. While the king would certainly have chafed at the less than complimentary references to himself, time proved that he found consolation in them, even hope—enough so that he ardently desired his own copy.

In 1642 and 1643, a troubling string of events built to the point of boiling and drove the desperate king to seek Sor María's spiritual counsel in person. Early in 1642, as the calamitous Thirty Years' War raged without apparent end, Spain had again thrust headlong into war with France. Felipe was discouraged and simultaneously chaffing at the contrived isolation that Olivares so frequently engineered upon him. Amid great fanfare and pageantry, he defied his prime minister and made an uncharacteristic personal appearance at the front in the north-eastern Pyrenees, at Roussillon. Driven farther and farther south with each battle, Felipe found himself retreating to Zaragoza. There, without the normal layers of protocol and formality, one of Spain's allies, Neapolitan general Torrescusa, had bullied his way in to see him.

All would be lost, Torrescusa brashly informed him, unless Olivares was removed. The prime minister could not be trusted, he said, among allies or even his own people. If Felipe did not remedy the situation, Torrescusa would no longer guarantee the loyalty and cooperation of the Italian army. Speculation quickly flew from Zaragoza to Madrid about the possible demise of the tyrannical Olivares.[8]

For a time Felipe had ignored the advice and encountered defeat after hopeless defeat in the struggles with Catalonia, and even among his former loyalists in Aragón. At long last, however, even he could no longer overlook the impact of his long-standing adviser's tyrannous role in these painful losses. He decided that when he returned to Madrid, he would regain the control that he had lost to Olivares. Instead, after he arrived at the Royal Palace at the Alcazar in Madrid, he was met with even more flagrant offenses by his prime minister.

A courier delivered a most disturbing letter to the king. Olivares, Felipe read, had personally insulted the royal family. The king immediately and uncharacteristically fled to the queen's apartments on the other side of the castle. While the exact words of the letter did not come to public light for some months hence, that afternoon the sounds of Queen Isabel and Prince Baltasar Carlos carried throughout her wing. She had reluctantly endured Olivares's dangerous erosion of their nation's standing and solvency, all the while fearing that there would be no country left for her son to rule. After Olivares's egregious personal insult, however, the queen could bear it no longer.

"My efforts and our son's innocence must serve you for eyes," Isabel had cried with her arm around the shoulder of the now-adolescent prince Baltasar Carlos. "For," she said, "if [you] look through the eyes of the count-duke much longer my son will be reduced to a poor King of Castile instead of King of Spain."[9]

As the dilemma unfolded, the king learned that his cousin, the Duchess of Mantua, had arrived in Madrid and requested lodging and food from Olivares. Since the count-duke had long since banished her from Madrid because of her role as vicereine of Portugal, he felt no compunction in turning her away again. His rude treatment of the king's own family sent shivers of dread through staff and servants alike.

After Olivares's contemptuous treatment of the duchess, members of the court sent word to Ana de Guevara, the king's childhood nurse and—as the monarch lovingly referred to her—his "foster mother." Olivares had cruelly disparaged this woman, too, and had banned her from the castle when Felipe was still a crown prince. Sensing the travail of her former charge, the loyal woman had somehow gained access to the grounds and was seen in the corridor kneeling before Felipe, imploring him to "listen to those who loved him best," and to dismiss Olivares.[10]

The conflict had been unbearable for all involved. Over the previous twenty-two years, the count-duke's power over the king had risen steadily, causing even the strongest of allies and adversaries to fear his judgment no less than the king's. During that time, whenever the king and he had verged on a serious conflict of opinion, the count-duke manipulatively implied that perhaps the king could do without him temporarily while he took a long overdue leave of absence. Predictably, this always sent the inexperienced king into an immediate panic at the thought of ruling without him, and a truce was always achieved without an interruption of the count-duke's services.

Over time, however, Olivares's despotic practices had increasingly estranged him from many factions within and beyond the borders of Spain. Finally, to these ample political grounds for disaffection, he had added personal affront to the king's own cousin as well as his childhood nurse, once and for all estranging himself from the king.

Felipe soon took a stand. The count-duke's long-standing hope to retire, the king informed him in writing on January 17, 1643, was now granted.[11] The good news was that Olivares—presumably—was out of the picture. The bad news was that the king was now in dire need of a new adviser. Fortuitously, this spurred more reliance upon the queen's counsel, but the gap left in Olivares's absence was considerable.

Celebrations nevertheless abounded throughout the kingdom, and nowhere was joy more boisterous than in Madrid. There, a lane called Liar's Walk (Mentidero) ran the length of the long, high path along the wall of San Felipe's Church, from High Street to Puerto del Sol opposite the palace. Along it, potentates traditionally seeded manipulative gossip and satirical verses, and peasants harvested palace news.

Often the despotic machinations of Olivares or the clandestine activities of the king provided salty scandals for those who ambled along the path or observed it from the shadows. Finally, however, later in the day on January 17, crowds along the walk had shouted "We have a King again!" when they dared to believe the hive of whispers swarming around the announcement of the fall of Olivares.[12]

Soon the count-duke's vacant position of principal chamberlain reverted to an honorific role more servile in nature, but still accorded to a nobleman. As for the count-duke's other informal role, the king staunchly announced his intention to rule without the aid of a privado, a privileged insider and court favorite who spoke for the king.[13] Felipe also declined to appoint anyone to fill Olivares's formal role of prime minister.

Unfortunately, Olivares—having sensed trouble in the offing—had drafted numerous decrees in advance, for the king's signature. Even after his dismissal on January 17, these papers made their way through normal channels to the king's desk. As Felipe reexamined the voluminous stack of papers that had accumulated during the transition, in April of 1643 he despairingly discovered that he had already signed several without reading them.

In particular, Felipe saw that he had signed two documents that buttressed Olivares's maneuvers to maintain some vestige of a power base, should the rising tide prevail against him. One letter dismissed Inquisitor General Sotomayor, who had served as Felipe's confessor since he was a boy, and banished Sotomayor from Spain with a pension of twelve thousand ducats per year for life, on condition of his resignation and quiet retirement to Cordova. The other, in a clear attempt to cement new loyalties, appointed Padre Arce y Reynoso as the new inquisitor general.[14]

Whether from weariness or reluctance to overtly cross Olivares, Felipe let the documents stand. Nevertheless, he determinedly set about the job of ruling on his own. Sensing his countrymen and court's need to put the debacle of Olivares behind them, he valiantly attended meetings in person at the Council of State, reviewed documents personally in advance of taking action, and resisted any temptation to establish a privado in the court.

This was, of course, a losing battle. Every head of state benefits from wise counsel, and Felipe IV was no exception. Court favorites emerged, among them a politic courtier named Don Luis de Haro, the nephew of none other than Olivares.[15] Yet there were differences.

Where Olivares had assumed a masterly role over the king, de Haro insinuated his way into friendship with the monarch. Where Olivares was arrogant, de Haro was modest. He soon filled much of the vacuum left in Olivares's wake, thus absorbing a great deal of Olivares's power through sheer mediocrity, according to some scholars, although he did not formally fill the position of prime minister until 1659.[16] Whether this was by Olivares's own design or by default is inconclusive. What is known is that the gap left after Olivares's demise was so immense, and the king's needs were so extensive, that he inevitably sought additional counsel from many sources. Eventually his search led him to seek wisdom from a humble nun in Ágreda.

Felipe remembered a manuscript he had read, shared by a Franciscan official who had received it from a priest serving as confessor of an extraordinary saintly woman. For a brief time members of the court had fluttered curiously about the king and the manuscript, but events leading up to Olivares's downfall quickly absorbed their fickle attention. Then, the king realized that the abbess in Ágreda might shed some light on his dire plight and even put in a word for him with a higher—more celestial—authority.

In July of 1643, Felipe IV was still mired in the administrative changes he had wrought in recent months, following the painful separation from his former prime minister. Since he did not correspondingly reduce his nightly philandering, he was in sore need of rest and a ray of light. He determined to meet the unusual nun—Sor María de Jesús, abbess of the Convent of the Immaculate Conception in Ágreda. His staff was to arrange it soon and to coordinate it with the army's upcoming journey to the frontier where they would mobilize troops in Tarazona and then move on to the battlefront in Zaragoza.

How much advance notice Sor María received about her upcoming prestigious visitor is not known. Yet between her friends at the Convent of the Caballeros de Gracia in Madrid and the viceroy, Don Fernando de Borja, we can be reasonably sure that she knew the king had reviewed some copy of the in-progress manuscript of *Mystical City of God*—and that some impressions about her writing and its value had wended their way from the palace to Ágreda.

Another certainty, although one rarely aired in this context, is the abbess's likely concerns about the king's less than exemplary reputation with women.

PART FOUR

ADVISER TO THE
SPANISH KING
1643

"The king . . . commanded that I write to him"

EVEN AT THIS POINT IN SOR MARÍA'S LIFE, AT THE AGE of forty-one, her place in history was secure—as a mystic, a visionary, and a writer. Her supernatural appearances in the American Southwest would generate speculation and invite mention through the twenty-first century and probably beyond. Her visionary experiences of Mary would inspire untold thousands of spiritual aspirants worldwide. And her prolific baroque writing would be studied in university departments of Spanish literature and language in perpetuity.

Yet even before the ink was figuratively dry on her many sheets of parchment paper, Sor María was soon to add another component to her already glittering résumé—that of spiritual and political adviser to the king of Spain.

Theirs was an unlikely relationship from the start—a friendship between a philandering king and an ascetic nun. Yet the rewards to each were unmistakable. Felipe IV was in dire need of counsel and encouragement, and Sor María was soon to suffer intimidation and danger from an elderly priest and the Inquisition. The king, according to many historians, benefited from Sor María's prudent spiritual and political advice.[1] While according to latter-day Inquisition specialists, Sor María owed her safety, and perhaps even her life, to the protective patina of royalty.[2]

FIGURE 22. King Felipe IV of Spain in 1652. Oil on canvas, by Diego
Velázquez. Courtesy of Convent of the Conception, Ágreda.

With Felipe's dismissal of the count-duke, he more frequently stepped into the outer realms of his kingdom, albeit with the tired dignity and reserve that had overtaken his persona as he wearied from the demands of his reign. In July of 1643, the thirty-eight-year-old king was on his way to war at the Aragón frontier beyond Zaragoza. He was determined to meet Sor María in Ágreda en route, before engaging in battle. It was a long and arduous journey, additionally burdened with a torrent of attention from his pent-up subjects along the way.

Since all the shouting on Liar's Walk after January 17, wherever Felipe went, his overly grateful subjects threw themselves before him with new hope for relief from the overbearing policies and taxation of the count-duke and for long overdue access to their monarch. It had been, after all, over two decades since his people had access to the king. Felipe's appearances, therefore, often caused an exhausting stir wherever he went.

En route to Ágreda, his party traveled from Madrid in a northeasterly direction. They skirted the mountains to the north and east and aimed their cavalrymen and carriages diagonally across the countryside. As they journeyed, Felipe likely recalled the many unfulfilled promises issued by his ailing father to go boar hunting in the foothills near Ágreda, a sport that regained its prominence there in the twentieth century.

As the king ventured out to reestablish a presence and remedy the disastrous deterioration of affairs in the far reaches of Aragón, peasants and nobles, padres and monsignors alike welcomed the king to their town or region. Some regaled him in a pageant on the bumpy cobbled streets, while others eagerly waited the passage of the entourage beside their castles, palaces, and homes.

Unlike the king's younger sister—wife of Holy Roman emperor Ferdinand III—who in 1631 traveled to Carinthia in a two-seated velvet-lined carriage with glass windowpanes, Felipe chose for extended travel the shutters and drapes of the stalwart boxy carriage he used on boar hunts. During a summer journey, it would have retained the heat far more than his sister's smaller, sleeker carriage, although he had outfitted it with the new suspension inventions of the Germans.[3] As the miles passed slowly by, between cascades of adulation from monarch-starved subjects, the king must have sagged in his hot, mobile confines.

Felipe had also carefully instructed his staff concerning all travel arrangements, according to his new circumstances. They would have a retinue, he informed them, but it would not be extravagant, as in the days of Olivares. A full complement of servants would not be necessary, he specified, merely a few to manage the household suites in the two attendant coaches.[4] The royal cavalry would also accompany them, sufficient to interact with Aragonés officers and army, yet only in reduced numbers. Absolutely no more than thirty, Felipe commanded.

Two soldiers likely rode on the royal steeds behind the carriage so that Felipe—an avid horseman—could elect to ride at any time. After that the servants' coaches would have labored, carrying personal attendants and a handful of additional manservants, as well as the household needs for the journey. While sumptuous looking to the poor, it reflected little of the ceremonial train the count-duke had usually required. Still, it afforded Felipe some basic comforts over the forty leagues to Soria, thirty beyond that to Ágreda and Tarazona, and on to his encampments at the front in Zaragoza.[5]

With the bulk of the journey behind them, they likely bivouacked near the city of Soria, a few hours short of Ágreda, then left before dawn. Given the distance and the pacing of the retinue and its stops, they would have seen the Moncayos just as the range burned with the promise of new life, as flames of dawn pulsated behind its peaks. The high, rolling curves of the peaks, dark as deep water, no doubt undulated against the pale pink dawn rising behind them. Nestled in their foreground lay Ágreda.

Riding in from the south and west, the small country road rolled alongside the mountains like a ribbon. As they neared Ágreda, Felipe may have ruminated about the fact that the strategically located village had belonged to the Crown in the days of his grandfather. Later it came under the protection of the noble Castejones family and became the administrative seat of the region.[6] Ágreda had been a logical choice for the seat because of its strategic location at the farthest reaches of Castile, marking the borders separating that province from Navarra and Aragón.[7] Small wonder, he may have mused, that this lively atmosphere spawned the likes of Sor María de Jesús. For at the intersection of these points in his earthly kingdom, she reached for and wrote of the heavens.

Then, on the outskirts of Ágreda, the entourage rode along on Calle los Manzanos probably just as the city sweepers removed the dust from the walks of the Municipal Palace overlooking the village's central courtyard, the Plaza Mayor. At the Convent of the Immaculate Conception, the nuns would have completed their predawn prayers, and most would have returned to their cells to sleep until 6:00 a.m. Perhaps some maintained vigil with Sor María as they awaited the arrival of the king, or perhaps that is when Sor María penned the following passage in *Mystical City of God*: "If the Catholic princes, of both Church and state, would use the proper diligence, aiding as it were this heavenly Lady, She . . . would not fail to help them, conferring upon them happiness in this life and in the next."[8]

At that moment, a cavalryman likely leaned over his horse to ask a city sweeper the directions to the convent. The king no doubt paused his entourage to send a messenger on to the convent as a courtesy to announce his imminent arrival. Then, as they resumed their ride to complete the distance to the convent, excited men and women assuredly emerged along the way to greet the royal train, as the tiny village quickly awoke.

The nuns, however, remained cloistered. The king's carriages and cavalry thundered onto the narrow stone access path alongside the convent, only greeted perhaps by the friars of the neighboring Saint Julian's convent and Sor María's confessor, Padre de la Torres. Sor María, meanwhile, likely sat behind the small window cut between the visitors' room and the convent's waiting room, the same two-feet-by-two-feet speared opening through which the nuns conversed with any visitor, king and commoner alike.

Sor María made notes about the details of her first conversation with the king. Also, in the correspondence that was soon to ensue between them, they each referred enough to their meeting so that the essence of their exchange clearly emerged. As the beleaguered king unburdened himself, Sor María quietly listened, occasionally offering a cheerful or encouraging word. During the meeting, however, she made a pivotal decision that affected the balance of their relationship, despite the disparity of their stations in life and the fact that—at that point—she had no idea whether she would ever hear from him again.

"Our Lord the King entered our convent on July 10, 1643," she wrote in convent records. "He commanded that I write to him, and I obeyed. . . . I begged him to forbid the wearing of unchaste clothing which encourages vice, and I offered all the prayers of our community on his behalf."[9] With the phrase "unchaste clothing" Sor María referred to the *guardainfantes* so prominent in Madrid at the time, a scoop-necked hoop-skirted gown similar to the farthingales worn in England and France. If up until this point the king had any mistaken notion that Sor María or any of her nuns bore any similarity to the nuns of San Placido or other unreformed convents, it was most likely dispelled at that moment.

FIGURE 23. Formidable spiked grille in convent's *locutorio* through which Sor María conversed with King Felipe IV and others. Photo by author.

Sor María's courageous stand with the king did not offend or anger him. Instead, impressed with her vision and integrity, after he left Ágreda he assembled a list of his concerns, for which he asked her prayers. These he entrusted to his new friend, Don Luis de Haro, who personally carried them back to Ágreda and recited them to Sor María.

While from the king's viewpoint, he may have initially wanted to delegate the responsibility for saving himself to a pious nun whose job it was to pray—without appropriate reforms on his own part—Sor María did her best to offset this pattern from the beginning. She did so in a deferential yet truthful manner that was to be the hallmark of her communication with the king, differences in position notwithstanding.

"Señor," she wrote to the king on July 16, 1643, "I strive to overcome my timidity and to deserve your bidding to correspond. I do so now as your faithful servant. . . . Please know that from the depths of my heart I have presented your concerns and aspirations to the Lord. . . . Ever since you were here, and under your obedience, I and the entire convent pray for the Lord's help in guiding all your efforts. In this request I will persevere always."[10]

At the same time, Sor María took care to clarify her position on individual responsibility. God is compassionate, she told him, but the king must be strong of heart and act in such a way as to deserve the Lord's protection. Emboldened as she went along, Sor María asked the king to exhort his company to good behavior during their encampment in Zaragoza.[11] In doing so, she was evoking common knowledge of the rowdy behavior in Zaragoza of the king's courtiers and soldiers the previous year, and the failure of some to pay for their lodgings.[12]

Finally, she assured him of her prayers for the successful return of the silver-laden fleet from America and mentioned that indeed she had received the list of the king's needs for her prayers from Don Luis de Haro. "All these," she wrote, "I place at the feet of the Most High to petition." Although she privately feared, and rightly so, that de Haro might soon carry on in the devious tradition of his uncle, the count-duke, she made no inference about her misgivings. In closing, she made a special gift to the king, writing, "Please accept the enclosed fibers that I have cherished, from a rope thought to have touched the wrist of Christ. . . . From the Servant of Your Majesty, Sor María de Jesús."[13]

Sor María wrote to the king a few more times during the summer and early fall of 1643. In August, after hearing of some of his achievements, she assured him of her prayers on his behalf. "Even as your successes mount," she wrote, "I continuously clamor to God." In September she entreated him again to take action against "the vices that contaminate Spain and the costumes that foment incendiary behavior."[14]

With her lifelong hallmarks of honesty and diplomacy, Sor María also took care to mention any of her contacts with others that might have a direct or indirect impact on the king. "The Duke of Hijar advised me that the army has gone out to battle [against Catalonia]," she wrote to him, expressing her confidence in Hijar's "good zeal and faithfulness" to the king.[15] In communicating this with the king, she implied without saying—a skill she developed into an art form over the years—that she supported the duke's political aspirations, perhaps over Olivares's nephew de Haro. Time proved her mistaken in her regard for Hijar, an error that would send the Inquisition to her door in a few years' time.

In the same series, she told the king that she had heard from Queen Isabel, through her long-standing friend Don Fernando de Borja.[16] Sor María and de Borja—viceroy of Aragón and Valencia—had corresponded since 1628. In September of 1643, he had been in the service of Isabel and Felipe's crown prince, Baltasar Carlos, as a gentleman of the chamber.[17] As such, he had the ear of the prince and his mother. The queen, no doubt concerned with the king's questionable relationships with nuns, and learning of de Borja's high estimation of Sor María, desired her own communication with the celebrated abbess.

"The Queen ordered me to correspond with her," Sor María wrote to the king, "regarding the great responsibility to which you have obliged me. I acknowledged her mandate, and assured her of our community's continuous prayers."[18]

For the most part, however, Sor María reimmersed herself in the manuscript of the biography of Mary. She was close to completing *Mystical City of God* in 1643. Books 7 and 8 comprised the last volume, entitled *The Coronation*. During this latter part of Mary's life, the history of Saint James's evangelical work in Zaragoza, Spain, represented an important episode to her Spanish "daughter." The king's proximity on military maneuvers in Zaragoza no doubt enlivened Sor María's treatment of the legend even more.

"Joyfully I will confess to all that shall read this history," she wrote, "that I consider myself extremely fortunate in being permitted to write it in a place which is only two days' foot-journey from the city of Zaragoza."[19]

As Sor María wrote about the story of Saint James at the end of Book 7, she knew from her meeting with the king that he wanted his own copy of *Mystical City of God*. Yet her procedures for achieving a final copy involved several stages. First, she wrote her material. Then, it was discussed with her superiors, primarily Padre de la Torres. After this it was reviewed and edited for any potential error and the inclusion of appropriate biblical references in support of what she had written. It was an arduous process, considering that every page was handwritten and then hand-copied, whether by Sor María herself or the scribes at Saint Julian's.

Sor María debated the merits of sending the king any early copy while he was in Zaragoza. In the meantime, she relished writing about the account of Saint James as it intersected with the life of the Heavenly Queen. Mary, according to Sor María's visions, was transported by a host of angels to Zaragoza and commanded Saint James to build a church in her honor. The angels instantly "set up a column and upon it the [Heavenly Queen's] sacred image." Saint James and his disciples completed the construction and made "the first dedication of a temple instituted in this world under the name and title of the great Mistress of heaven and earth."[20]

To this day, Our Lady of the Pillar Cathedral is a famous historic and religious monument in northeast Spain, featuring the legendary angelically created image of Mary. Like the annual pilgrimage to Santiago de Compostela in Spain where Saint James is said to be buried, the Zaragoza cathedral draws tourists, historians, Marian devotees, and admirers of Saint James from around Spain and the world, most notably in recent history to Zaragoza's 2008 hosting of the World's Fair.

Between her writing about the Queen of Heaven and her prayers for the earthly king, Sor María continued to advise and guide the nuns in her charge and to eagerly join her voice with theirs in the memorable polyphonic hymns so appealing to all who heard them.[21] "She was so punctual at all the offices and exercises of the community," Ximénez Samaniego attested, "that she was the model and admiration of all the nuns."[22] As was obvious to all, they revered her for her kindness and her piety. The nuns also frequently commented on the beautiful fragrance that seemed to accompany Sor María throughout the convent. "Oh, what a good smell, Mother!" they were known to fondly say. "There are angels here; Your Reverence is with the angels."[23]

In the midst of this refined religious atmosphere, a most unusual letter for Sor María arrived from Zaragoza.

CHAPTER 14

"I believe your intentions are good"

"SOR MARÍA," THE KING PENNED, IMMEDIATELY SETTING
the tone for their six-hundred-letter correspondence as a genuine dialogue, "I write to you leaving a half margin, so that your reply may come
on the same paper. I further enjoin and command you not to allow the
contents of this to be communicated to anybody."

As he wrote these words on October 4, 1643,[1] the king demonstrated
what he meant, writing only on the right portion of the pages and leaving a full column of space to the left. In these spaces, Sor María was to
respond to his dilemmas, and then she was to return the selfsame pages
to the king. Often, during the twenty-two years of their correspondence,
the king instructed the royal courier to wait while Sor María stopped
whatever she was doing to immediately write her reply and furnish it for
return delivery. In this way, the king hoped to embark upon a confesso-
rial relationship with the wise abbess and to maintain utter secrecy. It
was an uncommon testimony to his high opinion of her.

"Since the day that I was with you," he wrote, "I have felt much
encouraged by your . . . earnest attachment towards my well being [and
the] success of my realm." The king explained that he received advice
from many religious people, even some who claimed to have revelations.
Yet, too often their advice proved false or harmful. Sometimes, he said,

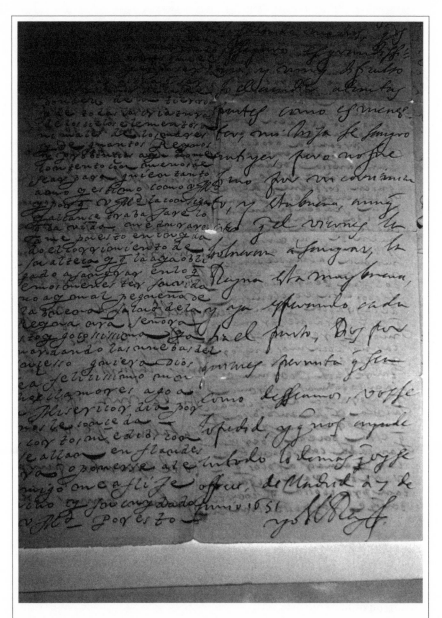

FIGURE 24. Original letter between King Felipe IV and Sor María. Right column written by king, dated June 12, 1651, left by Sor María. In convent archives. Photo by author.

he was advised to punish or dismiss people in his court who had done nothing wrong. Other times, he was advised to promote individuals without merit. "Their truth cannot be depended upon," he wrote to Sor María, asking her to respond to him "with all frankness as to a confessor" and not to "be influenced by what the world says."

When he had left Madrid for the battlefront, the king wrote, he lacked "all human resources" and looked "only to divine help" to solve his failure and misery. He blamed himself for his country's woes. In fact, he confided in her, he wished that he personally could absorb all of God's punishment for his errors, rather than causing "afflictions . . . upon these realms," because he felt that Spain's problems "all arise from my having offended our Lord."

On a more positive note, he reported that since he had met Sor María, "Our Lord has already begun to work in my favor, bringing in the silver fleet and relieving Oran [a Spanish fortress under siege in Africa, and] . . . affairs in Aragón have somewhat improved with my presence." He was quick to remind her, however, of his and Spain's ongoing needs: the Portuguese rebels, the risk of an uprising in Flanders, and the deplorable lack of money in his treasury.

"I do hope you will console me with your reply," he wrote in conclusion, "and that I may have in you a true intercessor with our Lord, that He may guide and enlighten me, and extricate me from the troubles in which I am now immersed." In the tradition of his father and grandfather, he did not sign his name, but simply closed with the signature "Yo el Rey," Spanish for "I, the King."

Although the letter was delivered by a monk traveling on foot, the royal seal no doubt indicated to all that Sor María had received a letter from the king. Yet he had commanded the absolute confidentiality of the contents of their correspondence. The directive proved a challenge for a nun bound to her superiors by the vows of obedience, as well as to her king by virtue of her citizenship.

Sor María did not receive this letter until the tenth of the month. Despite the delay, she did not respond immediately. Instead, she prayed, reflected, and likely consulted her confessor, Padre de la Torre. To disobey the king, she knew, was folly. Yet not to have a record of such important correspondence was unwise. And so, relying upon a technicality, she made a plan.

Sor María would respond to the king as directed, in the left margin of his original letter. Then she would personally copy the contents of each and maintain these copies in secrecy. If she felt as though she needed Padre de la Torre's priestly counsel before making any response, she was fully capable of referring obliquely to certain issues, without technically betraying the king's confidences. With this plan in place, she penned the following reply on October 13, 1643,[2] with the hope that she might avoid the disadvantage of its return delivery by foot.

"With humility and obedience," she wrote, "I accept the favor that Your Majesty has endowed on me. I have composed my reply without anyone else's license, reserving these secrets in my heart." Sor María did not make this commitment lightly. While she did indeed maintain her own file of the king's letters and her responses, this was not made public until after each of their deaths, in 1665. At that time, the king's copies were revealed, as well as hers, and the identical sets of six hundred letters became part of the historical record of their friendship and the times.

As always, Sor María assured the king of her and the convent's continual prayers and their "deep affection for your monarchy and your person." Then she quickly delved into the issues at hand. Responding to his misgivings about having left Madrid for the battlefront, she wrote that she did not think his decision to do so was wrong because God's favor was evident by the success of his silver fleet. Not even human frailty, she advised him, could impede "the marvelous work of the Lord."

"Your Majesty, I believe your intentions are good," she assured him in the beginning of the letter, "and that you give yourself too little credit." Then she proceeded with her characteristic honesty to tell him that the peril of his monarchy was a punishment in direct correlation with his wars with other Catholic kings and the country's lack of moral reform.

Typically, after making a particularly difficult point, Sor María offered some mitigating comfort. "Punishment is also a sign of God's love," she told him, suggesting that "your Majesty *can* change," and that when the king renewed himself in God, God would in turn renew his blessings and guide the king "to punish evil and administer justice equally over all."

While Sor María had been forthright thus far, in this letter and in the letters she had written to Felipe before his first letter to her, her communication generally applied to the spiritual ramifications of his actions or her prayers for his specific requests. In this first shared correspondence, however, she dared to offer the king some sage political advice.

FIGURE 25. Etching of Sor María by Bartolomé Maura in 1884, as published in first edition in 1885 of letters between Sor María and King Felipe IV. In convent archives. Courtesy of Convent of the Conception, Ágreda.

"God distributes talents unequally among us," she wrote to him. "I do not approve of discrediting one person to the advantage of another, especially when it may impugn someone's honor. Yet there are some near you who possess a great capacity to help you, while others are not only useless in the science of governing, but they fatten their own larders at the cost of the common good and that of their prince and king."

He must sort these people out, she told him, or his kingdom would continue in its downward descent while some of those men grew rich, crowding "close to the warmth of your fire for the power of its heat in enriching their own fortunes. It would be better to level the ranks of all such persons," she wrote, to hold equal audiences with each courtier, and then to make his own decisions without showing favoritism.

In her innate pragmatism, however, Sor María advised caution when dealing with powerful men. She acknowledged the problems the king faced because of his former administration, referring to Count-Duke Olivares without mentioning his name. Yet in contrast to many people of the time—perhaps even her friend Don Fernando de Borja—who felt that all the king's problems originated from Olivares and most likely continued with the ascension of Olivares's nephew, Don Luis de Haro, Sor María took a different approach. She advised him not to shut out de Haro, but to take advantage of his resources.

"It is not a mistake," she wrote to him, "to give prudent satisfaction to a man of the world because, after all, you do need worldly resources." With that, she opined that she couldn't say much more "when confined to the pen," praying that he would dilate his heart to God, wherein the Lord would prosper him and fill him with peace, "rendering the king happy and blissful." She signed off as "Your Majesty's humble servant, Sor María de Jesús," no doubt praying for herself in the process that her bold reply would be well received.

The die was cast. Sor María had committed herself indelibly in writing. In more ways than one, her fate would depend upon the king's reaction to her letter. Had she gone too far? Would he take offense at her presumption to offer political advice in addition to the spiritual consolation he so obviously craved? If so, had she incurred the wrath of the Defender of the Faith as well as the king of the land? His reply was not long in forthcoming.

"I was very comfortable with your response," he wrote from the

Zaragoza battle camp on October 16, 1643,[3] "since as you advised, I have dilated my heart." Her prayers had "reached the Lord," he wrote, intimating improved military success and encouraging signs of peace with Catalonia. Regarding her daring advice on how to approach his courtiers, he said that he was doing his best to achieve a balance in administering justice with fairness and honesty.

"Yet while I am decisive in distancing myself from the former administration, it is not possible," he wrote, "to quickly remedy damages that took so long to amass." Too, because of the deceit of so many former favorites, he expressed concern that he would not be remembered well if his new efforts did not come to light. If he had to be faulted, however, he wrote to Sor María, he preferred to be remembered "as a weak man, and not a malicious one. And, if you understand with any more specificity what is God's will for me, you must advise me. For I would gladly offer my life," he added, "for the restoration of my kingdom and peace throughout Christendom."

"Your letter gives me great consolation," Sor María replied on October 25, 1643,[4] "for what your monarchy needs the most is peace. . . . Truly a dilated heart tackles great challenges. With God's help it is a good day's work in the infancy of human capacity!"

In this letter, she admonished the king for his hesitancy in dispensing justice, reminding him that a "faithfully served prince" must himself internalize the fear of God and rule himself with rigorous prudence in order to be successful. Yet, she counseled him, it was equally important not to drown in regret over past mistakes. Rather, she advised him to "learn from past pain, by making an amendment in the future."

Reminding him that she kept abreast of news from the front, she shared her dismay that many nobles had refused to bear arms on his behalf, an implicit obligation to the Crown in exchange for their formal freedom from taxes. She wrote that she hoped they would soon support him again, not only for the increased numbers of armed forces, but for the encouragement it would give to the soldiers. In the meantime, she told him in closing, he should be encouraged that the location of his afflictions was for the moment centralized in Zaragoza, because the Lord had promised all who devoutly invoked his help in this place honoring the Heavenly Queen that he would "favor them with a liberal hand." To that end, Sor María enclosed another "poor gift," the recently completed pages on the story of Saint James.

"Know of my affection and the license I take," she cautioned him, "in showing these pages to you."

While Sor María always kept her commitments, she was unwilling to undergo this risk entirely alone. According to one annotated collection of the correspondence between her and the king, by November 25 of that same year her confessor—Padre de la Torre—also participated in providing the king with early copies of Mary's biography.[5] It was an extension of the confidentiality of the agreement between the king and the nun, to which both parties agreed.

For his part, the king continually reminded Sor María of her commitment to pray for him. "I remind you of it in the greatest necessities," he wrote to her from Madrid on December 29, 1643.[6] He expected any hour, he told her, the arrival of more silver-laden galleons from Mexico. So much was at stake, he reminded her. Too, he said that he hoped to succeed in carrying out her advice for him in his court, now that he was back in Madrid.

He specifically referred, he said, to the sixth point in the letter to which he was responding, her supplication that "Your Majesty make yourself thoroughly versed in everything touching you . . . with full knowledge of facts."[7] To do so, she counseled him to find an adviser in the court in whom he could trust, suggesting that the enhanced understanding he received would help to offset many difficulties in the court.

"When you have learnt [sic] the truth, the execution should be rapid," she wrote to him, "for the evil is great and the remedy needs resolution." "God assist your Majesty," she added, "and rule your heart."[8]

The king's troubles, however, were only beginning.

In early October of the next year, 1644, Sor María wrote in a private notebook that she had learned from Don Fernando de Borja that the queen had fallen gravely ill in late September. He had asked for her prayers on behalf of the queen, a request Sor María filled with great concern.

"The following Saturday at midnight I saw the earth divide," she wrote, "and I heard many cries from an enormous cavern. I recognized the soul of Queen Isabel. She moaned desperately."

The next day, on Sunday, October 9, a courier from Madrid pierced the quiet of the convent. He brought letters written the previous Wednesday (October 5), indicating that the queen's condition had improved.

"With this information I was rather confused, worrying for a while that I had been influenced by a demon, but Padre de la Torre said to write

it all down," she wrote. For several days, the disturbing visions continued, showing the queen bemoaning her moral passivity and suffering
penance in what appeared to Sor María to be a scandalous netherworld.
"The queen appeared from what I later knew to be purgatory," Sor María
wrote later in the month, "having received the confirming news of her
death [from sources other than the king], although not until ten days
after the fact."

"I worried about how and when to tell the king what had happened to
her soul," Sor María wrote, consulting her confessor about the implications of her visions regarding the queen's death. He "obliged me through
obedience to pray and work on her behalf and not to stop until I had success. So, I passed many days without noticing anything."[9]

"Sor María—" the king finally wrote from Madrid on November 15,
1644,[10] "I find myself in the most oppressed state of sorrow possible, for I
have lost in one person everything that can be lost in this world; and if I
did not know . . . that the Lord disposes for us what is best, I do not know
what would become of me."

Isabel, weakened earlier in the year by miscarriages, had on September 28 fallen sick with cholera and a streptococcus skin infection. After
the doctors copiously bled her with leeches, her condition worsened, with
symptoms that today would likely be recognized as diphtheria. The king
rushed home from the battlefront off southern Catalonia to be with her
but was met fifty miles outside Madrid with the news of her death. In
shock, he diverted to El Pardo, just outside the city, to grieve with his
son, fifteen-year-old crown prince Baltasar Carlos, Felipe's only legitimate heir.[11]

With Isabel's death, Felipe also lost the hope of heirs beyond his two
surviving children, Baltasar Carlos, and the now five-year-old princess
María Teresa. Felipe loved his son enormously and now looked to the
prince for comfort. At Sor María's prodding, he had begun to tutor his
son in the ways of ruling. Now, without their mother, a most capable
and lovely queen, he worried about his children, whom he called his
personal angels.

"I ask you to entrust these two angels to God," he implored Sor María
on their behalf on November 15, 1644,[12] "that He raise them in His holy
service, and enlighten me that I may provide what is most suited for
them." "I confess much need for divine comfort in resigning myself to
this terrible blow," he added, writing, "please remember your promise

to send the missing pages of the Blessed Mother's life, which despite my [sorrow and] schedule, I will not fail to read."

Perhaps it was a request she had agreed to, thinking how unlikely it would be that the monarch of her country would follow through with it. She knew, as she read his letter and as she had known when he made the request, that circulation of unapproved copy would be frowned upon. Yet she had given her word.

Sor María, of course, began her November 18 letter of response with every possible assurance of her sympathy about the queen's death.[13] "There can be no greater loss for you and our monarchy than the death of the queen," she wrote to him, encouraging him to offer his suffering to God in "real resignation."

"I know more than I can say about your sorrow," she wrote, acknowledging his "pain and solitude in the midst of so many afflictions." Then she advised him patience and trust in the Almighty's compassion and reminded him of her prayers for him. True to her forthright nature, however, she felt obligated to tell the king about the rampant negativity of popular opinion circulating about him.

"There is wide sentiment throughout our kingdom that the queen's death is a chastisement from the Lord," she wrote to him. As a remedy, she advised reliance on those of his "faithful ministers who are God-fearing and zealous, and who would—without ulterior motives—assist in the reformation of the vices and other dangers threatening our realm." "At the same time," she wrote, "you must focus on the spiritual education of the prince and princess, for all the good you give them will benefit Christianity."

In these two letters, Sor María and the king also discussed the election of the new pope in Rome, Innocent X, as related to their efforts on behalf of the doctrine of Mary's Immaculate Conception. Felipe told Sor María that he had engaged many learned theologians in the issue, appointed ambassadors to the pope, and already sent considerable documentation on the Immaculate Conception to the Holy Father. "They will do everything possible to accomplish what [you and] I desire," he wrote to her, "and I would die happy knowing I had participated in this service to Our Lady."

Sor María, of course, couldn't have agreed more and reiterated her hopes to the king that the "new Holy Father will bring universal peace to the Church, and . . . settle the definition of the mystery of the conception of the Queen of Heaven." She advised the king to rely on Mary and to "not to limit his devotion and faith in the Mother of Grace for anything." As for further progress on the manuscript of *Mystical City of God*, she said she had written much more in it, but that "because of my confessor's other duties with the prelate, he has not gone through the copy very much." It was her way of asking him to be patient about receiving his own copy.

Thus far in her November 18 letter, Sor María had not yet mentioned anything to the king about her visions of Queen Isabel. These were not easily put in a letter, yet she wanted to be honest. Finally she settled upon a note toward the end. "There is nothing more I can say [in a letter] about the queen," she wrote, intimating that in "the secret of my heart" there was much more to share.[14]

She did, in the future, confide in the king about her visions of the queen, but not until she saw him again in person. In the meantime, the two continued to correspond, the king confiding his afflictions and needs, and the nun providing a steady stream of encouragement. Somewhere along the line, Sor María was pleased to note, her exhortations seemed to actually take root.

"I now trust that God in His mercy . . . will not allow [these realms] to be ruined utterly," he wrote to her from the battlefront in Aragón on March 25, 1645,[15] even though he still felt that his "faults alone are sufficient to provoke the ire of the Lord." Nevertheless, with his newfound hope, he assured Sor María that "the greater the punishment the greater will be my appeal to faith and hope, as you say."

In this letter, Felipe told Sor María that he had brought Prince Baltasar Carlos with him to the battlefront. Unlike his own initiation into reigning, with an ailing father and tutelage under the thumb of Count-Duke Olivares, Felipe hoped to more properly educate the prince, by involving him personally wherever possible. It was a good plan, except for Baltasar Carlos's fragile constitution. "I have brought him with me," he wrote, "and have confided his health to the hands of God."

The king could not know, at that time, of the prince's risk or the additional heartache it would bring upon him in the not too distant future. He was also unaware of Sor María's difficulties, so absorbed was he in his own.

CHAPTER 15

"I am beside myself, Your Majesty"

ALTHOUGH THE INQUISITION'S FIRST INQUIRY IN 1635 into Sor María's unusual experiences of bilocation had been set aside, she knew the file on her existed. She was understandably wary of any undue attention.

Yet, she had already been asked to sit for the first three of many portraits that would comprise an impressive historical iconography of Ágreda art still on display today around the world. She had also caught the attention of the Franciscans relative to both their missionary work in the New World as well as their advocacy of the Immaculate Conception. And, she had—for good reason—attracted the attention of the king.

Sor María's fame was not the low profile for which she had hoped, and it also generated detractors. In 1645 an old confessor insinuated to her that women in the church should not write and hinted that the Inquisition may have planned sanctions to silence her.[1] At the same time, well-meaning friends encouraged her to focus more on her duties as abbess and her new role in advising the king.[2] It was enough to fan the flames of her own "natural disposition" of self-doubt and generate a sense of personal jeopardy.[3]

FIGURE 26. Sor María at age thirty-six, in what became her signature pose with writing paper and pen. Oil on canvas, artist unknown. On display in—and image courtesy of—Convent of the Conception, Ágreda.

"Overcome by fears and difficulties," she wrote, "I resolved not to continue [the biography], and to use all possible means to adhere to this determination."[4]

Discontinuation, however, was not her only remedy. That spring, Sor María burned a significant portion of her writing and refrained from producing any more.[5] Padre de la Torre chastised her roughly and ordered her to rewrite the missing material. Sor María did try to comply, but it was a difficult order for the priest to enforce, as he had been promoted to head his region as provincial, and he was frequently absent. During those absences the old confessor reappeared, as did Sor María's self-doubt. The most serious incidents of book-burning, however, were yet to come late in 1646 and again in 1649.

Meanwhile, the demands of the king added to Padre de la Torre's prodding, as Felipe continually asked Sor María for his own copy of *Mystical City of God*, as it was written. He had received an edited copy of the first part—Books 1 and 2—in November 1643, an early draft of the second part—Books 3 through 6—in May of 1645,[6] and even as she destroyed parts of it, he was clamoring for more. In addition, he planned to visit her again in the spring of 1646 with his son, and she knew the pressure would increase as his visit neared.

"Help me, Sor María," he wrote to her on November 6, 1645,[7] "because ultimate ruin threatens every part of the monarchy this year." He would work hard, he told her, and she must pray incessantly. After all, it had been an effective strategy thus far, as the number of soldiers at the front in Catalonia had increased from fifteen thousand to twenty thousand in the past year, and with her help he had already been "freed from the snares of treachery forged against my person."

Despite his urgent portrayal of the situation, the king wrote his November letter from the seaside in Valencia, where he had taken Baltasar Carlos for a welcome rest with family and friends. They had gone there directly from the front in Catalonia and planned at the prince's urging to return to Madrid before the end of the year.

Eight more letters passed between Sor María and Felipe, during which time the king had indeed returned with his son to Madrid. Because the king's presence at the front, however, had so lifted morale and generated success, unrest grew at his absence, and the battlefield soon recalled them to Catalonia. Once again, Ágreda was an important stop en route to the frontier.

Sor María looked forward to seeing the king again and to discussing in more depth the subjects they did not feel comfortable entrusting to their regular correspondence, which always bore the risk of interception.[8] In advance of his visit, she sent another reassuring letter, knowing of his propensity for discouragement.

"Although the water comes close to the throat," she wrote on March 28, 1646,[9] "threatening to drown the small ship of Spain, do not fall prey to distrust, as your faith safeguards so many. . . . The threats against Italy, Spain and other parts are from men. I have been acquainted with divine anger for years, and I assure you, it is more prudent to fear heaven." "Take heart," she nevertheless comforted him. "You need to dilate [your soul] to accomplish great things, neither saddening yourself with blame, nor succumbing to it, [mistakenly thinking] that that is what will obligate God to forgive you [rather than proper reform and atonement]."

Finally the king and Prince Baltasar Carlos arrived in Ágreda.

"Our lord the King passed through this place," Sor María wrote in 1646,[10] "on Thursday April 19, and he entered this convent with his son the Prince."

Sor María decided that this visit was an opportune time to tell the king about her visions following the death of Queen Isabel. She did so with great concern for his emotional state, and that of his son, despite legendary accounts of the king's own father and grandfather appearing after death to venerable religious figures of their day.

"He commanded me to write to him soon, and also the prince," she wrote, "with my paper on the death of our lady the Queen and later events."

Sor María sent the paper to the king and in it described her visions of Isabel's death and relegation to purgatory and the queen's ultimate passage to heaven. She wrote that God had detained the queen in purgatory for "passively ignoring the [moral] state of the monarchy" more than any egregious sins on the part of the queen, then ended with a vivid description of the angels carrying Isabel to her "eternal rest in the Lord."

While the scribes at Saint Julian's were nearly finished that summer copying for the king the third part of *Mystical City of God*,[11] Felipe wrote to Sor María in July that the prince had caught "tertian fevers" in Pamplona, after leaving Ágreda. Frantically, he begged for her prayers, remaining stalwartly at his son's side despite the clamoring of the Aragonés at the front for the king to personally direct the campaign. Two months later, the prince was well enough to travel, and they finally arrived in Zaragoza only to learn of the king's sister's death—Empress María.[12]

The king had little time to mourn, however, for soon after learning of his sister's death, imperial ambassadors arrived in Zaragoza, proposing Baltasar Carlos's marriage to the daughter of the emperor who was also Felipe IV's niece, Archduchess Mariana of Austria. The prince, he told Sor María in mid-June 1646,[13] was "very much pleased with his new state," and for Felipe's part, he was happy to welcome his niece as his new daughter-in-law. He was certain, he told Sor María, that the marriage would produce "very beneficial effects to the Catholic religion, which is my sole aspiration."

Sor María penned immediate letters of congratulations to the king and the prince on June 19, 1646.[14] She reminded Felipe of the Lord's role in his success and in the prince's life and health. She also responded to his complaints about the situation in Lérida, reminding him that his former minister had alienated the natives there, leading the way for the French to recruit "many of the king's own citizens."

"I cry out to the Lord," she wrote, "that the people of Lerida will understand their jeopardy . . . before the enemy is fortified even more. If I could rescue them with my own blood, I would."

Sor María received a polite response from the prince, acknowledging her letter of congratulations and their meeting in Ágreda, and asking her blessing and prayers for his upcoming marriage to Mariana of Austria. Before July was out, Sor María forwarded to the king the third and final part of *Mystical City of God*, Books 7 and 8 of the original Spanish version.[15] In September Felipe IV wrote to her saying that he was trying to devote two hours a day to reading the material and that publishing it would aid their efforts with the pope on the issue of the Immaculate Conception.[16]

Sor María demurred to the king, implying that no one would be interested in the writings of a poor ignorant scribe such as herself. In truth, the idea of publishing the biography terrified Sor María.[17] Padre de la Torre was absent more frequently, and she had not forgotten the incident with the old confessor the previous year. She set aside her fears in October, however, when she received shocking news from the front.

"I am not in a condition to reply to [your last letter]," the king wrote to Sor María on October 7, 1646,[18] "for our Lord has placed on me a trial through which I can hardly live. Since yesterday my son is oppressed with very extreme fever . . . and now he is delirious." The doctors, he told her, thought that the prince's condition might progress into smallpox, which ironically would perhaps present a better chance of recovery. "I know, Sor María, that all the punishments that I receive in this life could not possibly atone for all my sins," he wrote to her, "but I appeal to God's mercy . . . and I entrust you to help me with all your prayers."[19]

Sor María must have received his letter the next day. She responded immediately. "Your pain pierces my heart," she wrote on October 8.[20] "I will prostrate myself unceasingly . . . and our entire community will do the same, praying that the Lord will not take away your son, if it is his will." Soon, however, she learned that it was not to be so.

"Since petitions for my son's health did not move the Lord," she read in the king's letter of October 10,[21] "last night between the eighth and ninth hours he died, surrendering to the most violent illness the doctors had ever seen. My only consolation in the midst of such sorrow is that for more than an hour he became very calm, confessing and receiving the Last Sacraments with all lucidity of what was happening."

"I am in shock," he wrote to Sor María. "I have lost my only son. You have seen him, and know what a comfort he has been to me in the midst of all my troubles. . . . I am trying to offer up this blow to God, but it has penetrated my heart and I am in such a state that I can't tell what is a dream and what is really truth."

"The king's son is dead. Long live the king's sons," were likely thoughts echoed throughout the land. Blasphemous as it sounded to Sor María's delicate sensibilities, she knew it was true. Like the rest of the country, she grieved for Felipe's and Spain's loss in the death of the only legitimate male heir to the Crown just two years after the death of the queen. Yet she was all too aware of the prodigious number of bastard offspring generated by the monarch. She knew that thirty had been counted from many sources, though only eight were acknowledged, and only one of those—Don Juan José of Austria, son of the actress Calderona—was given rank within the military.[22]

Sor María lifted her pen to write her condolences as honestly as she could.

"I am beside myself, Your Majesty," she wrote to him on October 12,

1646,[23] "seeing your resignation at your loss, when I must reprimand myself for my bitterness on this occasion. Truly you have dilated your heart, and gained wisdom with your sacrifice."

Sor María went on to console the king, telling him that God had called the prince to him "during his tender years, protecting him from the dangers of a leadership position in this vale of tears." She reminded Felipe that that the prince was not gone forever, "but rather that he has gone to where Your Majesty hopes to go, that celestial homeland where there is no sadness, anxiety, or pain." There, she told the king, the prince was now like an angel, especially in light of his spiritual lucidity at the end.

En route to Madrid for the prince's funeral, Felipe found solace in Ágreda on November 5, 1646, while the body of the prince continued on with the retinue. This visit was to be the last personal meeting between the king and the abbess although their correspondence continued regularly, until each died in 1665. During this meeting, mindful of Sor María's experiences after the death of the queen, the grieving king commanded her to write to him about any visions she might have of the prince after his death.[24]

Soon, however, Sor María faced considerable tribulations of her own.

CHAPTER 16

"I remain alone
and fearful
of making mistakes"

AFTER SOR MARÍA COMPLETED THE LAST OF MYSTICAL CITY of God, Padre de la Torre was frequently away on provincial matters. Sor María felt particularly bereft during an extended two-week absence in 1646 when she was again subjected to the harsh judgments of the old interim confessor. Her fears and insecurities flared in the "dark night."

The old confessor ordered her to burn everything she had written. Her friends continued to advise her to concentrate on her duties as abbess and adviser to the king rather than the risky path of writing. The conflict was unbearable. "My mind was hindered," she wrote, "[by] such tempests of contrary thoughts and suggestions within me, that, deeming it the greatest presumption to have attempted such an arduous task, I concluded to burn it."[1]

Accordingly, Sor María burned her copy of Mystical City of God, along with copies of everything else she had written. Upon returning, Padre de la Torre was furious with Sor María. He accused her of using obedience itself to disobey. He ordered her to begin immediately to rewrite it, even as his health began to fail and he was unable to adequately follow through on his instruction.[2]

In the meantime, Sor María solicitously continued in her consolation of the king in the wake of the prince's death. They exchanged several letters in which she offered countless prayers and well wishes. She also wrote down many pages of her visions of the prince's progress in the afterworld, which she did not send to the king until early January 1647.

"These visions were not imaginative or physical," she wrote,[3] "but rather intellectual. In them, I recognized and heard the soul [of the prince] and his angel, to whom I responded."

"When I lived as a mortal," the prince in this way told Sor María on the twenty-sixth of October,[4] "I was ignorant of divine science, because materiality can often cause a darkness in the soul. But as I died, I entered a new light. There, my angel told me many things. . . . I have great compassion for my poor father as I know he is surrounded by lies, and treachery."

The prince cited injustices at the palace and concern for his sister and the house of Austria. "Many at the palace do not serve my father because they love him, but for their own advantage." If the king didn't maintain an even hand in governing, the prince told her, "he will not be loved by his good vassals, nor feared by the villains."[5] Sor María dutifully noted the prince's communications, as well her own observations, and sent them to the king in mid-January of the following year.

"Your letter, and the lengthy enclosure regarding the soul of the prince, consoled me beyond words," Felipe wrote to her from Madrid on January 30, 1647.[6] "I have read it two or three times, Sor María. And while I recognize God's compassion, I am all too aware of my offenses. This terrifies and exhausts me."

The king acknowledged Sor María's advice not to overdelegate to one person, but reminded her that he was just a boy of sixteen when he assumed the throne. That was the cause of his reliance on "the departed," he wrote, referring to but not naming Olivares, who had died a year and a half earlier.[7] He grappled in this letter with the demands of being a monarch, citing the need to delegate in the context of the system of government set in motion by his grandfather, Felipe II. He alluded to Don Luis de Haro's fine character, also without naming him, and then went on to name de Haro's duties. Still, he found it necessary to assure the abbess of his diligence.

"I, Sor María, embrace all of my work," he wrote. "As everyone can tell you, I am continually seated in this chair with my papers and pen in hand, examining and managing all the issues of my court and dispatches from near and far."

The rumors of his favoritism, he assured her, were generally lies put forth by ambitious men less interested in proper service than their own advancement. He asked Sor María to share any firm information she had about the identities of these individuals, to facilitate his ferreting out the suspects. Then, he said, he would remove them and bring them to justice.

In another letter earlier in January, the king had written to Sor María about an unexpected development resulting from the prince's untimely death. Apparently the emperor, after imparting condolences over the king's loss, now offered Mariana of Austria as a bride to Felipe himself. Without an heir, and at the precarious age of forty-two, Felipe readily accepted the offer in service of God and country.[8] "Agreement on my new marriage with my niece is settled," he continued in his letter to the nun on January 30.[9] "You must beg Our Lord to bless it for the good of the monarchy."

He also reminded her of a secret she had mentioned to him and assured her to be without concern since he would hold it inviolable. He referred to his copy of the manuscript of *Mystical City of God*, the only remaining copy after she had burned her own copies. While some members of the court had learned of its existence, the king guaranteed to Sor María that he would hold its contents confidential. Two weeks later Sor María penned a response to this letter with great concern that the relay of couriers who delivered it may have been diverted and its contents read. She worried about all the confidential matters at court, as well as her own secret.

"I did not receive your letter until two days ago," she wrote on February 15, 1647.[10] "Its delay worries me," she wrote, concerned about the hands it may have passed through before reaching her.

Regarding his request that she identify corrupt members of his court, she declined, admitting that she—sadly—knew much of what transpired at the palace but that the role of judgment fell alone to God and by extension to the king as God's emissary on earth. "My intent in writing that to you," she clarified, "was to encourage you, and to remind you of the abuses that will result from the appointment of more favorites."

In a rare moment of self-revelation, Sor María thanked the king for his generosity in safeguarding her secret, admitting that she needed his help. She decided, too, to share her fears about Padre de la Torre's illness. "My confessor is very sick and in danger of his life," she wrote worriedly.

"I miss his advice terribly. Without him I will be left most alone and surrounded by great troubles. I have obeyed you in giving you this news through this letter and I know you will guard it carefully."

As usual, she attended fastidiously to the king's needs, writing that time was critical in his army's efforts in Lérida and that the French were hard at work to undermine his forces there. "I beg you to immediately appoint a general to conduct your military exercises," she wrote, "because to billet your troops in distant parts he will need time to assemble and prepare your campaign. And the later it gets, the more you relinquish the ability of an offensive war for the perils of a defensive one."

With that, she gave her affectionate congratulations on his engagement to his niece, the Lady Archduchess, and her prayers that together they would prosper for many happy years.

In mid-March Sor María had another powerful visitor from Madrid—commissary general of the Franciscans, Padre Juan de Palma.[11] De Palma had served as Queen Isabel's confessor and remained in that capacity to Felipe's daughter, María Teresa.[12] He had learned of the king's copy of *Mystical City of God* and hoped to read it. The king, however, remained steadfast in his promise to Sor María to keep the document confidential. As a result, de Palma now made his request directly to Sor María. With great trepidation, Sor María agreed to let de Palma read the king's copy.

Meanwhile, Padre de la Torre's condition worsened. As his health dwindled, so too did the solace and protection he had so readily provided to Sor María for the past twenty years. Soon, she feared, she would be alone again and subject to the old confessor's harsh judgments of women. Perhaps the old confessor was right, she no doubt thought, remembering her own words in the opening of *Mystical City of God*. "I acknowledge myself to be a weak woman wanting in all virtue," she had written when she first embarked upon the effort. "Therefore, it should be far from my thought to approach such a work."[13]

De la Torre had been her mainstay, her compass, a guiding light encouraging her on her mystical path. Even in the face of imminent death he likely urged her to continue in her work to rewrite the biography of Mary's life.[14] For her part, acknowledging her timidity and great fears, she admitted that she "was much enamored by the security which the ordinary paths of the other nuns seemed to offer."[15]

Ordinary nuns, de la Torre likely told her, don't counsel kings. Yet

Sor María knew—better than most—that monarchs had their own temptations and vulnerabilities in addition to the danger of battle and corruption in their courts. That knowledge, and the knowledge of her own difficulties, led her to the succinct understanding that the greatest battle ever fought is the battle for oneself. "Él que se vence, vence," she was known to advise her nuns throughout the years. "He who conquers himself conquers all," she told them.[16] For the Heavenly Queen taught her that "all these combats, and those we shall yet speak of, are spiritual."[17]

Girding herself for the struggles to come, Sor María prayed for Padre Francisco Andrés de la Torre's peaceful passage to the next life. By nightfall on March 20, 1647, the body of her confessor and ecclesiastic protector lay inert, as church officials gathered to pray for the final consecration of his soul.[18]

"I remain alone and fearful of making mistakes," Sor María wrote on March 30, 1647,[19] to the king about de la Torre's death. "When Padre Juan de Palma was here, I asked him to advise and protect me, even from faraway, since he knows about the books. . . . [I thought] that with the authority of the prelate he might be better able to protect me from curiosity-seekers and publicity than those in lower positions." Meanwhile, Sor María anxiously awaited word of de Palma's judgment of her work in *Mystical City of God* and for any word on the assignment of a new confessor. Unfortunately, the prelate was not a well man himself, and the king was preoccupied with his own troubles.

"I ask you, Sor María, as your friend," Felipe wrote to her on April 3, 1647,[20] "to beg God to take pity on our monarchy, for I assure you it is in the most precarious state imaginable." He referred to his inadequate defenses against the French, in Catalonia.

Later that spring, de Palma reviewed the king's copy of *Mystical City of God* and declared his amazement at its marvelous content and his certainty that it had been divinely inspired. The king was pleased, of course, as was Sor María. However, the commissary general's ringing praise was unofficial, and the situation soon became more complicated.

Encouraged by de Palma's opinion, the king thought it best to gain a broader endorsement of the book, especially in light of some of its more controversial content, such as Sor María's treatment of the Immaculate Conception. In light of his careful dealings with de Palma, and his care in gaining her permission for a review of the book in 1649, her compliance with the king's approach can be assumed. Felipe therefore inquired privately to the Franciscan minister general, who quietly arranged for a group of ecclesiastical authorities to review the king's copy.[21]

Even if this review were technically in confidence, knowledge of the manuscript and its contents was certainly on the rise. In addition, the length of time needed for all the participating readers to complete their reviews generated a long period of uncertainty for the bereft nun. During this time, she still did not have a permanent confessor, something she mentioned periodically to the king. One of his responses that summer was not particularly comforting.

"Padre de Palma told me that one who has such [divine] teachers has little need of human help," the king wrote to her on July 10, 1647.[22]

Almost a year later, Sor María had not yet heard from the Franciscan minister general about her writing or the assignment of a new confessor. Finally, after learning of Padre de Palma's death in the spring of 1648,[23] she wrote to her friend Don Fernando de Borja on June 12 for his assistance.[24] She implied concern about the anticipated ruling of the minister general on her book. She hoped for a good ruling, of course, yet she had no desire to publish the work, thinking—albeit unrealistically—its best use would be the inspiration of the nuns in her charge.[25] And while leaving most things unsaid, she knew her good friend would understand.

"It makes me tremble with fear to think of getting a confessor who would want to publish my works," she wrote to de Borja. "If you communicate with the general of our Order, please convey to him the inadvisability of my publishing. But it is important that he does not know that I have negotiated this."

In this letter, uncharacteristically, she also bemoaned the seeming uselessness of her correspondence with the king, after learning about his continual adulterous affairs. Some knights of the court visited her in Ágreda, she told de Borja, and they spoke of the king's many diversions with women and entertainment at the palace, and of people's speculation about a successor even as everyone awaited his marriage to the new queen.

Despite his social life, however, the king worried mightily about his military efforts. He wrote to Sor María on June 17, 1648,[26] about the successful defeat of a rebellion in Naples but still asked her to redouble her prayers to fend off other potential losses. "Since in addition to war," he wrote, "the plague now anguishes much of Valencia and Murcia." And whether or not the king learned of her letter to de Borja, he was aware enough of his own faults to admit them to her without any additional prompting. "I fear, Sor María, that I am the one who wastes all the pains you take," he wrote to her two weeks later, on July 1, 1648.[27] "Because in the measure that your efforts increase, my sinfulness increases."

Despite her discouragement about the king's infidelities, Sor María remained loyal and consistent in her advice to him. When from de Borja she learned of potential threats to the king from none other than the Duke of Hijar, about whom she had spoken favorably to the king, she was devastated and wrote to him immediately to warn him.

"I am anguished," she wrote on September 11, 1648,[28] "for I have heard rumors that there is a plot against Your Majesty and that some suspects have already been imprisoned."

"Nothing came of it," he reassured her on September 30.[29]

Yet Sor María knew that her previous correspondence with the Duke of Hijar might be misconstrued and turned against her by those in the king's court who were jealous of Felipe's reliance on her. She was also motivated to fully disclose to the king any of her other activities that might, even peripherally, relate to him.

"He wrote to me in May of this year," she told the king,[30] "but I didn't reply because I was behind in my correspondence. He intimated that there might be some troubles emerging which I thought might be related to Granada."

As the plot unfolded later, everyone learned of Hijar's interests in replacing Don Luis de Haro or assuming independent power over Aragón, thereby splitting the country.[31] In this letter, however, the duke merely tried to gain Sor María's intercession of putting in a good word for him with the king.

Owing to Sor María's disconsolate sorrow after the loss of Padre de la Torre, she did not respond to Hijar until July of that year. When she did, she assured the king, she advised Hijar to report his allegations directly to the king.[32] While she waited anxiously for the king's reply to her letter of September 11, Sor María finally learned of the minister general's determination in the review of her manuscript.

"At His Majesty's command," Minister General Juan de Napoles wrote to her on September 12, 1648,[33] "your book has been examined by ecclesiastical authorities both outside our Order and within it, and, thanks be to God, there has not been found in it anything, however trifling, that ought to be deleted."

Before Sor María could begin to feel anything akin to relief, however, the minister general begged her to ensure that no copies of the manuscript were lost or confiscated.[34] He was concerned that many of the passages might be misinterpreted and then used against either her or the king. Her feelings of vulnerability and anxiety justifiably increased.

CHAPTER 17

"Others have
died for this"

THE KING—UNAWARE OF THE INQUISITION'S PLANS TO
interrogate Sor María—assured her that he held her blameless in the
Hijar scheme. He had been aware of the plot, he wrote to her in his
September 30 letter,[1] saying that it had been ill-conceived and not directed
against his own person. Hijar and his accomplices, the king wrote, would
be fairly tried later in the year.

In early December, Sor María first learned from the king of the duke's
imprisonment and the executions of his accomplices. Then Don Fernando
de Borja wrote to her of the sinuous procession into the plaza ending
in the bloody decapitations of the offenders. The descriptions were so
frightening that she began to make notes in the margins of her copied
correspondence with the king about Hijar, fearful that her name was in
any way associated with the debacle. In these notes she painstakingly
chronicled inferences and deductions, omissions and implications in her
correspondence with the duke and related events. She used these notes
in her mid-December response to the king, as she laboriously reported
again on her interactions with the duke.[2] In the king's next letter, he
reassured her of his estimation for her.

"I do not doubt your pain at the mention of your name in the Hijar
case," he wrote on December 29, 1648,[3] "because I know how foreign such

things are to you. Please be assured of my complete confidence in your character, for I know more than others how God favors you."

The Supreme Tribunal of the Inquisition did not agree with the king's assessment. In the wake of Padre de la Torre's death, the Inquisition examiners dredged up the old testimonies put forth about Sor María. To these they added suspicions about her involvement in the Hijar plot.

On January 8, 1649 four *calificadores*—Inquisition examiners—gathered years-old statements about Sor María, including Padre de la Torre's reports about her life and works and depositions taken from Sor María in 1635 regarding her bilocations to New Mexico. They added to these copies of her early writings, which had been confiscated and filed long ago, and the testimony of additional witnesses.[4] The prognostication was ominous. "It was very difficult," they concluded, "to convince themselves that it was God's doing and not a passive or active illusion," exacerbated by "credulity on the part of those who have governed her."[5]

Three additional examiners consulted on the case. The first—Lucas Grandín—questioned the virtue of Sor María's trances, claimed her visions were diabolical delusions, and said that the Inquisition, not her own order, should appoint her confessors and control the shameful publicity she had received.[6] Despite these damning diatribes, he said there was as of yet insufficient evidence for a final determination.

The second and third calificadores—Alonso de Herrera and Tomás de Herrera—also reserved final judgment, pending further interrogation of Sor María. As explanation for all the improbable phenomena she experienced, they proffered that passive diabolic delusion and her overwhelming desire to be a missionary could explain what might have been illusions of her visits to New Mexico.[7] Sor María was all too aware of their efforts.

"Everything I have done to keep my secret has not been enough," she wrote to the king on August 20, 1649.[8] "The few words I have spoken about it were compelled under obedience. I do not find the religious establishment very artful in handling matters like this."

She was so worried, she told him, that she had just burned the remainder of her writings, most likely copies of those that had been in the possession of Padre de la Torre. Trusting the confidentiality of her correspondence with the king, she cautiously begged Felipe to maintain her most important secret, that is, his own copy of *Mystical City of God*.[9] She worried that the Inquisition would make inquiries about other copies, yet expressed her reliance on the king's discretion.

"I am confident that it will not be revealed by Your Majesty in any circumstances," she wrote, "even if the Inquisition asks for the book."[10]

The forty-four-year-old king, however, was greatly distracted by reports of the arduous six-month journey of his niece and bride-to-be from Austria. When he finally responded to Sor María's letter, it was to deplore his moral laxity and implore her prayers that he might be faithful to his new wife.[11] Sor María dutifully responded with affectionate prayers for his marriage and a firm reminder about the importance of faithfulness in order to generate an heir. "All your subjects cry out for the fruit of your new marriage," she wrote to him.[12]

"Try, Your Majesty," she urged him, struggling to find the right words for such an indecorous thought "to focus all of your attentiveness and longing upon the Queen, without turning your eyes to other alluring objects of desire."

The king assured her of his good intentions, but he worried whether such a young woman would be ready to bear children, "although others of her age, which is fifteen years, do so."[13]

By early October 1649, both king and nun strained with impatience. The king eagerly awaited the arrival of Mariana outside Madrid in Navalcarnero, while Sor María wrote to him hoping for some assurances from him about the implications of the Inquisition's recent inquiries. When he did respond, he did not address her concerns, having recently returned from his honeymoon smitten with his young bride.

"I do not know how I can thank our Lord," he wrote on November 17, 1649,[14] "for giving me such a companion. I am extremely content."

In the meantime, the head of the Spanish Franciscans visited Sor María in Ágreda—Vice Commissary General Padre Pedro Manero, who had learned that the Inquisition might soon interrogate Sor María.[15] He interviewed her in detail about her visions, particularly her missionary experiences in New Mexico as the Lady in Blue. The meetings with Manero went well, and he left her with instructions to write a full report,[16] in order to settle the claims made in Benavides's memorial letter.

Sor María wrote again to the king soon after Padre Manero's visit, on November 26, 1649,[17] asking his permission to write her congratulations to the queen and expressing regret that he had not answered her previous letter. This particularly worried her, because in the earlier letter she had shared her concern over hearing that prelates in her order were talking about transcribing her manuscript, and she did not think the time was right to publish it.[18] In cautioning him, she had hoped the king would be spurred to more carefully guard his own copy.

"I received your letter last night but at an hour too late to respond," Felipe replied to Sor María on December 5, 1649,[19] "but I have very much wanted to write to you, and I always look forward to your news! . . . The other letter you mentioned to me, however, has not come to my hands. I will enlist a search for it, although it may not be easy to find. . . . I appreciate your happiness at the arrival of the queen. Please know how much I value your advice—the advice of a good friend."

Felipe shared how favored he felt with his new marriage and assured Sor María that he would take all possible measures to generate succession. "Your writing directly to my niece is fine, too," he told Sor María, "as I believe she will very much enjoy your letters." Then he told Sor María to direct her correspondence to the queen through the Countess of Medellín, her lady-in-waiting.

"Padre Manero was with me the other day on Church business," he continued. "He said he had visited with you three times, and that he had a very good opinion of you."

Unfortunately, Sor María learned from this letter, Manero told the king that he knew of the existence of Felipe's secret copy of *Mystical City of God*. Later, the king and Sor María determined that this breach of security arose from Manero's predecessor, Juan de Palma. At this time, however, Felipe was obliged to ask Sor María's permission to let Manero read it in confidence. "Because," the king wrote, "Padre Manero said he has much practice in these matters."

"I responded vaguely," the king assured her, "finding it necessary to warn you, so that you could respond calmly and frankly. Since I said that I would not to show it to anyone without your permission, I want to fulfill my word." Hoping this would not further agitate her concerns, he closed with the familiar refrain requesting her prayers and assuring her that "with God's help, I fear nothing."

Almost paralyzed with panic at Manero's request through Felipe, Sor María responded numbly to him with well wishes and a separate enclosure for the queen, commiserated about the bloodletting of the princess, and then made several suggestions about a court-related matter that had been plaguing the king. Stifling her feelings of betrayal, she gave numerous assurances of her prayers and those of the entire convent. Finally she found some peace on the issue and responded to the request.

"Others have died for this sacramental knowledge," she responded on December 18, 1649,[20] referring to many of the teachings in Mary's biography. "I am helpless without your defense . . . and I appreciate with what loyalty you guard over me. . . . Yet to write to Your Majesty is a favor I do not deserve, and it is not mine to judge why you were late in answering me. I am merely grateful that you do," she wrote to him. Yet, she intimated that even with that security, she suffered great anxiety because of the scrutiny of the Inquisition, owing mainly to her phenomenal exterioridades in earlier years when she was called by some the Lady in Blue.

"I begged you in the letter that got lost, and in an earlier one, not to give them the book," she wrote. "Yet Padre Commissioner General Manero is learned and perceptive in these matters," she told the king. "Therefore, if it is your pleasure to give him the book, I simply beg you to impress upon him to guard it with secrecy and caution, and to return it to you immediately. For our Divine Mother obligates Your Majesty to look after this work with affection, and I kiss your feet with humble gratitude for protecting it."

With that, Sor María wisely began a notebook, in preparation for any eventual interrogations and as a way of organizing her thoughts before writing the report to Manero about New Mexico. She had no idea how much the exercise would stand her in good stead.

Less than one month later, the quiet of the cloister was pierced with the fearful arrival of an Inquisition appointee in Ágreda. Calificador Antonio del Moral, a Trinitarian, was armed with eighty prepared questions determined to ferret out the guilt of the public's darling.[21] Primary subjects included Sor María's suspected involvement in the Hijar plot and her potentially delusional experiences as the Lady in Blue.

Neither the king nor Padre Manero—increasingly an advocate for Sor María—were consulted, although both were aware of the likelihood of an interrogation. Sor María lay ill in her cell, weak with fever and just having been bled with leeches.

PART FIVE

THE SPANISH INQUISITION
INTERROGATES THE LADY IN BLUE

1650

CHAPTER 18

"It felt good to my soul
despite the enigma"

SCHOLARS CREDIT SOR MARÍA FOR HER TALENT AND literary achievements. Historians credit her for her political acumen and the valuable chronicle of court life evidenced in her correspondence with the king. The Catholic Church honors Sor María as a venerable of the church, crediting her heroic life of virtue, as well as her tremendous fortitude, wisdom, and character. On these levels, we can easily see the prolific author, the diplomatic adviser to the king, even the harried prey of the Spanish Inquisition, and gain inspiration from her strength and achievements in the face of adversity.

Fewer serious observers, however, allow that as a saintly woman Sor María might have had visions, the occurrence of which fit into the church's niche of private revelations, a sanctioned grazing garden of spiritual delights. There we find evidence of a softer, subtler nature, a spiritual aspirant who dedicated her life to the quiet, unseen path of prayer and meditation and whose diligent hoeing of the spiritual garden yielded subtle, ethereal fruits. On that level, spiritual seekers gain inspiration from Sor María's visions of the life of Mary, insights about the spiritual path, and valuable encouragement on how to surrender to God's will.

Where is the frame of reference, then, for the other standout phenomena in Sor María's life—the audacious claims of levitation and bilocation?

Many people—scholars and religious and laypeople alike—say these are unlikely events. Others make a leap of faith and say they are conceivable because "with God all things are possible." Still others might try to understand these mystifying spiritual events by looking at them in the light of equally mystifying scientific ones. Holograms, for example, exist in fact, projecting through laser technology three-dimensional, 360-degree images before us physically. Few people on the street, however, could explain the inner workings of a hologram. Fewer still could explain the exterioridades of our subject, although this inability to explain does not per se discredit either.

In the case of the Spanish Inquisition, the interrogators had ample evidence of Sor María's levitation during prayer, as other nuns and the public had observed her doing so. Regarding her supernatural appearances in southwestern America, however, they had only the long-distance testimony of Padre Benavides quoting the Jumano Native Americans and Sor María's own accounts. In addition, the inquisitors also had to determine whether these manifestations—if indeed a reality—signaled the work of the Devil or the hand of God.

In light of this complexity, the additional line of inquiry about Sor María's involvement in the "Hijar plot" against the king seemed almost simpler to address, although her innocence in the matter was not necessarily assumed by the Holy Office.

Padre Inquisitor Antonio del Moral was well aware that the king had conducted his own investigation of what had come to be known as the Hijar plot. He knew that the king had fully exonerated Sor María long before Felipe wrote to tell her with relish of the execution of the perpetrators.[1] The acquittal—in del Moral's mind—was based entirely on their unlikely and somewhat questionable friendship, and he wanted no such interference in his assessment.

Yet, based on a review of the list of prepared questions, the Hijar plot represented only a small percentage of the inquisitor's concerns. Perhaps del Moral even admitted in advance the unlikelihood of a cloistered nun's desire or ability to endanger the king. The entrée provided by any involvement with the Duke of Hijar, however, was most convenient to the Inquisition's ongoing line of investigation on Sor María, which focused in the main on her alleged supernatural experiences and the state of her mind and spirit in the context of her visions.

Del Moral's arrival in Ágreda, therefore, was conducted in secrecy for the maximum effect of surprise and to thwart any advance preparation in Sor María's defense. He was armed with written instructions from "Santo Oficio," the Holy Office of the Inquisition, which also included provisions for a licentiate, or notary, namely Commissioner Juan Rubio, to document the proceedings. Del Moral's instructions read as follows:

Santo Oficio
Notice of the Convener:

To the Padre Presenter Antonio Gonzalo del Moral: on receipt of this notice, in the Convent of the Conception in the village of Ágreda, he will examine María de Coronel, alias de Jesús, professed religious there. He will do so with all caution and concealment, in the presence of Licentiate Juan Rubio, Commissioner and Notary of the Holy Office out of the city of Encino, in the tenor of the enclosed instructions.

He will question and cross-examine her replies as necessary. He will thus determine the truth and knowledge of her spirit, belief and intelligence. If her deposition results in references to any papers, crosses, beads or images, he must acquire them and accumulate them to this procedure. Thus we commission and bestow on him the power to weigh what sentence, warrant or edict is to be done.

Padre Diego de Arce y Reynoso, Inquisitor General
Bishop of Plasencia
January 10, 1650[2]

One week later, the convent's shocked housekeeper admitted the inquisitor and notary to the library, adjacent to the lower choir, where they set up their small court. The date was January 18, 1650. Sor María had been ill and was weak from just having been bled with leeches to reduce a fever. Two nuns set her on a chair and carried her down from the infirmary. They were quickly dismissed, and Sor María was instructed to kneel on a small Communion rail Rubio had taken from the lower choir where the nuns received Communion in the back of the church.

"At the command of the senior examiner," Rubio recorded, "the abbess Madre Sor María de Jesús was enjoined to swear an oath to God and the cross which represents his law, that she would speak truthfully and completely regarding all that she knows and all that she is asked, and to hold and guard secret all that transpires, on pain of complete excommunication in conformance with the order of our superiors."[3]

Suddenly, Sor María's worst fears had come to pass. She was immediately sworn not only to tell the truth, but to hold the proceedings in complete secrecy, on pain of excommunication. In addition, she no doubt fought her feeling of violation at being brought face-to-face with strangers without the protective grille usually separating nuns from visitors in the convent's locutorio, where conversations normally took place with outsiders.

There in the library, Sor María knelt before the inquisitors as a supplicant, without any barrier other than the kneeling bench at which she struggled to maintain her balance. Even in her fevered state, however, she had come prepared, having taken a moment to bring along the notebook she had begun in anticipation of an eventual interrogation.

She offered the notebook to del Moral and Rubio. She explained that she knew to keep it, because she remembered that before Padre de la Torre had died, he was asked by many inquisitors to present facts about her life and writings. He had told her, she said, that the examinations would eventually resume, and she kept the notebook to aid them in their questioning. When del Moral asked her about her other writings, she told him that she had burned them all, including the copies she had later found among Padre de la Torre's books.

Dismissing the notebook for the moment, del Moral pulled out a list of eighty questions that had been carefully prepared in advance. Many questions had multiple parts, examining specific details and perspectives on each topic and subtopic. The questions focused first on the alleged supernatural conversions of the Jumanos in New Mexico. These questions comprised over two-thirds of the interrogation. The Hijar plot was also covered, although minimally, as well as the nature of Sor María's visions and—of course—the issue of her writings.

Despite her illness, the notebook that Sor María had begun had helped to organize her thoughts. She was also gratified that she had made notations in the margins of her letters with the king regarding the Hijar plot, although the inquisitors did not know of her copies, nor did they presume to break the confidentiality of that correspondence.

Portions of the interrogation proceedings appear in a supplementary volume of contemporary Spanish editions of *Mystical City of God*, as excerpted from the notary's official report issued to her confessor after the fact. In it, the questions and answers are numbered according to the inquisitor's list. If a question had ten parts, it was still recorded in one paragraph, followed by an even lengthier paragraph comprising her answer. It is written in the third person, stating "he asked" and "she replied."

Painstaking as the record is, it does not reflect the give-and-take likely to have occurred in a personal interview. The treatment in this biography therefore converts the dialogue to the first person and splits the questions into more conversational parts, each followed in sequence by its corresponding reply.[4]

That said, del Moral began his rapid-fire questions.

"Answer under oath," del Moral enjoined her, as he embarked on the first series of questions. These dealt with Sor María's initial communications with her confessors about the bilocations, probing in detail how much she told and to whom.

"On the first occasion of your travel to the New World," del Moral demanded, "immediately after you returned, did you tell your confessor about it?"[5]

"Yes, I did," she replied. "I had just entered the religious life then, at about age eighteen. I had learned to show all my interior to the Holy Church and to obey."[6]

"When exactly you did tell him?" del Moral asked.

"At first," Sor María said, "before speaking to my confessor or anyone else, I was anxious about the good of those souls. Then I experienced some light and knowledge that helped me to understand that divine mercy shone on them with compassion."

"Did you call for the confessor?" del Moral persisted in asking.

"Yes," she replied, "but I did not send for the confessor just to talk. I asked only to confess."

Sor María, in her subtle way, was indicating that she thought she had communicated with her confessor under the auspices of confession, even though confidentiality was not a luxury frequently accorded to her during those tumultuous years. If del Moral understood her implication, there is no indication.

"Answer this," del Moral continued to read from the first inches of the long scroll. "Did an angel or St. Francis take your place while you were in the above mentioned kingdoms?"

Upon hearing this question, Sor María remembered the misunderstanding with Benavides, who claimed she had flown to the New World on the wings of Michael the Archangel and Saint Francis. She was gratified that she had clarified this issue in her report to Padre Manero, even though she was still stung that Benavides had so widely circulated a letter that she had thought to be private. In it, in referring to her mystical "flights," she was using terminology common among nuns to refer to the angel and saint as "wings," since their inspiration helped them "fly to God." The statement had been metaphorical, she clarified, whereas Benavides had interpreted it literally.[7]

Now, del Moral's question reflected, she knew, a presumption based on the earlier misunderstanding. No, her beloved teachers did not take her place, she simply clarified, nor had they ever prevented her going.

"On your way to being transported to these kingdoms," del Moral continued, "did you know what places you saw along the way?"[8]

"I could distinguish massive areas, but only briefly," Sor María said. "Mainly, though, I realized the multitudes of people in the world, and how few knew . . . the Gospel. With this knowledge, my heart came undone. It was not the purpose to know the names of the places, but the perdition of the souls."[9]

"Answer this," del Moral asked. "When carried to those kingdoms, or when you were there, did you get wet when it rained—you or your clothing—and if so, were you or they wet when you returned here?"[10]

"The light of the Lord was so abundant and fertile," she said, "that I did usually have some awareness of the effects of the elements. In some parts it was raining and in some it was drizzling, but regarding the matter of being wet myself, if it rained Padre, please forgive me, I don't remember."[11]

"If the Indians asked who you were, and from where, and in what way you had gotten there, how did you respond to them?"[12]

"I said that I brought them news from very far away," Sor María said, "and that I had come to advise them in the faith."[13]

Del Moral recalled the file on Sor María from 1635, in which the interrogators queried her about somehow transporting rosaries and other items to the New World. He wondered, no doubt, how she carried physical items through "the elements."

In Sor María's view, this was one of many mortifying instances in which the accounts of her experiences had been exaggerated. During the interrogation, she attempted to clarify for del Moral—as she did again later with Padre Manero—what she did and did not bring with her to the New World.

The missionaries, she reported, were often downhearted at their impoverished resources, complaining that they lacked even the sacramental necessities for saying Mass.[14] Sor María had mentioned this at the time to her confessors. They in turn had told the temporary convent administrators who later had ordered her to take a monstrance with unconsecrated Communion wafers to the mission fathers.

"But for my part, I was afraid to do something like that," she reported, "and touch the monstrance in which our Lord had been. I returned it to its place. . . . Then in the confusion, the nuns lost track of the monstrance and must have thought I took it with me."[15]

Her account of the rosaries, however, was another matter altogether.

"On one occasion," she continued, "I gave the Indians some rosaries. I had them with me and distributed them among them, then I never saw the rosaries again."[16]

"When you preached to the Indians," del Moral continued, "what was it that convinced them to convert?"[17]

"I understand that there might be some doubt about this," Sor María replied, "because there is no way for anyone else to verify it. Nevertheless, our discussions included . . . the theological virtues of faith, hope and charity, which would give them the light to understand God . . . and not be so attached to earthly things." Then she fully described her narratives to the Jumanos, including the infinite attributes of God, his unity with Christ and the Holy Spirit, the entire story of Mary's Immaculate Conception, and the story of humanity's redemption through her son. Then, she told del Moral, when she told them that the doorway out of darkness was through the church and baptism in the spirit, they were eager for baptism.[18]

When asked about how long she was there, she reported, "I was never there a day and a night, nor was it necessary."[19]

She was reminded in responding to this question that Padre Benavides said that she had been in New Mexico for three days. Later, in her letter to Manero, she clarified how he may have gotten that impression, explaining that she had often been ill for several days at a time during the period in question, and if she went for three days without eating or speaking that the other nuns mistakenly assumed she was in mystical transport to the American kingdoms for the entire time.

"Then answer this," del Moral said. "If time passed so quickly, as you seem to have said, how could you teach them so much about all of our sacred faith and principal beliefs in such little time?"[20]

"I never much noticed the passage of time," Sor María said. "If it seemed as though I was there for a longer time, it also seemed as though they gave me some shelter and sustenance. And whatever hours there were seemed to be enough."[21]

The questions resumed in the afternoon and continued each day for eleven days, for three hours each morning and afternoon except Sunday, until the twenty-ninth of January—from the inquisitor's scroll to the abbess at the Communion rail, always kneeling, never allowed to sit.[22]

"Answer under oath," del Moral asked one day, having reached the thirty-fifth in the long series of questions, "at what locations, and in what situations did you preach to the Indians? Furthermore, how did they assemble to listen, and did they arrange a pulpit or eminent place for all to hear?"[23]

"I still cannot say whether I went there physically or not," Sor María replied. "But no, I did not preach from a pulpit, because I am not that eminent." "Nor did I call to them, or make them join me," she said. "So, sometimes there were more Indians and sometimes there were less, but it does seem to me that the Lord arranged the means to suit the end he desired."[24]

"Yet how in these provinces, which are said to be barbarian," del Moral asked, "with people who do not know how to speak without grunting, could you communicate clearly and instruct them in such a way that they could understand you and you them?"[25]

Sor María had always described the Jumanos as "apt and competent beings" who were chosen by the Lord because they were the ones "most disposed to convert."[26] Yet she was too discreet to correct del Moral's opinion of them and potentially alienate him in the process.

"The way of speaking was certainly very different from what we have here," she testified. "Sometimes we used external gestures. Other times perhaps God used an angel to speak through me. It felt good to my soul despite the enigma of how it was happening, so that I never felt anything contrary to the faith or the truth."[27]

"Were you occasionally missed," del Moral asked, "in the time you ascended from the convent to the kingdom of the Indians?"[28]

"I don't think I was ever missed, Padre," Sor María said. "That would be impossible to hide among women [living together so closely]."[29]

"Who remained in your place, if there was no sense of your absence?

VENERABLE MADRE MARIA JESUS DE AGREDA
THE LADY IN BLUE 1620 1631

FIGURE 27. Twentieth-century mural of Sor María preaching to Jumano Native Americans, from original painting by Dorothy White circa 1960. On display in—and image courtesy of—Saint Anne's Parish, Beaumont, Texas.

An angel perhaps?" del Moral challenged her. "Did an angel come to substitute in your official role as abbess, or in the choir at matins, or even in the middle of the night sitting in your chair and writing in your room? If that is the case, how could the angel do so without the other nuns recognizing that something was different?"

"No, Padre," she said. "Even though I myself was very engaged with what was happening, feeling entirely diverted and suspended, it was all mainly during my first three years as a nun, and in fact I was not yet the abbess. Also, while sometimes I actually witnessed a [physical] presence, the visits were also sometimes intellectual, and sometimes imaginative."

"Tell me," del Moral asked, reading from the list of eighty questions, "in the conflicts between the Christians and the unbelievers, how many men took the part of the Christians. How many took the part of the heathens? And, how many of each were killed?"[30]

"I do not know the numbers," Sor María replied simply.[31]

"With what weapons did they fight?" he asked.

"Their weapons were different from those we have here," she told him,[32] describing their primitive slinglike devices for throwing stones, their crossbows and wooden knives.[33]

This line of questioning brought the interrogation to the issue of Sor María's physical safety in the midst of warlike conditions. It was particularly pertinent since stories had circulated in the 1630s about her having suffered fatal injuries at the hands of a hostile tribe.

CHAPTER 19

"Angels take on more of an aerial body"

THE INQUISITION'S MEMORY ON SOR MARÍA WAS LONG and its file deep. The letter Padre Benavides had written to the missionaries, in 1631, had revealed an account of her having been killed and martyred for the faith while in the American Southwest. "She herself was martyred and received many wounds," Benavides had written, "and her Holy Angels crowned her because she was granted . . . the blessing of Martyrdom."[1] Del Moral's pointed questions about the occasions of warfare among the Native Americans, and between some Native Americans and the colonists, now probed that possibility.

"Sor María," del Moral said, "you have said to me and also confessed in your notebook, that the people of the kingdom of Tixlas [Texas] were very fierce, and that many of the unbelievers were very hostile. You said that many Christians had died."[2]

"Yes," Sor María said, "I remember that there was a big battle in which the Christians suffered great losses."[3]

"And," del Moral continued, "you said that you stood on behalf of the Christians and you cheered them on in battle, and that there was no further damage to them," implying that she claimed responsibility for their victory.

"During the fight, I lifted my hands to God and cried out to his

Majesty. I asked him to help this cause," Sor María said, giving the credit to the Lord.

"Where did this battle take place?" del Moral asked. "How long was it, and who were the captains of the armies?"

"As for the length of the battle, and the exact location, I cannot say," Sor María answered. "Nor do I know the names of the captains of the armies."

"Were you visible to the Christians in the battle?" del Moral asked her. "Did you fight in their defense? If so, with which weapon, and in what part did you affect the outcome? Be clear, also, about whether you slew any infidels with your own hands."[4]

"Whatever assistance I gave," Sor María said, "consisted only of my poor prayers."[5] "And," she added, "I cannot say that I was present at the battle visibly. Just as in other instances that I have described [sometimes a physical presence, sometimes intellectual, and sometimes imaginative]. I can say that I have never had a weapon in my life, nor have I killed anyone. Always my greatest 'weapon' has been to preach about the Eternal Father and his holiest Son and to defend those who confess to him."[6]

"How do you suppose that you knew about the death and martyrdom of two of our religious?" he asked with stiletto-like precision.[7]

This was a difficult moment for Sor María, as she debated just how much to tell the inquisitor. The time of her appearances in the New World, after all, was a time of painful contrasts. Not only had she experienced the joy of ecstasy in prayer, levitation, and bilocation, during the same period she had also struggled against the sexual temptations that caused her such remorse that she always referred to those times as the "bad years." At the time, however, she likely transmuted her feelings of guilt—for even experiencing the temptations—into a desire to suffer and die for the faith in order to atone for her sins. She admitted later, in her summary of the interrogation, that she replied to this question most fearfully, grappling to remember exactly what happened and how to speak about it. Later in the year, in her report to Padre Manero, she would more frankly admit how Padre Benavides had embroidered the facts.

"I desire to tell the truth," she finally replied to del Moral. "During those times I myself longed to die [for the faith]. Yet it was more than 27 years ago," she said, "and as I remember it, my understanding of their martyrdom [seemed spiritual], through what I often describe as 'interior light.'"[8]

If del Moral had read Sor María's early writings, he indeed would have been reminded of her great zeal for the faith, from the time she was a teenager on. "Even at the cost of my lifeblood," she had written in "Face of the Earth and Map of the Spheres," "[I long to] spread the holy gospel from west to east and from north to south."[9] Several years later, she expressed similar sentiments in her letters to Benavides and the missionaries, writing to them that she would give her blood or her life in order to be able to evangelize.[10] Even after the interrogation, such was the depth of her feeling about missionary preaching that she wrote about it again to Manero, reiterating her fervor to die, if necessary, in order to work in the conversion of souls.[11]

"Whatever exactly happened," Sor María said to del Moral, believing the experience to have been more spiritual in nature than physical, "I affirm with all truth and certainty, that nothing of this circumstance happened with the intervention of the demon, whom I then detested, now detest, and will forever detest."[12]

Then as the days went on, gradually Sor María gained in strength, and she was better able to respond to the Inquisitor with her signature diplomacy.

"Answer this," Padre del Moral began on another day, "in the notebook you say it is clear that all the faithful and the infidels have guardian angels. How do you know this, and how can it be a [required] matter of faith that the heathens too have guardian angels?"[13]

Sor María would soon write in her report to Padre Manero that "the creatures most disposed to convert, the ones toward whom [God's] compassion was most inclined, were the New Mexicans and the inhabitants of other remote kingdoms in that part of the world."[14] She then reasoned that He would not withhold from them the very angels who would work with them toward union with Himself.

To del Moral she replied, "I know that this is not an article of divine faith as required by the Church. . . . Yet I also know that man must make his way on earth, and that God will judge all on the last day. Therefore, I believe with human faith that it is through divine mercy that the natives have guardian angels. Because God, in his divine mercy, provides the means so that we are not lacking, giving us each an angel to warn and direct us so that we may flourish."[15]

"What type of communication have you had with the angels?" del Moral asked.[16]

La V.M. Maria de Jesus de Agreda. Predicando
à los Chichimecos del Nuebo-méxico. Antt de Castro f.

FIGURE 28. Woodcut of Sor María preaching in New Mexico, by Antonio
de Castro in 1730, originally used for 1730 Mexican edition of Benavides's
correspondence with the missionaries. Courtesy of Catholic Archives of
Texas, Austin.

"As you might expect, the primary communication for a species that is abstract, is intellectual," Sor María said, "in that angels are of a spiritual substance. They infuse the soul with respect, fear, and reverence for the knowledge of God. Then they give light to the soul and reveal to it the will of God."[17]

"Do they have a body?" he asked.

"In a way," Sor María said. "Since we cannot see a spirit with our physical sight, because it has no materiality, sometimes they do manifest on more of a corporeal level. In this case, the angels take on more of an aerial body, which *is* possible to see."

"What was the condition or odor of their dress," he persisted, "and were they young boys, men, or old men?"

Sor María no doubt thought this question entirely irrelevant as applied to spiritual beings such as angels. Yet she replied patiently. "Because our minds always have images according to our understanding and experience," she said, "we envision the angels as a corporal species [like ourselves]. Usually it is an image of a lad, a beautiful young man, such as I have seen portrayed of Tobías." "Although," she added, "it is still possible to feel an angel's presence without seeing it, since it sends inspirations and warnings that we can feel. It is like being in a completely dark room, when we nevertheless somehow know that someone is there."

When she rewrote *Mystical City of God* in later years, Sor María included the following passage on angels: "God had created the angels [when he] . . . said: 'Let there be light, and light was made.' He speaks here not only of material light, but also of the intellectual or angelic lights. He does not make express mention of them, but merely includes them in this word. . . . But the metaphor of light was very appropriate to signify the angelic nature and mystically, the light of their science and grace, with which they were endowed at their creation."[18]

"Have you, Sor María, seen God clearly and distinctly?" del Moral asked later.[19]

Sor María no doubt reeled at the question. How could they think she had seen the Most High? She likely reasoned that any answer to this question could condemn her. If she answered affirmatively, she could be accused of spiritual pride and of claiming to have had beatific visions. If she answered in the negative, it would contradict her own visionary experiences as reported to her confessors over the years.

"Padre," she said, "of all your questions, none has devastated my heart more painfully than this one. I know even when I die that I will not be worthy to see God's face. This weighs more bitterly than anything else I have endured. Yet despite my faults," she added, "I sense his potency—not even intuitively, but more in wonderment."[20]

"What is there, that you see?" del Moral asked.

Sor María, who valued the clear essence of intuitive knowledge so highly, sadly confessed that her "vision" of God was indirect at most, not even intuitive. "It is as though I see through a veil," she said, "in a vision of an abstract and intellectual species for which there were no words. . . . I do, however, even with my shortcomings, see his infinite attributes and perfection," she added, "but not his presence. That is for those more blessed than I."

By then del Moral had asked the seventy-sixth question in the exhaustive series, and Sor María had apparently responded with composure and wisdom. At this point, however, he asked a three-part question so general that it took several pages to record Sor María's reply.

"Declare the exterior exercises in which you have engaged and the interior favors which the Lord then endowed upon you," del Moral demanded in the first part of question number seventy-seven.[21]

One can almost hear Sor María gasping for enough breath to adequately address such a sweeping question. It was, in fact, the essence of her spiritual life. Patiently, yet painfully aware that she was not yet out of danger, she went back to the beginning and began yet another narration of her life. She credited her parents with setting her on a spiritual path. She described the clear light she experienced at an early age when she prayed and followed the straight path. And she spoke of her early understanding.

"From my childhood," Sor María said, "the Lord showed me the mysteries of our holy Catholic faith with great clarity, but only inasmuch as grace also penetrated my poor weak mind."[22] She described the sustenance she received after taking her religious vows as a nun, her adherence to the scheduled spiritual exercises, and the love that the Lord enflamed in her heart, despite her imperfections.

"The light of the Lamb of God guided me during the day," Sor María said, "and during the dark nights of my ordeals. Even though I was sinful, lukewarm, ungrateful and imperfect, and the least of his creatures," she described herself disparagingly, "with a weak and imperfect nature that impeded me from attaining the perfection that I felt I owed the Lord, still he bestowed upon me benefits and favors. Thus faith became my sustenance, the column of my fortitude, the guide of my thoughts, words and actions."

"How have you been occupied and used your life, since the conversions [in New Mexico]?" del Moral asked as the second part of the seventy-seventh question.[23]

"After I prayed for the removal of the exterioridades, the light grew within me most abundantly," Sor María said. "This produced a gentle yet very strong [spiritual] intelligence. . . . It showed me the imperfection and misery of the senses, and that without that dependency I could understand the higher levels of the soul. That seems to me to be the greatest martyrdom, to die to the senses, to lose the affection for earthly things. Then," she said, describing how her soul simply opened up, "I understood the secret ways of creatures and the science of the Lord."

"Now everything manifests to me through the light of the Lord," she continued. "It infuses my duties as abbess, and increases my compassion for the needy," she said, referring to her convent's mission to feed the poor and hungry, of which there were many. "With all the poverty and hardship in the world, I believe that priests and nuns can do much to soften the suffering in the world."[24]

Then del Moral asked the third part of the seventy-seventh question, opening up perhaps the most perilous area of inquiry for Sor María.

CHAPTER 20

"I saw them all written out in a divine handwriting"

"WHAT ARE YOUR PRESENT CONCERNS AND STATE OF MIND?" del Moral asked her.[1]

Because they were so integral to all of her experiences, Sor María again described the nature of her spiritual visions and took this as an opportunity to "confess" her controversial writing activities.

"I still receive many favors from the Lord," she said. "These [visions] are sometimes intellectual, as I have mentioned, sometimes imaginative, and occasionally corporeal," she said. "Many of them pertain to the life of Our Lord and his Blessed Mother. Some of these visions were so memorable," she added, "that after I told my superiors about them, I began to write the biography of Our Lady."[2]

She cited her superiors' approval of her writing the biography, particularly her obedience to her long-term confessor, Padre Andrés de la Torre, in doing so. She mentioned Padre Juan de Palma—confessor for the royal princess—who had reviewed it favorably. And she told how she burned the biography, on the order of a temporary confessor during de la Torre's absence, began rewriting it on de la Torre's return, and again burned what little she had rewritten near the time of de la Torre's death. She did not, however, disclose a pivotal conversation she had with de la Torre before his death, regarding the king's secret copy of *Mystical City of God*.

Bishop Ximénez Samaniego recounts how de la Torre had severely reprimanded Sor María for burning her copy of the history. Yet, Ximénez Samaniego wrote, the confessor advised her not to access the king's copy for the purpose of making another original. Instead, he considered it prudent to keep secret the fact of the king's copy, perhaps not willing to compromise the history of Sor María's obedience, albeit to a temporary confessor.[3]

Now, without a confessor after de la Torre's death, Sor María carefully reviewed the circumstances surrounding the existence of the king's copy. She determined to maintain the strategy he had recommended. She therefore continued on with her narration, covering her correspondence with the king and her regrettable involvement with the Duke of Híjar. At this point, she no doubt hoped the interrogation was almost over and made a few summary statements.

"Since then," she said, "I have been alone [without a confessor], and no one has compelled me to resume [the biography]. So I have immersed myself in my daily duties, and I have not written anything but my own spiritual intentions, which I call the 'purpose of perfection.' As I said on your arrival, I put these in the small notebook that I would like to give to you now. That is all I have in my possession." "Nor," she added, "do I know of any more papers that anyone else may have, that I have written."[4]

In making this last statement, Sor María took a great risk in stretching the truth. After all, several other individuals could attest to the king's copy of *Mystical City of God*, since they had reviewed it. She counted, no doubt, on two things. First, the secrecy that she had begged the king to enforce, despite the fact that the word had spread about his copy, even if minimally. Second, in all likelihood, that some hand other than her own had actually copied or written the set of papers now in the king's possession. This was not a comfortable compromise for Sor María, yet she did it thinking to protect herself from further scrutiny. This half-truth would plague her until her death, ameliorated only by the counsel of a future confessor.

In the meantime, hoping no doubt to distance herself from that painful topic, Sor María mentioned one more thing about the present time. She told del Moral of her love of Latin.

"I have always felt a great affinity for the message of the Sacred Scriptures," she said. "I have not studied Latin, but on occasion in encountering a passage while saying the divine office, I seemed to understand the

Psalms and some great mysteries and parables. So occasionally I attempted to translate it into Spanish, even though without any particular insight. Then I might write some of it down for the other nuns when they seemed to be in need of encouragement."[5]

In mentioning this earlier writing, Sor María inadvertently provided an entrée for the inquisitor's next question and his seemingly endless follow-up questions reaching far into Sor María's past.

"Did you compile any litanies of Our Lady?" del Moral probed.[6]

"Yes," Sor María said. "During that time when I was about nineteen years old, there was a great drought in the land. Everyone in the village prayed a novena to Our Lady before the Virgin of the Martyrs."[7] Miraculously, she explained, their prayers were rewarded. At the same time, she was sick in her cell and asked to have the statue brought to her. Upon being immediately cured, she stayed up all night writing a litany to Our Lady in gratitude.

"Were you ordered or commanded by her to print it?" del Moral asked.

No, Sor María replied, it had merely been an exercise of devotion to the Mother of God, one not meant for other eyes, unless to inspire the nuns in her charge.[8]

"Then by the order of what person was it printed?" he asked.

Sor María explained how she showed the material to her confessor who, in his enthusiasm, had copies written for his priest friends. One of them, to her consternation, published it in Zaragoza without her knowledge, under the name of Don Miguel Coronel.[9] Yet she harbored no resentment for his having done so, she assured del Moral, and most likely admired the priests for their devotion to Mary.

"From what papers or books did you get the praises for Our Lady? Or, in what part of the Scripture or in which authors have you read any of them? Or, did any other person tell these praises to you so that you could write them down?"[10]

"Certainly I was inspired by the Sacred Scriptures," Sor María said, "particularly by Proverbs and the Songs [of Solomon]. But no one helped me to write them, and the real 'book' where I found them was in the light of the Lord and his divine intelligence. It was as though, at the instant that I thought of writing them, that I saw them all written out in a divine handwriting."[11]

Del Moral then delved into a series of questions involving specific titles of the Virgin, which Sor María had recorded in the document.

"What is the meaning," he asked incredulously, "of the verse which says: 'Immaculate and most perfect mirror of the divinity'?[12] How is this possible?"

"Sometimes when we look into a mirror," Sor María said, "we may observe something new. When we look at Mary—as into a mirror—we know the Most Holy Mother participated in our redemption by taking the flesh of the Son of God into her womb. We also know that God is said to have created man in his image and likeness. In partaking of man's redemption, it seemed to me that the Most Holy Mary helped to restore man's resemblance to God, and in doing so by virtue of her own immaculate purity, she acts as a mirror in producing the most genuine likeness of God."[13]

"What about the verse in which you describe her as 'Complement of the ineffable and most holy Trinity?'" del Moral asked, intimating the unlikelihood of a woman complementing the godhead.[14]

"As I understand it from the homilies of Saint Eusebio and Saint Ildefonso," Sor María said, "Holy Mary is not a complement of the Trinity intrinsically, since God is infinitely complete, and has no need of a complement. Extrinsically, however, this divine Lady gave the flesh from her own body to the Son. In doing so she surrendered to God's will and participated in the pleasure of the Divine Trinity in redeeming our souls."[15]

"What of the verse which calls her 'Sphere of the Divine Omnipotence'?"[16]

"In the celestial sphere of Our Lady's body," María said, "the Blessed Mother carried our Lord for nine months. Thus it is through this pure and admirable creature that we know the grandeur of divine omnipotence that is behind such works."[17]

Del Moral read the entire litany word for word, stopping to question Sor María on each entry. The process was exhaustive, in that the litany contained eighty-one entries coined by Sor María—each of which required explanation—in addition to some traditional titles of Mary that were also quoted. After Sor María clarified the last honorific title of Mary, however, an unexpected godsend rewarded her endurance—del Moral gave her the first concrete indication that the interrogation was going well.

"He was satisfied with the clarity of my explanations," Sor María wrote later, "and said that I showed an intelligent understanding of 'divine handwriting' and sacred Scripture. He said that God had communicated with me."[18]

Finally, when the last—eightieth—question was asked and answered, Sor María had every reason to believe that the eleven-day marathon had concluded.

She was wrong.

CHAPTER 21

"Of the history of the Queen . . . it is best to keep it a secret"

"AFTER ALL THAT WE HAVE ASKED," DEL MORAL NOW SAID, "do you have any other statement to make to the Holy Office in order to clarify these subjects? Do you have anything else to say in order to attain the purest truth regarding these matters?"[1]

The question was open ended and set a high bar to hurdle—the "purest truth." It gave Sor María one more chance to blunder or to add significant testimony in support of her previous responses. She was exhausted. Yet she addressed the issue of the final injunction thoughtfully.

"I said that it had been many years since the events about which I was being examined," Sor María testified, "and that there had been so many questions and cross-examinations, that in my state of illness my memory was weak and fragile. What if I had omitted something? What if this omission was due to my weakened state, rather than a lack of desire to express the purest truth in obedience to the Holy Tribunal that I respected and venerated as a daughter of the Church?"[2]

Del Moral likely agreed with her dilemma but did not offer a solution. Sor María did. "To ensure that I could determine what information might be missing or need amendment," Sor María continued, "I asked that they read to me everything that was recorded, from the beginning to the end. The Padre Calificador agreed, and the notary read everything back to me."

With a humble resiliency the likes of which the inquisitors must have rarely encountered, Sor María had deftly maneuvered herself into a position of relative control. Not only would this process help her to decide if there were any glaring omissions on her part, it would also serve to assure her that the inquisitors had correctly recorded her responses.

Perhaps offering a fleeting prayer of thanks, Sor María listened carefully to the entire record. At the end, she decided that it was accurate and mainly complete and that she would sign it. Before doing so, however, she required one more step for her own closure. With her typical diplomacy she made a request.

"The record is accurate," she said to del Moral and Rubio. "Yet—more for my own consolation—I beg humbly at the feet of the Holy Tribunal that I may profess my faith to you. It will be a comfort to me that will last until my death, that I confessed before the Holy Office which so unwaveringly defends the faith." Del Moral agreed, and Sor María dug into her reserves to deliver a powerful closing statement of her beliefs and religious fervor.

"Lord and immortal King of the centuries," she began, "for your glory and honor alone I want to praise you and to confess."[3] She covered her belief and adherence to all the articles of faith, commandments, creeds, scriptures, "sacraments, definitions, sayings, apostolic and ecclesiastic laws, and traditions of the holy Roman Church, with Christ as its head, as governed by his Vicar the Pontiff and sanctified by the Holy Spirit." All this she communicated with the baroque eloquence replete throughout her writing. "All that I have professed," she said in conclusion, "I affirm and revere to the extent that I would die for this truth."

Then, as though she herself had arranged for the event, Sor María thanked the calificadores for the examination. She assured them that it had allayed her fears, especially following the death of her confessor, and hoped that they would be instrumental in guiding her. She told them that they had taught her much in the process of the interrogation and "enlightened my ignorance, since no other creature needs correction and warning more than I."

"With that," Rubio recorded, "she stopped, declared the record was true, and ratified it by signing her name."

The inquisitors prepared to leave Ágreda on January 29 with a far different frame of mind than the grim attitude that had shrouded their arrival. While they provided neither copies to Sor María of any of the proceedings, nor even a brief statement of acquittal, it was clear upon their exit that Sor María had indeed turned the corner.

In contrast with the secrecy of January 11, del Moral and Rubio now spoke openly to the other nuns of the Convent of the Conception, saying what a treasure they had in Sor María. They praised her as well to the curious townspeople who had gingerly hovered nearby in the church, no doubt to pray for a good outcome for their cherished mystic.

As testimony to their newfound esteem for Sor María, the two inquisitors requested some religious articles with which she had prayed—crosses and items listed in the record of the event as "devotional adornments," in all likelihood medals worn by the nuns and perhaps rosaries. Like others who met Sor María, however, they hoped to maintain their acquaintance beyond their meeting. They asked to correspond with her, and indeed they did, throughout their lives.[4]

With that the two withdrew from Ágreda far differently than they had arrived. In their wake, Sor María no doubt lifted her heart in copious thanksgiving before taking a well-deserved rest and resuming her duties.

Meanwhile in Madrid, news of the surreptitious interrogation of the king's special correspondent had been rippling through the court. The inquisitor general, the king learned, had selected someone outside the Franciscan order to gain a less biased evaluation of the abbess's sanctity and her activities. Perhaps Felipe dove into the pile on his desk to reread Sor María's letter of January 21, thinking it might contain hidden clues about her recent trials. There were none.

"I admit to Your Majesty," she had written to him midway through the eleven-day interrogation, "that Divine Providence strikes a heavy blow when heretics are permitted to marshal their forces against the Christians." Then Sor María had shared a long account from the biblical Book of Judith, wherein Judith braves enemy forces and helps to recapture her city from the Assyrians at the battle of Bethulia.[5]

How could she have mentioned nothing of the interrogation he may have wondered in amazement, then perhaps speculated that since she had been sick, perhaps her illness had not yet abated and she was clouded with fever. Or, perhaps he realized that the story of another brave woman gave his friend strength during her trials.

This clearly left the king in ignorance about what had transpired during the interrogation about the biography of Mary. Although distracted because of the installation of his new bride after their honeymoon, Felipe quickly grew concerned about Sor María. Had she encoded the letter for him, he may have wondered, looking again for a secret message to decipher. Could that be the meaning of her conclusion about Judith when she had written, "moved by prayer, Almighty God gave the victory using as his instrument a weak woman"?[6]

Try as he might, there was no message to decipher about the inquisitors or her book. Nevertheless, he no doubt appreciated, despite the circumstances, that she still had the presence of mind to quote for him an inspiring passage from the Bible. "For God has said," Sor María had written, "'with charity and everlasting love have I loved you.'" "And God's love," she wrote, "is not changeable like human love, because it is the essence of his Being. God *is* love."[7]

Juan Rubio prepared the report for del Moral's signature on February 4, 1650. The notary included a transmittal note to the inquisitor general expressing their newfound admiration for Sor María and crediting her "sublime holiness" and "supernatural understanding."[8] Inquisition General Diego de Arce y Reynoso examined the report in detail and consulted the Inquisition's prosecuting attorney. The two agreed with del Moral and Rubio and approved the report. Soon—probably in the first half of February—the inquisitor general gave an account of it to the king.[9] Sor María, however, would not learn of the formal findings for several weeks.

"In fulfillment of my commission," del Moral wrote,

I took a deposition from the Madre Sor María of Jesus, Abbess of the Convent of the Conception, town of Ágreda. I recognize in her much virtue deeply rooted in charity, and a great intelligence of the Sacred Scriptures. It appears to me that she has acquired more through continual prayer and interior surrender with God, than many accomplish with study and great exterior work. . . .

She satisfied all principal essentials of the examination with humility and truth. In my estimation, those who initiated this line of inquiry embellished and made unwarranted suppositions, because they did not have reasonable cause to begin with. . . .

Regarding what she signed under [Benavides's] order, we consider it an "indiscreet obedience," and attribute it to the inexperience of youth and gender. As for the subject now, I say that she is a catholic and faithful Christian, well-founded in our holy faith. She embroidered no fiction into her accounts, nor was she deluded by the devil.

This is my best judgment, which I humbly yield.[10]

In the absence of any direct disclosure about the interrogation from Sor María, the king appears to have written a short letter to her about his problems in Córdoba and the plague in Andalucía, encouraging her to safeguard her health. No doubt he hoped to hear her own account first and then to send his hearty congratulations.

"Señor," she wrote to him on February 18,[11] "please accept my humble and affectionate gratitude for your compassion regarding my illness, amidst all your own concerns. Right now my health and my life seem so useless that my only consolation in this valley of tears is that I may offer them up for Your Majesty and your reign."

True to their established rapport, Sor María did not hold back any tough advice after the affectionate greeting, especially if she thought the king needed some compelling reason to turn to God. "Happy is the monarchy whose heroic prince is steeped in virtue, moderated in his passions," she wrote. "Then the heart of the king [will be] held and protected in God's hand, appeasing his anger. . . . Thus I was so sad to hear of the onset of the plague in Andalucía and its fury in Córdoba," she added, ". . . and I shed many tears on your behalf. We must do everything possible to invoke divine remedies."

According to form, she also assured him of his place in her prayers and her hopes for the birth of a successor to the throne. Then, when she had covered all the other matters she thought important to the king and could avoid it no longer, she knew she must tell him about the Inquisition's visit. She had written him on February 4, a few days after del Moral and Rubio had left, but at that time she was still recovering from her illness and had not adequately internalized the import of the events enough to write about them. Two weeks later, however, she was thinking more clearly about it and knew the king would soon learn of it anyway, by virtue of his position as Defender of the Faith.

"And now, my dear sir," she wrote, "I cannot keep this secret from

Your Majesty, for I love and esteem you so, and for the confidence that I have in you, more than in any human creature. During my illness, a party of the Inquisition arrived here to evaluate the Litany of Our Lady, (which I believe I have shown you) that I had written [long ago]. I responded to their questions, even the most difficult ones; and they interrogated me about many other events."

She referred, of course, to her supernatural visits to the New World, the conversion of the Indians, and the Hijar debacle, although she did not go into detail on those questions. "I declared the truth," she wrote, "and it was important to do so, because the variety of priests and confessors who attended me had added and removed so much in the story. . . . I only worry that my responses were correct, because I was alone, without counsel, and so many years had gone by."

She took time to share with her friend, however, how she felt personally about the interrogation and how it had actually helped her. She didn't mention how effusive the inquisitors were upon their departure. Rather, she wrote about what mattered most to her about the exhaustive process.

"None of this saddened me," she told him. "In fact, for the security of my conscience, I really wanted to give a truthful account of the events that caused so many difficulties." "Now, advancing through fire and blood," she wrote dramatically, "I have achieved that security." "As for the inquisitors," she added, "they proceeded with such great piety and secrecy, that I have become a great admirer of the Holy Tribunal and the integrity of its proceedings."

At this point in her letter, Sor María knew that she had to write something to the king about *Mystical City of God* and in what context it may have come up during the interrogation. Since the inquisitors had asked no formal questions about it, and the only mention came so briefly from Sor María herself—and since she had so adamantly enjoined the king to maintain the secrecy of his own copy—she opted to write a carefully worded caution to the king, knowing he would understand and respect her wishes. "Of the history of the Queen of Heaven, they said nothing. They must not know about it. Until this storm passes," she enjoined her royal friend, "it is best to keep it a secret."

This secret, necessary as it may have been, disturbed Sor María deeply. She longed for a permanent confessor, to whom she could unburden herself.

CHAPTER 22

"I was alone,
without counsel"

KING FELIPE IV, WHILE CONCERNED ABOUT THE WELFARE
of his treasured spiritual adviser, in no way associated Sor María with
the more egregious cases of the Spanish Inquisition. Yet, his own prothonotary, Geronimo de Villanueva, Marqués of Villalba, had repeatedly suffered arrest and imprisonment for years under the censure of
the Inquisition.

Villanueva's vulnerability was associated mainly with the Convent of
Placido in Madrid, which he founded in 1623,[1] and whose abbess became
his mistress. The king himself, much to Sor María's dismay—and that
of most of the religious establishment—had been no stranger to illicit
liaisons with the San Placido nuns. Villanueva was not cited, however,
for his licentious affairs, but rather for being an accomplice to, or at least
complicit with, alleged heresy. Initially, in 1638, the convent's spiritual
director was prosecuted and found guilty, and the abbess, nuns, and
Villanueva were cleared.[2]

Reversals of Inquisition acquittals were unfortunately common,
however, casting an uneasy shadow on even the most positive rulings.[3]
Pius V had long ago decreed during his papacy (1566–72) that no acquittal
for heresy should be considered permanent. And indeed, in Villanueva's
case, the Inquisition kept an active file on him and the Convent of Placido

for many years, well after the royal prothonotary received even more favorable royal appointments to prestigious councils in 1639 and 1643.[4] By August 31, 1644, Villanueva was arrested on the order of Inquisitor General Arce y Reynoso, the same inquisitor who six years later ordered the surreptitious interrogation of Sor María.[5]

The king was conflicted over Villanueva's case, desirous of protecting him yet strongly influenced by Arce y Reynoso—to the extent that some said the king was completely under his domination.[6] Eventually the case came to the attention of Pope Innocent X, who demanded that complete documentation be sent to Rome. The laborious task of copying the papers took several months, producing a heavy trunk laden with over forty-six hundred pages.[7]

The intrigues, feints, diversions, and delays that followed were so intricate, over a number of years, that they warranted a treatment of over twenty-five pages by Inquisition authority, church historian, and Harvard University doctor of laws Henry Charles Lea in his definitive four-volume compendium on the Spanish Inquisition.

Though we do not know how much of this activity was apparent to Sor María, she likely knew something of it, and probably other examples as well. And it all played out in the late 1640s and early 1650s, the same period during which her own case came to a head.

Nevertheless, unlike Villanueva, Sor María's interrogation did not constitute a trial per se, but rather an investigation. So, one might have reasonably expected that del Moral's glowing account of the Ágredan mystic would stand her in good stead, perhaps for the rest of her life—if, that is, she did not engage in any other controversial matters.

That her case did not go to trial was a strange double-edged sword. On the one hand, her activities had not warranted a trial. On the other hand, the Inquisition was only obligated to provide advance warning to the king—and no one else—if a case had escalated enough to require a trial. Thus Sor María had indeed been "alone, without counsel" as she had previously written,[8] not only without a permanent confessor since de la Torre's death, not only facing the inquisitors for eleven days without counsel, but also without the knowledge of the very one who might have intervened, had he known about the interrogation.

Now, when Felipe read in the space of a few weeks the inquisitors' findings, and Sor María's own account of the interrogation, he was doubly confounded. First, that the event had taken place without his knowledge, and second, that Sor María did not seem privy to her official exoneration as evidenced in del Moral's report.

In Ágreda, Sor María opened the correspondence from the courier. The king, she saw, was responding to her most recent letters, in the second of which she had mentioned the examinations of the Holy Office.

"Today I received your two letters, of the 4th and 18th of this month," the king wrote on February 26, 1650.[9] "I know I am late in responding but . . . it is a pleasure that we write to each other, and I am thankful, in all truth, for all that you say and what you exhort me to do."

There were three days left before Ash Wednesday. Felipe explained to Sor María that he was spending them by himself at del Retiro, the park and palace retreat he had built just outside the walls of Madrid. The queen and his daughter, he wrote, were elsewhere, attending festivals permissible to the pre-Lenten season. He enjoyed the solitude and the beautiful environment, he told her, especially after all the battlefront exercises when he and his troops were encamped on the frontier. Then he no doubt relished the rare opportunity to provide assurance to the holy woman who had unfailingly advocated his best interests for the past seven years.

"I sense the travails which God has given you," he wrote, obliquely referring to the interrogation, "and I am very grateful for the secret that you entrust to me. But truth never fails, and all these clouds will one day clear so that the light of your virtue will shine even brighter."

He told her that Padre Manero recounted his visit with her and that Manero had already read the first part of Mary's biography. Manero hoped, he told her, that sometime soon she would provide to him the latter part of the account that bore her signature. In withholding that portion, Felipe explained, technically Manero had no way to confirm her authorship until such time as she decided to officially disclose it herself.

"Then later," he wrote, "if it seems right to you, you might write to him concerning this." "In the meantime," he added in the artful ambiguity they so frequently employed in their letters to each other, "it does not need to be disclosed (as you say, and as it seems to us) that I have it. So that when it comes to light, no repair will be needed [in defense]."

This passage proved a forewarning of future complications over Sor María's writing, particularly *Mystical City of God*, to which the pair obliquely referred. Much of the criticism and censure, however, would occur in the decades and centuries after the book's publication, which took place five years after Sor María's death. It would evolve into a centuries-long debate in which pope after pope took contrasting positions on the work, issuing approvals and censures in alternating succession. For the time being, however, the king felt triumphant and optimistic on Sor María's behalf and advised her in kind.

"Nothing, not even the devil, will overshadow this most worthy work when its time comes to be published," he vowed. "We do this for Our Lady, in whom I hope for all my remedy. [Signed,] I the King."

This represented quite a turning point for Sor María. Her exoneration provided no fanfare of vindication, such as might be the case in a public trial. Yet, it cleared her of suspicion over those specific issues that the interrogation had addressed, such as the bilocation and the litany. It also served to ease her mind about her controversial past and the attendant misconceptions.

It did not, however, resolve her oppressive secret regarding the king's copy of *Mystical City of God* or provide her with a clear spiritual direction. For someone as complex and refined as Sor María, this was no small consideration. As a result, she continued to experience a compelling need for a permanent spiritual director and confessor. Fortunately, help was on the way. Sor María soon received another crucial letter, from the Franciscan minister general, Padre Juan de Napoles, with welcome news indeed.

Padre Andrés de Fuenmayor, Napoles wrote, had recently been appointed as her permanent confessor. Fuenmayor was from Viana near Logroño and was an intelligent man somewhat her junior, with a high level of expertise in Latin and the Scriptures, which she might find helpful in her writing. He was also related to the Fuenmayor family of Ágreda, which had founded the Augustinian convent across the road from Sor María's ancestral home. Napoles assured Sor María that the priest was most capable and that the appointment was serendipitous because of the proximity of his family.

Because of Fuenmayor's youth, Napoles decided to augment his efforts with the seasoned experience of the retiring provincial, Padre Miguel Gutiérrez. The combination, he said, should provide the abbess with ample spiritual guidance and finally close the unfortunate discontinuity she may have experienced since the death of Padre de la Torre.[10]

By April 1650, Fuenmayor and Gutiérrez had been comfortably installed in Saint Julian's, next door to the convent, when a delivery arrived for Padre Fuenmayor. It was a transcript of the Inquisition's interrogation, he informed Sor María, and it had been delayed because it was mistakenly sent to him in Viana and held there in some cases he had left behind for shipment later. It was an inspiring account, he told her, and one she might want to include when she captured her own impressions of the event.

For the first time in several years, Sor María found new hope.

PART SIX

FRUITS OF A MYSTIC'S LABOR

1650

CHAPTER 23

"For God's sake . . .
I beg you to . . .
avoid oppressing the poor"

THE OPPORTUNITY FOR A NEW BEGINNING EXHILARATED
Sor María, and it evoked in her a deep longing for complete spiritual cleansing. She was, after all, almost forty-nine years old. In seventeenth-century terms, she was about to embark upon her later years. And throughout her life, she had already brushed close to death several times. Now she wanted to completely reconcile her conscience with the will of God. This was all-important to her—her avowed reason for living—and she determined not to leave this life without complete preparation for the next.

Yet, Sor María had much to focus on in the wake of the inquisitorial flurry. The administration of the convent called for renewed attention, as did the guidance of the spiritual devotions of the nuns under her supervision. For many, that would have been challenge enough. She also needed to continually apply herself to the concerns and correspondence of the king—another substantial and ongoing responsibility, as Spain continued to war with France and conflict blighted the Catalonian countryside.

In addition, before the January 1650 interrogation was too distant to remember, she hoped to complete the promised report to Padre Manero about the bilocations to New Mexico. With Fuenmayor's support and encouragement, she accomplished all this by early 1651.[1] Then, she directed her attention to her deepest concerns—her spiritual life.

She had, she reasoned, diligently served as abbess since the age of twenty-five, beginning in 1627. Now, she longed for an opportunity to immerse herself more fully in spiritual pursuits. With Padre Fuenmayor's support, she wrote to the *nuncio*—papal ambassador Julio Rospigliosi, who was a great admirer of hers and had visited her in 1643—for release from her duties as abbess.[2] Privately, she hoped the change would be permanent, knowing she had many capable replacements among the nuns in her charge. Rospigliosi granted a three-year sabbatical, the only interruption in her administrative duties as abbess until her death.

Fuenmayor's participation was significant in obtaining the sabbatical. He also had a crucial influence on Sor María from the beginning, despite his inexperience—or perhaps partly owing to it. So respectful was he of her spiritual attainment, and so concerned was he that her story might be lost, that he mandated her to chronicle her spiritual experiences from then forward. At a later date, he would also insist that she write an account of her life from the beginning. On June 24, 1651, Sor María obediently began the first of thirty-six notebooks, a series that would continue through 1654.

Sabatinas—translated literally as "Saturday Masses," but more accurately interpreted as a sabbatical from her duties as abbess—chronicled a deeply moving period in Sor María's mystical life, one in which she reembraced her spiritual path with a vigor determined to break new ground. During this time, she went inward to search her soul, to confront her past, and to face her eternal future. She planned to make a general confession.[3]

This was not unlike the process novices undertake today as they approach their religious vows. In these general confessions, novices review the spiritual momentum and sins of their entire lives. Today this process takes only a few days.[4] In Sor María's era, however, Spain abounded with lengthy "confession manuals" for the religious and layperson alike. Then, confession was an elaborate process, compounded by the fact that by this time in her life, Sor María was no novice.

In this context, general confession bears no resemblance to today's brief "incremental" confessions often sandwiched in between Saturday errands, in which the practicing Catholic confesses only those sins committed since the most recent confession. Rather, the sacramental opportunity of a general confession affords spiritual aspirants the chance to evaluate their entire lives in light of their spiritual failures and successes, and their relationship with God. Sor María began this process on August 18, 1651.[5]

"I began my preparations for a general confession," she wrote, "as if I were going to die then, at age 49. . . . It took until October 18 of the same year . . . to contemplate my sins, to examine and write about them, and to prepare for the disposition of my soul."

She was scrupulous to a fault in the examination of her conscience. "Great anguish erupted," she wrote as she contemplated her shortcomings. "I longed to prepare for my death." One day, as she fought with self-doubt and yearned to be at peace, she reported that an angel responded to her cries. The angel told Sor María that he would help her to prepare for the painful transition from this temporary life to the eternal one. With his help, she saw a parade of humanity, from the beginning of human history as she understood it.

"I saw all the deceased, from Adam to the present," she wrote, "their bodies and their bones. I saw the ends of so many pontiffs, monarchs, princes and kings, eminent doctors, ecclesiastic and secular, poor and rich, gentlemen and plebeian, men and women, all turned into dust. Many of the nobility were thrown into hell, whereas lesser people were saved. Virtue alone prevailed. Only the righteous were blessed."

In order to prepare to die properly, the angel told her, she must shed everything she knew and did and cherished. She must die to sin and all its effects. "I realized that sin caused the disorders of nature," she wrote, "volatility of tempers, corruption, undue passionate appetites, beastly anger, violence, and all sorrow and anxiety." In order to die to this glut of sin, the angel counseled her, she must die a mystical death. In the process, he warned her, she would suffer physically, too. "I had a serious illness," Sor María wrote. "I believed I was indeed dying."

In this vulnerable state, Sor María asked herself and God what she could do to improve her life and her confession. The angel spoke, describing the perilous nature of life, replete with opportunities to go astray. Sor María saw that people far more eminent and learned than she had been condemned and that the prudent course of action was to surrender to God's will completely and without hesitancy. The angel in turn described the brevity of life, comparing it to a single step in a far longer journey.

She realized that one of her potentially greatest offerings in this life—her writing about Mary—could be the very thing that might endanger her anew and for which she felt adamantly unworthy. "I begged the Lord with tears to uproot me from this world," she wrote, no doubt hoping to physically die rather than risk further controversy about her visions of the Heavenly Queen. Then she voiced her misgivings to the angel.

"God is your truest friend," the angel replied. "He will guide your steps with intention and love." Even as she pondered the angels' relationship with God and humankind, a response was immediately forthcoming. "Light emanates from God's immutable being, as the origin of all," the angel said, "and we administer the light to you."

Thereupon Sor María made a decision. "I offered, if need be, to [re]write the History of the Queen of Heaven," she wrote. Immediately she felt comforted. All her introspection and heartfelt surrender led to a deeply satisfying and lengthy confession. "The Lord forgave my sins," she wrote. "He purified me and my senses. [Through the angels] He anointed me with light, saying it was the Holy Spirit. Then I 'died' and was 'buried.'" "I spent thirteen days confessing and making acts of contrition, until All Saints' Day, November 1, 1651. From then on, I remained 'deceased,'" she wrote, referring to her mystical death.

Sor María's rarefied state of mystical death persisted beyond her general confession. Temporarily freed from her duties as abbess, she engaged in convent activities with the other nuns, but her soul reverberated continually at a level of spiritual peace that transcended her senses. And although she and the nuns practiced their devotions in a cloistered convent, visitors and correspondents were always quick to spread the word about the Ágreda abbess and her convent.

So revered was Sor María's advanced soul and the spiritual exercises at the Convent of the Conception that requests arose for a new facility near Zaragoza. Sor María immediately set to work with the temporary abbess on the arrangements, although in order to do so, she would have to send some of her own nuns as founders.

In the meantime, the king continued to press Sor María for advice and prayers. She always replied graciously and frankly, even when she was in the midst of extended spiritual introspection. One time, when Felipe opined at length about his tribulations and weaknesses, Sor María replied boldly to him.

"He is not king, who is not first the king of himself, his appetites, and his passions," she wrote, concluding with what had become one of her signature aphorisms. "Él que se vence, vence," she told the king many times, as well as her nuns. "He who conquers himself, conquers all."[6]

"Your letter is of great comfort," he wrote to her on May 29, 1652.[7] "It gives me the respite to rise above my cares, in anticipation of the days when Our Lord will set me free from them."

He updated her on the revolts in Andalucía, the riots in Córdoba and Seville, and the setbacks in Barcelona, still a part of the separate Catalonian territory. He reviewed the progress of his nineteen ships off the coast of Majorca, there to fend off other aggressors by sea. His detailed descriptions vividly portrayed the conflicts he sought to control. "The riot in Córdoba abated, by the infinite compassion of Our Lord," he wrote. "But then Seville erupted in riot on the 22nd," he added, explaining people's reactions when they heard the announcements about the devaluation of the currency.[8]

Sor María's reply was reminiscent of the language of *Sabatinas*, her ongoing account of the spiritual exercises following her general confession. "The King of the ages, creator and preserver of the universe, is infinite in wisdom and kindness," she wrote to the king on June 1, 1652.[9] "All his works are measured with fairness and justice, and an immense love for the creatures he brought from nothingness into existence."

She wrote that it was not harshness when God seeks to save us from dangers leading to eternal death, but love, just as a loving father takes a knife from his young son, so the son will not be hurt even though he may cry more. Yet, she opined, mankind too often chooses "the poison of vice and despises the antidote of virtue." She proceeded to connect the riots in Córdoba and Seville with ongoing activities in his court, deftly interweaving spiritual admonitions with practical advice.

"Your vassals have taken to vice," she wrote. "Wickedness is applauded and virtue outraged.... The powerful pursue the poor.... For God's sake, Your Majesty, I beg you to relax the changes you are making [in your taxation policies]. If you avoid oppressing the poor, they will not revolt."

Sor María well knew the Crown's financial difficulties, because the king made sure to apprise her of his every problem. She was quick to empathize with his perpetual need for more resources and agreed that it would take powerful means to remedy the deficits. But she did not want him to extract taxes at the cost of peace in the kingdom. "Yes, be exacting," she wrote to him, "but as gently as possible. Also, do not neglect your requests for help among the rich and the powerful, as they have more to give, and it will not provoke them as much as the poor."

In this letter, Sor María also shared her personal feelings about an event at the convent. She was about to send off four of her nuns to found another convent in the province of Aragón, in Borja near Zaragoza. "These days I walk between great enthusiasm and sorrow," she wrote to her friend. "I am greatly consoled because we will dedicate another monastery to the worship of the Most High and the devotion of the Immaculate Conception. But this has left a huge tender gap, in losing these nuns with whom I have lived so long."

"I am not surprised how much you miss the nuns who have left," he replied on June 12, 1652.[10] "But I also know that you can offer up the good fruit that they will reap, and be comforted by their results." Then, of course, he regaled her with his woes.

The previous year, Queen Mariana of Spain had given birth to a daughter, Margarita María. Although the event was greeted with great fanfare, and the king's older daughter María Teresa stood as the infant's godmother, the king was discouraged. Since Baltasar Carlos's death, he still had no son as male heir to the Crown. The birth of his daughter, a frail shadow of her older half sister, contrasted painfully with the heroic success of Felipe's most renowned illegitimate son, Don Juan José of Austria.

Don Juan José—by 1652 a charismatic army commander—had proven himself in battle, excelled in the siege of Barcelona the previous year,[11] and received many substantial and honorific titles. He had captured the hearts of many Spaniards, and although there was a fringe movement to maneuver him toward succession to the Crown, it was untenable given the political climate.[12]

The queen, jealous of Don Juan José's popularity, watched helplessly as the king's eye once again wandered to other women. Felipe rarely referred to Mariana as his wife, but rather as "his niece," and when speaking of his daughters and young wife in tandem, he often called them "the girls."[13]

To Sor María he confessed his anguish at the growing affronts to God throughout his kingdom and all of Christendom and blamed himself as the potential cause. As usual, he was quicker to embrace his weaknesses than his strengths. "I wonder increasingly if all this is born of my sins," he continued in his letter of June 12. "God knows that I want to be right, and that I try not to offend him, but I am afraid of my weakness. Help me with your prayers, so that I can please God, and reform."

Despite Sor María's occasional doubts that she could effect any change in the king, some positive indicators occasionally leaked out in Felipe's letters. Historians posit that her influence helped him from falling into complete indifference,[14] even though he battled an insurmountable financial depression dating back to the reign of his grandfather, Felipe II.

"As you say," he wrote, "I will try to limit the burdens of [tax] debt on business, so that it does not further damage the economy. And I assure you that I will do everything possible for the relief of the poor. My ministers shall treat them with love and gentleness, within reason. Further, I will work to equalize the burden between the rich and the poor, as this is undoubtedly very suitable." Although "the situation in France was more of a mess every day . . . the riots in Andalucía seemed to be calming down," and there was other good news that year in the Spanish recapture of the French seaport town Gravelines, site of the ignominious defeat of the Spanish Armada in 1588.

Despite Felipe's continual transgressions, and his reliance on Sor María's prayers to pluck him out of harm's way, he also began by this time to show signs of internalizing some of her spiritual advice. "I see more clearly," he wrote, "how damaging the offenses to Our Lord are to all of Christendom."

Sor María found herself encouraged by his admission. "Your letter evokes two different effects in me," she wrote to him on June 21, 1652.[15] "I experience supreme sorrow, and extreme pleasure. Pain pierces my soul, to see the heart of your anxiety and your embattled crown. If I could lessen your suffering, loading everything onto my shoulders, it would alleviate my sadness. Yet the storms toss you into pain, and motivate you to amend your sins."

As usual, Sor María had to remind the king that his responsibility was to follow through on his inclinations to reform. To help bring that about, she suggested that he make a thorough confession, followed by Communion.

"With such a divine sacrament," she wrote, "Your Majesty can strengthen his weakness, in order to walk the laborious path that remains to you." Sor María then extended her "humble thanks for trying gentler means with the poor" and commiserated with his various military challenges, acknowledging that some of the delays he was experiencing caused the depletion of the army's energy and supplies. "I will cry out of the depths of my heart to the Most High for you," she wrote in closing. "May the Almighty prosper you for many happy years."

Soon after Sor María wrote this letter—the 379th in the 600-plus series between her and the king—she prepared to use her sabbatical to further her spiritual quest. As Bishop Ximénez Samaniego wrote, "She plunged herself into the immense sea of divinity."[16] Her journey is faithfully recorded in *Sabatinas*. It began with a major shift in her relationship with the Blessed Mother.

CHAPTER 24

"I have come undone in affection"

IF PERHAPS WE HAVE DIFFICULTY IMAGINING SOR MARÍA'S unquenchable desire for increased spiritual perfection, the virtuosos of the ages may provide some insight. Johann Sebastian Bach by 1735 had already written his famous Brandenburg Concertos and the Mass in B Minor, yet even on his deathbed, having already composed over one thousand works, he dictated a choral prelude for organ. Albert Einstein published four papers in 1905 that built a new foundation under modern physics, including his famous formula, "$E = mc^2$." Yet he forged ahead, relentlessly pursuing his theory of general relativity and the Unified Field Theory through his later years.

Sor María applied this universally recognizable fervor to the "science" of her spiritual life, knowing the opportunities for development to be virtually unlimited. She called it *ciencia infusa*, or "infused science," in recognition of its spiritual—yet no less real—origin.[1] Her three-year sabbatical provided a forum for her impassioned forays into this science or discipline of the spirit, guided by her visions from Mary and the Christ.

On November 21, 1652, the feast day of the presentation of the young Virgin Mary at the temple, Sor María began a sort of apprenticeship that she termed her "novitiate of the first level of perfection."[2] It was a period of prayer, contemplation, and application of spiritual principles received from Mary in visions. This would last through Easter of the following year, at which time she entered a second novitiate. By the spring of 1653, on the day of the Blessed Trinity, Sor María began her third novitiate. Yet there was more to come. Each novitiate Sor María completed would eventually reap a new state of spirit, or "religion," as she called it.

Pages fell from Sor María's pen as she poured upon them the vivid accounts of her spiritual experiences. In her first novitiate, at the invitation of the Virgin, her approach to spirituality was to change dramatically. In contrast to the way she practiced her religious exercises for many years, as a disciple, now she was to engage upon a path of imitation. "I was led to understand that I must copy the Heavenly Queen's virtues and interior practices according to my impoverished ability," she wrote, "in remuneration for having written her life."[3]

Sheet by sheet, Sor María chronicled the tutelage of the Virgin and these new initiations into the mystic realms of the spirit. Mary portrayed her virtues, practices, and prayers to Sor María in detail, very much like the sections of personal instruction at the end of each chapter in *Mystical City of God*. She exhorted Sor María to renew her religious vows and told her that this new state would adorn her more richly than untold jewels. Sor María embraced anew her religious convictions and worked diligently to imitate her queen and teacher.

However, as Sor María well knew, the greatest rewards often were preceded by the greatest challenges. On one occasion, she felt she had been invited by Mary and Christ to continue in her quest, when she saw a fierce dragon with seven heads blocking her way.[4]

"I was troubled," she wrote, "asking 'How is it possible to get past such fierce figures without getting killed?' 'Come, come,' they said to me. 'Step on them, step over them, and enter [heaven].' I answered, 'I do not know how,' and was instructed that, similarly, when Christ told Saint Peter to walk on the waters, it was not as formidable as it seemed."

After many tests, Sor María seemed to reach a plateau of fulfillment. "Then an infused spiritual essence adorned my head like hair," she wrote. "I wore a necklace with three gemstones of faith, hope and charity. The virtues embroidered my habit, with chastity girding my waist, and my sandals were made of diligence."

Sor María continued on this esoteric pursuit for almost two more years. She describes in *Sabatinas* how her novitiate into the second level of

perfection elevated her from the imitation of Mary to the imitation of Christ. This stage began early in 1653.

"Do you believe," the Son asked in her heart one day after she received the Holy Sacrament, "that I am here, in you, transubstantiated?"[5]

"Yes, my Lord," was her reply.

"And that I am a priest according to the order of Melchisedech?"

Again she agreed, describing how she prostrated herself on the ground and called herself a vile worm. Then it seemed to her that two angels lifted her from the earth, she recounted, and presented her before the divine tribunal. Sor María cried out, "Lord, Lord, transform me. Let me die now so that I may live."

"In his heart of love, I have come undone in affection," she wrote in 1653 after the Paschal feast of the Resurrection, when the Lord granted her wish. "I have been made new, with the result that in Holy Week I suffered and died a happy death with Our Lord and was resuscitated with Him, from that day forward to follow him."[6]

Thus Sor María died yet another mystical death, a pattern that would continue throughout each novitiate, into the three "levels of perfection." Her deaths represented the death, in stages, of her lower self. This she would shed and leave behind, in favor of the higher levels she had yet to ascend on the quest to obtain her desire, the divine Lord, separation from whom remained her greatest fear and equaled a living hell.

"I feared that all the terrors and threats of hell would befall me were I separated from the Lord," she wrote, "and I thank the object of my love for giving me this understanding."[7]

Garbed in this protective psychological armor, only to have to divest herself of it, Sor María was invited to take another step, on to the third level of perfection, to contemplate God within her soul. "To enter these infinite spaces, you must be washed in the blood of the Lamb," she was told, "dressed in purity alone, stripped of everything. Thus enter the misty light, and surrender to our love. Climb, climb, climb, knowing that this novitiate with Mary Immaculate entails also a novitiate with your husband Christ, because the way to enter the Godhead is through his only begotten Son."[8]

She continued in these exercises through the remainder of 1653 and well into the next year. Her charge this time, Bishop Ximénez Samaniego explained, was to immerse herself in the divine essence of the Most High himself, "her celestial sovereign." "God established these degrees," Ximénez Samaniego wrote, "to enable all souls to ascend to the height of perfection."[9]

Sor María aspired to this charge with all her heart and soul, despite her frequent bouts with low self-esteem.[10] How could such a "vile worm-let" as she, she wondered, even presume to embark upon such a path? Yet she persisted, and, as Ximénez Samaniego reports, she relayed all these events to her confessor, Padre Fuenmayor.[11] The allotted time for her sabbatical would soon run out, and she hoped that he would help her to renew it. In the meantime, she persisted in the rigorous discipline of the spirit.

Again, there were exercises to complete and tests to pass. Again she faced the decreasing yet no less frightening nature of her limitations and faults. And again she conquered even more of her sensate self in favor of the divinity to which God called her. "Él que se vence, vence," she often thought. "He who conquers himself, conquers all."

Her efforts were amply rewarded.

"It is my pleasure," revealed the Lord, in a passage that later appeared in *Mystical City of God*, "that you dwell in the infinite regions of my Divinity and that you roam about and disport yourself through the infinite fields of my attributes and perfections. There the view of the intellect is without any restraint. There the will is delighted without shadow of misgiving, and there the inclinations are satiated without bitterness."[12]

By the middle of 1654 Sor María had completed the third level of perfection and felt invited by Mary and the Lord to enter the states of religion corresponding to each of her three novitiates. She was humbled and stricken with her unworthiness, yet she persisted into the divine abyss. Ximénez Samaniego describes her experience of being transported to the throne of God. "In the year 1654, on the feast of the Assumption of the Blessed Virgin Mary," he wrote, "she was taken (whether in the body or out of it she could not say) before the throne of the most august Trinity."[13]

"I felt useless and weak, terrified and ill," she wrote. "The Lord said my faults were grave, and that even with all the benefits I received that I was slow in putting them into action. Mary intervened on my behalf, pledging my reform, and asking the Lord for my pardon. . . . Then they commanded six angels to uplift me: two to purify me of imperfections, two to fill me with the power of light, and two to ready me for the [spiritual] benefits I would soon receive."[14]

Words often failed Sor María in recounting these events despite her diligence in recording them. After the ministrations of the angels, she merely says that in the presence of Mary she sat at the feet of Christ and he washed her in his blood. For her, it represented a fulfillment beyond comprehension. "I professed to that path," she concluded simply, "as the daughter and imitator of the Most Holy Virgin."[15]

Sor María emerged from her three-year sabbatical glowing with spiritual fulfillment. Yet she felt that she had so much further to go. She requested a renewal of the sabbatical, originally granted by Cardinal Rospigliosi, the future pope Clement IX. She longed for the continued freedom to pursue the spiritual discipline that she considered her primary vocation and an infinite path. *La ciencia infinita*, she now called it, "the infinite science."[16]

Padre Fuenmayor regretfully informed Sor María her that he had queried the provincial—and beyond—and they had refused an extension of the sabbatical, having too high of an opinion of her exemplary leadership abilities. Resigning herself to obedience, she lovingly reembraced her duties as abbess.

Meanwhile, as Sor María battled her spiritual demons, King Felipe IV continued to wrestle with threats to the Spanish throne.

Bad news assailed the king from every direction, he wrote to Sor María. The French pressed more dangerously in Flanders, and his Irish mercenaries in Catalonia deserted to join the French. He couldn't even trust the remaining mercenaries, he told her, because they mutinously threatened to sell the Spanish fortress to the French.[17]

"My cares increase every day," he had written to her during her sabbatical, describing how he had taken to visiting the crypt beneath El Escorial.

Witnesses later recounted how the king had spent two hours kneeling in prayer on the hard stones of the mausoleum, in front of the very niche reserved for his own body. When he emerged, they saw that his eyes were "red and swollen with weeping."[18] Many suspected that the lack of a male heir, and the queen's sequential births to several daughters, each of whom died at birth, were major factors in his depression. Others knew that financial difficulties plagued him and that the king and queen's household often lacked food, even bread.[19] Yet, the king experienced a strange comfort, he told Sor María, to be in the presence of the bodies of his ancestors.

"I saw the corpse of the Emperor," he wrote to her in 1654. "It helped me much, especially as I contemplated the place where I am to lie when God shall take me."[20]

"Señor," she replied on April 9, 1654,[21] "everything in life announces that we must die. We have only to look at the ground to know this—eventually green countryside goes brown, flowers wither, trees go barren, and we see that all creatures are mutable and impermanent. In meditating on death, we are led to understand the deepest causality. Then . . . if we heed the admonition of the Holy Spirit to 'remember your last years and you will not sin' . . . death becomes the portal to eternal life and ultimate happiness."

While the king had apparently found peace with his mortality, the abbess's admonition not to sin remained a distant hope. Felipe never directly confessed his extramarital affairs to Sor María. His references to his "sins" sufficed for their mutual understanding.

"I trust you Sor María, to plead on my behalf for Our Lord's grace, so that I can truly repent of all my sins, and take advantage of all the troubles he sends to me," he wrote on September 9, 1654.[22] "And please," he added, "do not forget to entrust us to God for the succession to the throne."

Sor María was ill and had been further weakened when bled with leeches, so she did not reply immediately to the king. In the meantime, she ruminated about his perpetual malaise until she was well enough to reply.

"I would have written to you sooner, Your Majesty, but illness and bloodletting prevented me," she finally replied on September 18.[23] "The delay to your succession saddens me. I will clamor fervently for this necessity, with particular prayers and exercises."

For the next several months, their correspondence continued as usual. The king's letters reflected his grave circumstances, and Sor María's replies sought to counsel and console. Because he did not have much of an education in the Scriptures, Sor María looked for opportunities to include biblical passages in her letters to him, as well as summaries of inspiring biblical tales. His responses made it clear that most of the biblical references beyond the obvious were new to him and very much appreciated. Yet he was so beset by the calamities of his reign that he was not nearly as prone to dialogue about spiritual matters as he was to portray his continual jeopardy.

On June 30, 1655,[24] he wrote to her that the English had attacked the Spanish silver fleet off the Atlantic coast, at the same time attacking in Mexico and Santo Domingo and unexpectedly capturing the Spanish territory of Jamaica. "If [war broke out]," he wrote, "it would be the final ruin of this realm."

"Our state is so desperate, although we work incessantly to do everything possible," Felipe continued on August 18, 1655,[25] "that if Our Lord does not intervene on our behalf, our defense is lost. So please, Sor María, beg him to set aside his wrath at our offenses, so he will defend our monarchy against any more dire threats."

In stark contrast to how hard she was on herself, Sor María's approach to the king was kindly and indulgently maternal. However, a response to his requests was difficult even for her, having just heard rumors that the king had wounded the Duke of Veragua after being discovered *en delectación* with his wife the duchess.[26] Sor María searched her soul for

FIGURE 30. Baroque alarm clock sent to Sor María by King Felipe IV, to ensure that she awoke early each day to pray for him. On display in— and image courtesy of—Convent of the Conception, Ágreda.

the right approach in her response to the king. In the process, she recalled one of her visions of Mary.

"The Lord commands us to forgive the offending brother," the Heavenly Queen had counseled Sor María, "although they may have offended seventy times seven."[27]

After much deliberation, Sor María decided to write cryptically yet pointedly to the king, to shock him into attention. She knew how much he counted on her prayers, so she threatened him with their ineffectiveness in the face of his continual moral transgressions. "Señor," she wrote to him on October 8, 1655,[28] "God's cause and Your Majesty's is my own burden, too. It awakens me each day, and draws me into prayer on your behalf. Yet I am but human, insufficient in the face of such a great undertaking. My clamoring to God's tribunal may spur divine fury."

This response was as close as she would get to issuing a rebuke, and it signaled her frustration in her dealings with the king. It was also one of the few evidencing anything close to harshness toward another person on the part of the gentle, humble nun. She was uncomfortable with the turn of events and began to doubt the utility of her correspondence with the king. Yet she felt honor-bound to continue.

To gain perspective on the deplorable drama of the king's latest affair, Sor María determined to write soon to her other friend at court, Don Fernando de Borja. In the meantime, she knew it was time to address the question of the biography of the Queen of Heaven.

CHAPTER 25

"Your trials are my own"

SOR MARÍA'S TESTIMONY TO THE INQUISITION BOTH exonerated her and entrapped her. Despite the existence of the king's secret copy of *Mystical City of God*, she could not lay claim to it without admitting her duplicity. The half-truth she had told to the inquisitors was on record, that she knew of no copy in existence of the book that she had written. This strategy—initially advised by her now deceased confessor, Padre Andrés de la Torre[1]—was a rationalization likely based on the possibility that a scribe had actually penned the king's copy and others from the original manuscript.[2] Now that the Inquisition had exonerated her, however, Sor María had no way of gracefully admitting the book's existence without also uncovering the subterfuge.

In a quandary, Sor María consulted her new confessor, Padre Fuenmayor. After careful consideration, he agreed with Padre de la Torre's guidance, that the king's copy had served to protect the last remaining copy of the manuscript in the event that Sor María was punished by death after the interrogation. If that had been the case, the king's copy would have ensured that the book would not have been lost to the world, thereby justifying the subterfuge.

When Sor María had been exonerated, however, it still seemed unwise to disclose the existence of the copy. Not only would that reveal the duplicity, but doing so might also leave her vulnerable to a revision of the Inquisition's judgment, or further investigation. Therefore, Fuenmayor concurred with another of de la Torre's injunctions, that Sor María must rewrite the book from the beginning, without the benefit of the king's copy. After praying over the dilemma, Sor María felt that Fuenmayor's guidance was confirmed. "The Lord . . . in sheer mercy, spoke to me," she wrote, "[saying] 'Write it a second time in order that thou mayest supply what was wanting and impress her doctrines on thy heart.'"[3]

Sor María felt great relief. While the existence of the king's copy would not be resolved until the saintly abbess extracted a promise on her deathbed from Bishop Ximénez Samaniego, at least her current difficulty was resolved. "I felt in my interior a most powerful change accompanied by abundant light," she wrote. "The Mother of God also spoke to me," she added, describing this as an opportunity to write her life "with less attention to the material and more to the spiritual and substantial part of it."[4]

Therefore, on December 8, 1655—the feast day of the Immaculate Conception—Sor María began anew to write *Mystical City of God*. This labor of love would take another five years to complete. In some ways, it would resemble the original manuscript, many parts of which Sor María recomposed from memory. In other ways, it would reflect her heightened spiritual growth in the intervening years. And, because she was not hurried by a king who desired all the new pages even in rough form, rewriting afforded the opportunity to more carefully edit the final copy.

At the onset of the new year, however, Sor María still had old business to attend to, regarding the king's flagrant affair with the Duchess of Veragua. She sought advice and clarification from her friend Don Fernando de Borja.

"I cannot possibly write all that I have to say," Sor María wrote to de Borja on January 14, 1656.[5] "To you alone I declare that the correspondence with the king continues despite my sorrow over two things. First, I hear he is back again to his old youthful flings and that he has wounded someone in his haste [to flee]. Tell me, dear friend, if this is true, and if so, how to maintain my will to write to him? Secondly, this crown is in great danger, and . . . so many around him are blind. No matter how I weep over this and how clearly I write, it is as though an oak and a diamond try to converse."

To her dismay, although she was not naive enough to be surprised, de Borja soon verified the illicit liaison and the king's assault on the aggrieved husband. Although Sor María would never abandon or condemn a friend, the situation pained her, and she questioned her adequacy to the challenge. In praying for guidance, she was reminded of the importance of faith, in relationship to her prayers. "Whenever souls come to thee . . . harassed by the demons," Mary had guided her, "thou [must] pray for them with lively faith and confidence."[6]

Additionally, as she searched her soul for the rhyme and reason behind her responsibilities to the king, she felt certain that she had been specifically called to intervene in his life, regardless of any particular outcome. "Although thou must pray for all souls," the Heavenly Queen had counseled, "yet thou must pray more earnestly for those whom the divine will points out to thee."[7] Accordingly, Sor María decided to reference the king's fixation on death, as evidenced by his long meditations in the mausoleums.

"Señor," she wrote on February 17, 1656,[8] "your continual desire even though directed at a perfect end [salvation], is violent to the will and painful to suffer if you do not put it into action [with virtue]. This only increases the anguish and bitterness of your soul because there is no reason to stop its vehement longing."

Thus the correspondence continued—the king's increasingly morbid confessions and Sor María's patient though pointed replies. In the meantime, she assiduously applied herself to the arduous task of rewriting *Mystical City of God*. Padre Pedro Manero, the helpful church official who had encouraged her to clarify her mystical experiences of bilocation, had been made bishop of the nearby Tarazona. In his new capacity, he again visited Sor María in Ágreda and urged her to prioritize the book's completion, above all else.[9]

Despite her cloistered existence, life was never dull for Sor María. The life of the spirit—for her, the ultimate frontier—provided abundant challenges, and her patriotic duties often catapulted her into rarefied political realms as well.

During the summer of 1656, emissaries from France had begun to make overtures to the king for peace between the two perpetually warring nations.[10] With Don Luis de Haro, Felipe had entertained a French diplomat at the Palace del Retiro. Although the meetings came to naught at the time, the subject had been broached, even as far as hinting at a marriage between the French heir to the throne, Louis XIV, and Felipe's daughter, María Teresa, to solidify an alliance.[11] The talks were poignant for Felipe whose first wife had been the French princess, Isabel de Bourbon, and whose sister—Anna of Austria—was now the queen regent of France, widowed by Louis XIII and mother to the proposed groom.

With Felipe's failure to produce a male heir, however, María Teresa was first in line to assume the Spanish throne. Felipe, therefore, considered her marriage to Louis XIV an untenable option.[12]

So widespread was the knowledge of Sor María's influence upon the king that the French efforts for peace extended even into Ágreda. The Duke of Gramont, an important figure in the French court, and one who had a family member enrolled in Sor María's convent, wrote to her and asked her to intervene with the king. Ever discreet, Sor María immediately wrote to the king about the duke's overture, inserting the duke's letter with her own into the courier's pouch. In her letter, she asked the king what action she should take, if any.[13]

"The Duke of Gramont does well in seeking to correspond with you," Felipe replied on April 18, 1657,[14] reflecting that he did not think it prudent to refuse the request.

The king asked Sor María to engage in active correspondence with the duke, but to do so without exceeding the limits of her state as a nun. She might, for example, hint about how much she longed for peace and that she knew the king desired it, too. Felipe told her his good opinion of the duke, assuring Sor María that he thought Gramont was sincere in his intentions for peace. Then he marveled at God's hand in the event. "Perhaps Our Lord is opening a way to bless Christendom with peace," he wrote to her, "that we could not achieve on our own."

In May, Gramont was elevated to ambassador extraordinary to the Frankfurt court, which was about to elect a new emperor.[15] With the augmentation of Gramont's position, Sor María and the king's hopefulness also rose. Gramont, however, temporarily spurned the Spanish Hapsburgs. Then England entered the war with France against Spain, and before long alternate marriage proposals were tentatively circulated between Louis XIV and England's Margaret of Savoy.[16]

Sor María wrote in frustration to Pope Alexander VII. "Que haga paces!" she wrote emphatically to him. "You must make peace!"[17]

While in a few years' time in 1661, Alexander VII would thrill Sor María with the papal bull considered the turning point in the development of the doctrine of the Immaculate Conception, he did not impress her with his ability as a peacemaker. He responded politely, yet took no action. Meanwhile, with the birth on November 20, 1657, of a son to Felipe IV and Mariana of Austria—Prince of Asturias Felipe Próspero— María Teresa was no longer in line for the Spanish throne.[18] Soon the bargaining chips for peace reconfigured internationally.

"The new-born babe is well," Felipe IV wrote to Sor María, "and I implore you to take him under your protection, and pray to our Lord and His holy Mother to keep him for their service, for the exaltation of the faith and good of these realms." "If this is not to be," he wrote, thinking of his bitter loss at the death of Baltasar Carlos, "then pray let him be taken from me before he reaches manhood."[19]

In 1659 Don Luis de Haro was officially named as Felipe's prime minister.[20] Felipe dispatched him to the Isle of Pheasants in the Pyrenees, a small island equally divided by the border between France and Spain. There, de Haro met for five months with the French representative, Cardinal Jules Mazarin, as the two bandied about the terms of the truce between the two countries. De Haro's correspondence with the king documents the treaty negotiations that ensued. When they reached sufficient agreement, the Duke of Gramont again played an ambassadorial role, this time in officially requesting the hand of the Spanish princess in marriage, on behalf of Louis XIV of France.

"I am personally very pleased that the French are sending the duke," Felipe wrote to Sor María on September 23, "both because he is acquainted with you and also because he is friendly towards the Spanish people."[21]

Gramont arrived at the Spanish court in October 1659 and was met with somber dignity.[22] Most of the concessions in the treaty, after all, were Spain's. She retained Catalonia and reserved the right to reconquer Portugal, which was excluded from the treaty along with England. Yet Spain lost Luxembourg, the region of Roussillon (at the eastern edge of the Pyrenees), and many principal areas in Flanders.[23] Thus, while the marriage—which was scheduled for the following summer—signified an end to well over thirty embittered years of poverty-inflicting war between the two countries, it also painfully signaled the rise of France and the decline of Spain.

Thus came about the Peace of the Pyrenees, owing in some small part to the diplomatic intervention of a humble cloistered nun.

Although Sor María's fellow countrymen, lay and religious alike, would always consider her an extraordinary servant of God, she was no longer plagued by the embarrassing notoriety that had accompanied the exterioridades of her earlier years or by inquisitorial investigations. Her health, never very robust, weakened even further as she aged, yet her spirit remained strong. For five years, she worked to rewrite the manuscript of *Mystical City of God*. She also lovingly directed the nuns under her care and diligently continued her correspondence with the king.

"Your trials are my own," she assured the king, always reminding him to "animate and dilate" his heart.[24]

Finally, at long last, her volumes were complete. And while Sor María experienced a certain relief, she also knew that the review process would be lengthy and arduous. Each ascending superior in her organizational line would no doubt read it, perhaps annotating it as he read. She submitted the manuscript through channels, then wrote about it to Padre Pedro de Arriola, an adviser specially appointed by the bishop to examine the book. "I handed over the manuscript to the Father Guardian with reluctance," she wrote very frankly to de Arriola on June 11, 1660,[25] "because I was sure that additions and deletions would be made."

The prospect of revisions reminded Sor María of the tumultuous years during her first writing of the book and the stern judgment of the old temporary confessor that "women in the Church do not write." Though she was far from being ordered to burn the manuscript, her old insecurities again surfaced. "My dear Father," she continued in her letter to de Arriola, "[tell me] if it is right that this work should be given up and burnt, or if I should continue and complete it. I will obediently follow either course."

So wary was Sor María of a complex revision process, she wisely organized the material in the clearest manner possible. She divided the manuscript into eight books, which were further divided by chapters. Additionally, each chapter contained numbered paragraphs, cumulative to the end of each volume, a common format of the era.

"If I am to go on with it," she concluded to de Arriola, "I entreat you, Father, to send me a report on what you have read, making a list of the faults with their paragraph-numbers." Yet she took care to assure de Arriola that his corrections would be welcome and asked the priest to remember her before God.

Even as Sor María began this lengthy process, the king embarked upon a long journey of his own, to give away his daughter in marriage.

On April 15, 1660, María Teresa left Madrid with her father for two royal wedding ceremonies. One would take place—for Spanish pomp and pride—in San Sebastian, Spain, with a proxy standing in for Louis XIV. Thereafter, she would continue on to the Isle of Pheasants, for the official handing over of the bride. A second wedding would subsequently take place on French soil.

Felipe led the vast wedding train, a cavalcade of hundreds of courtiers and servants, in a long line of carriages that extended for twenty miles. Along the way peasants cheered, marveling at all the wealth and hopeful for an improvement in their own straits as a result of the new peace with France.[26]

At a rate that today would equal about six miles per day, the cavalcade arrived in San Sebastian near the French border on June 2. The Spanish ceremony took place on the following day, with de Haro standing in for Louis XIV. The church was packed, not only with Spanish nobility, but with many French dignitaries in disguise, there to view the first ceremony and anticipate the second.

Two days later, on the Isle of Pheasants, Felipe saw the series of pavilions specially constructed for the wedding parties. The buildings straddled the border between Spain and France with a corridor in the center, on the dividing line between the countries. He entered through the Spanish entrance and saw a regal woman awaiting him inside the French entrance. There he had a tearful reunion with his sister, Anna of Austria, queen regent of France, whom he had not seen for forty-five years.[27]

On June 6, crowds of people on either bank watched as two flotillas landed on opposite shores of the island, each bearing a king. Troops numbering over twelve thousand lined the two shores. The couple was united amid great fanfare, as the monarchs swore on a missal to keep the terms of the peace.[28] A few weeks later Felipe wrote about it all to his friend in Ágreda.

"I was very happy to receive your letter of the twenty-third [June] and through it you have accompanied me on my journey," Felipe wrote to Sor María on July 6, 1660. He regaled her about many aspects of the events, but especially wanted to tell her about seeing his sister, after such a long separation, and his interpretation of the reception he received from the French. "It was a great joy to see my sister," he wrote to Sor María. "The king [Louis XIV] seems like a very kind young man," he added in fatherly relief, having just described the young bride to his new son-in-law as a "piece of my own heart."[29]

"I am heartbroken that the definition of the Immaculate Conception has made no progress," Sor María wrote to Felipe on July 23. "Yet your letter consoled me greatly. I am glad you have safely returned, in good health, after successfully negotiating for the peace, with the marriage of [your daughter now] the Queen of France. I give to God great thanks, and to Your Majesty affectionate congratulations."[30]

CHAPTER 26

"Punish the rich and powerful people who oppress the poor"

MANY MIRACLES HAVE BEEN ATTRIBUTED TO SOR MARÍA during her lifetime and after her death. Some are more accurately described by the church as favors received from God as a result of contact with a holy person. Such would describe the Queen of Aragón's return from vice to virtue and the spiritual conversion of many individuals who encountered Sor María or who were the fortunate recipients of her prayers.[1] Others involved such a refined vision on her part that people testified—as recorded by Ximénez Samaniego—that she could see into the future, mainly about a person's health or the time of their death.[2]

According to Sor María, these insights occurred when she received "divine light," which she utilized to see into people's hearts. In her auto-biographical material, she cites particular passages in *Mystical City of God* that explain the phenomena.[3] "The light," she wrote, "makes clear the distinction between good and evil, and discloses the hidden and profound. I see . . . all the secrets of men . . . the dangers in which they live, and the errors of their ways . . . even as far as pertains to separate individuals and circumstances."[4]

Still other examples of her extraordinary gifts involve actual cures brought about by her intervention or by the faith of a person touching one of her belongings. Accounts of these cures affecting local individuals during Sor María's lifetime are recorded in Ximénez Samaniego's biography.

At Sor María's touch, Ximénez Samaniego wrote, Mary Mendoza was saved from amputation and cured of paralysis. After touching a cloth of Sor María's, Doña Ildefonsa Orovio's painful tumor completely disappeared. As someone touched Sor María's rosary to Peter Villa, the dying man revived long enough to take the sacraments before succumbing again to delirium. Upon touching Sor María's rosary, John Zamorra was healed of a fatal wound from a poisonous viper's bite.[5]

When the situation required more of a spiritual solution, Sor María—cautiously reluctant to judge—guarded exactly how much she disclosed to others about her perceptions of them. Instead, she weighed the responsibility, listened for guidance from God, then carefully spoke, not with the full nature of her cognition, but rather "speaking to the heart" of the person and using "charitable persuasion."[6]

In one extraordinary report that her prayers were instrumental in the temporary restoration of life to a dead man, the humble nun swore the witnesses to secrecy until after her death. The following account derives from witnesses' sworn testimony in official records documenting the apostolic process in her cause for canonization.[7]

In 1660, with the bulk of writing behind her and a certain slowing in the intensity of correspondence with the king due to each of their increasing ages and health concerns, Sor María frequently retreated in quiet devotions. On one such day, she knelt in prayer in the lower choir adjacent to the church. Unbeknownst to her, or any of the other nuns, two workmen approached the minor sacristan who assisted the priest in caring for the church. The men asked for and received permission to set a large chest just inside the church door, indicating only that it contained merchandise for safekeeping.

Deep in meditative prayer, Sor María heard "sad moans and profound lamentations." In the report, she indicated that she had been frightened and disturbed because the sighs sounded horrible and seemed hopeless. She told how she approached the church doorway and saw the chest. The crying, she realized, came from there. Then she realized that the chest was a coffin harboring an anguished soul, one that had died impenitent. To Sor María there could be no worse fate. She prayed for God to put new life into the soul, so it could repent before facing judgment.

In struggling for more understanding, Sor María said she realized not only that the coffin had been placed in the church in secret, but that a more astounding secret lay within: the body inside was none other than that of her brother, Padre Francisco Coronel. He had at one time held a position of authority at a Franciscan college in Madrid, but in later years he had felt that his efforts were not sufficiently rewarded and had returned to Ágreda, discontented, ambitions thwarted, bitter toward God and the church.[8]

Sor María grieved for her brother. She called upon God's "infinite omnipotence and divine justice" to concede "new life for a brief time and space," so her brother could confess his sins. In response, she felt prompted to arrange for a confessor to hear her brother's confession. She left immediately to do so and did not return to the church.

A neighboring priest responded to the call, almost frightened to death himself, he later reported, at the prospect of attending to a dead person. He was accompanied by another—perhaps the sacristan—who later served as a witness.

Coronel, they attested, stepped out of his coffin and prostrated himself cruciform before the altar. After some time, he "came to the feet of the confessor, and made a painful confession." The witness, who had left during the confession and penance, returned and saw Coronel reenter his coffin, arms raised toward the choir platform in gratitude to his sister. Then he reclined, the lid was closed, and the same two workmen carried it away.

The priest who took Coronel's confession made a complete record of the event, including his initial death and the witness's testimony. Then he sealed the record. It remained a secret throughout the lifetimes of the three remaining participants. Finally, over a century later, church officials broke the seal and added the amazing account to Sor María's growing file for sainthood.

Sor María's dedication to the king notwithstanding, she not surprisingly tried to minimize public exposure about any miraculous cures attributed to her. Considering the attention and prayer she already devoted to the king's dilemmas, for to her to presume that she could control the volume of tragedy and illness contained in his family would have been unthinkable. For her, this was where dutiful prayers intersected with surrender to God's will.

By September 1661, she learned that three-year-old prince Felipe Próspero had suffered many illnesses that weakened his already frail constitution, and Queen Mariana was again pregnant. Padre Fuenmayor, while in Madrid on church business, made an appointment to visit the king and to extend his prayers and well wishes to the royal family.

"I am glad that your confessor visited me," Felipe wrote to Sor María on September 21.[9] "He seemed to be a very good person. We spoke quite a bit about you, and I was very pleased with the conversation, since he emphasized the affection and love with which you entrust me to God."

Felipe's mood was soon soured, however, by bitter news. Later in 1661, Don Luis de Haro failed in a critical campaign to gain power over Portugal and died soon after. To complicate matters, King Charles II of England took a Portuguese wife, bringing all of England's force to Portugal's defense. Felipe had now lost not only his trusted minister, but any remaining hope that his bastard son Don Juan José of Austria could succeed where de Haro had not.[10]

In October, young prince Felipe Próspero again fell seriously ill. This time he did not recover. King Felipe, having married off his daughter María Teresa to Louis XIV, wept at the death of his only legitimate heir, as María Teresa had had to foreswear any rights to the Spanish throne upon her marriage. The fragile princess Margarita María, born in 1651, was not considered adequate to the throne, but the queen was again pregnant and approaching full term.

"After losing such a jewel as this," Felipe wrote to Sor María on November 1,[11] "I see clearly that I have angered God, and that these punishments are sent in retribution for my sins. . . . Help me, as a true friend, with your prayers to placate the ire of God, and supplicate Him, since He has taken away my son, to send a safe delivery to the Queen."

Before the king could sign his letter and insert it in the courier's pouch, the queen went into labor, and Felipe was called to Mariana's bedside to view his new son. "Our Lord has deigned to send me back my son," he added on November 8 at the end of his letter, "by bringing me another. . . . The Queen and the child are well."

"With tears and tenderness I know how much you must have suffered at the loss of a son," Sor María wrote to him on November 25.[12] "Yet you must take heart and dilate your soul to the consideration that these blows and tribulations help to fashion a crown of eternal rest . . . and [increase] our worthiness of God's grace and glory." They may also earn us some consolation in this life, she intimated, referring to his new son, the infant Don Carlos.

Despite the dire topic of death, and her own failing health, Sor María did not relent on her continual advocacy for the poor. "Your Majesty," she added, "you must expressly order your ministers to punish the rich and powerful people who oppress the poor by seizing and usurping their property. . . . So many changes in the coinage, too, are most injurious to the economy."

Though the king knew how interested Sor María was in the status of the doctrine of Mary's Immaculate Conception, he had no updates for her in his next letter from his sources in the Vatican. Not until December 8, 1661, did Pope Alexander VII write his papal bull clarifying the doctrine.

"I am most content with the Pope's bull," Felipe finally wrote to Sor María on January 10, 1662,[13] "and that he has conceded to us regarding the Immaculate Conception of Our Lady."

Multitudes of people, including Sor María, were ecstatic upon hearing the news as it unfolded in the following months. Although it would not be designated as official dogma of the church until 1854, Alexander VII's distinctions have been considered by Marian scholars to be the conceptual turning point that paved the way for final interpretation and acceptance.

Indeed, in 1854 Pius IX credited King Felipe IV for his advocacy on behalf of the Immaculate Conception. He did not mention Sor María, whose lobbying efforts were more behind-the-scenes. Yet, there is little doubt that she urged and inspired Felipe on the importance of the doctrine.[14]

As for Sor María, she was content to credit the king. "You, Venerable Majesty, had the motivations and the means to affect the Bull," she wrote to him on March 11, 1662.[15] "For that I give repeated thanks to God, and affectionate congratulations to you."

"I am sure that you feted this holy Mystery with great devotion and solemnity," Felipe replied on April 3, 1662,[16] "[knowing] how many great difficulties were conquered for the enactment of the Bull."

Celebrations soon erupted throughout the country, and Ágreda was no exception. There, on September 10, 1662, luminaries and nobility flocked to Ágreda to march in a long procession that ended at Sor María's Convent of the Conception. A festive Mass and sermon echoed from the convent's packed church, followed by music and dancing throughout the little town.

CHAPTER 27

"To God, the past and future are both now"

INEVITABLY OVER TIME, THE EARTHLY ENTITY KNOWN AS
Sor María de Jesus de Ágreda succumbed to failing health and the toll of
age. She suffered two serious illnesses in 1662, leaving her with palsy in
her right arm. Padre Fuenmayor encouraged her, nonetheless, to write an
autobiographical treatment of her life from the beginning. She succeeded
in chronicling her early experiences, from the age of two through the
founding of the convent in 1620, adding much rich detail to her growing
legacy of spiritual writing.

During this time, the delicate atmosphere of the convent was more
hushed than usual. The nuns gentled their footsteps on the polished
wooden and brick corridors as they increased their vigilance in caring for their beloved founder. They muted the peals of the Angelus
bells, hoping to deter the ailing abbess from adhering to her usual
devotional exercises.

As 1663 and 1664 unfolded, her condition worsened, often resulting
in long gaps between her letters to the king. Typically during this time
she began her letters with an apology for the long delay in writing to
him, owing to her illness. As for the king, by the end of 1664 he had to
dictate his last four letters to Sor María because of his own maladies.[1]
The two spiritual warriors were about to lay down their arms.

"I assure you that I only want what is best for the service of God," Felipe wrote to Sor María on March 3, 1665,[2] "not better health or anything else, except that divine will is executed in me."

Sor María replied that she was tenderly moved by the king's inclination toward divine will, even at the cost of his own health. Typically, she again offered comfort to the ailing monarch, writing a lengthier missive to him on March 27, 1665,[3] than she had in quite a while. She praised his heroic patience in accepting God's will, even above the natural concern for his own health. She assured him of the solicitude with which she prayed for him, "such that I am dedicated to work for your salvation like my own . . . as long as I live."

Because Easter was approaching, Sor María reminded the king about the passion and death of Christ. She also regaled him about the source of grace as "the immutable Being of God" and reminded him that the sacraments were the "fountains of grace," through which "the divine power pours its abounding waters." "Go to them," she urged him, "to satisfy your righteous cravings for the justifying grace that comes to us through the sacraments and may Your Majesty keep the beauty that grace brings by having a pure conscience."[4] Then she closed with copious prayers for the king and his family, specifically mentioning them all.

As Sor María went to seal the letter, she likely sensed that these might be her last words to the king. Perhaps that is why, facing her own eternity, she included another reminder to him. "To God," she wrote, "the past and the future are both *now*, the present."[5]

Sensing the end was near, Sor María's confessors did their best to attend to her spiritual needs and to put her mind at rest about her life's work. In particular, they debated how best to seek a definitive judgment on *Mystical City of God*, before her death. To that end, Padre Gutiérrez in 1664 had provided a copy of the book to Bishop Miguel Escartín of Tarazona, without Sor María's knowledge. No word was forthcoming by the end of 1664 and well into 1665. Then in April the bishop's conclusion arrived.[6] Although Escartín admitted astonishment at reading "such deep theology" as written by a woman, in his letter of April 21, 1665,[7] he praised the book as "so sublime, powerful and effective that it penetrates the heart with love for God and his most pure Mother."

The bishop's praise could not have been more effusive. He admired the style with which Sor María had portrayed Mary and her son. He cited her clarity and precision in communicating divine wisdom. He credited her with teaching the reader how to know and honor God and to practice virtue and detest vice. Most importantly, he wrote that in his estimation, *Mystical City of God* was "in perfect conformity to the evangelical law. Hence I see nothing which could give rise to the suspicion that this production is not the work of God."

Indeed, he wrote, the book would particularly enrich the souls of the faithful, especially those who are devoted to the Mother of God. "We must render grateful thanks to the divine Majesty," he concluded, "for having manifested to us in the present century this hidden treasure . . . through [the] faithful servant Sor María de Jesus of Ágreda." His letter, dated just thirty-three days before Sor María's death, marks the beginning of the book's deluge of endorsements by church luminaries throughout the centuries.

Just as Sor María sometimes foresaw the deaths of others, after Easter 1665 she saw her own death fast approaching. Her confessors did their best to minimize her rigorous spiritual practices, but she grew adamant at their increased importance under the circumstances. "I cannot do otherwise," she said. "I practice these exercises to prepare myself for a happy death."[8]

When the other nuns bemoaned their impending loss as well as her pain and suffering, she reminded them that "my death will soon occur" and that the future of the convent would fall to them. When the news spread throughout Ágreda, people gathered to pray for the prolongation of their beloved mystic's life. Clergy from surrounding towns walked in droves to the convent. Each person wept, Ximénez Samaniego wrote, "as if the dying nun had been his own mother."[9]

Knowing the end was near, Sor María agitatedly made her confession several times each day, praying for God's mercy "as if," Ximénez Samaniego wrote, "she had previously done nothing good, and was just beginning to do so at this late moment."[10]

Mercifully, she asked for the sacrament of Extreme Unction, long termed the "sacrament of the dying," and today more aptly called the "sacrament of healing." In it, the priest prays for the recipient, often exhorting him or her to focus on the expansion of the spirit beyond the boundaries of the body. Then an unction, or oil, is applied to the eyes, ears, nose, mouth, and hands, or sometimes just the forehead, in order to heal or close off the body's earthly portals, according to God's will.

All the nuns were present at Sor María's deathbed, as well as her confessors—Padres Fuenmayor and Gutiérrez—and the minister general of the Franciscans, Padre Alonso de Salizanes. Also present was Bishop Ximénez Samaniego, who—as became evident a few years later—made a deathbed promise to the dying abbess about the disposition of the king's copy of *Mystical City of God*. At the time, however, he merely commented on the effect on her of the sacrament. "When the sacrament was administered to her," Ximénez Samaniego witnessed, "the thick veil which seemed to obscure her mind was removed and the serenity of her spirit shone on her countenance which became beautiful and smiling."[11]

"Do not weep," Sor María said to the nuns. "Remember [instead] . . . that we must accept from the hand of God whatever He is pleased to send us." She spoke for several moments, encouraging them to serve the Lord, to obey his laws, to be faithful in their spiritual exercises, and to live above reproach so their actions would be "worthy of the daughters of the most holy Virgin." Wisely, she also shared the pragmatics of the moment, advising them to always "do good while you have time, and never defer anything until the last moment, for then disease and exhaustion will present many difficulties."[12]

Another world glittered in Sor María's eyes on May 24, 1665, as the nuns filed up to her bed one by one to ask her special blessing and to receive any special advice for the last time. She blessed each of them with a small sign of the cross and a whisper of kindness or counsel. Finally she fell back upon the pillow, ready.[13]

Around Sor María's peaceful form the nuns and priests gathered. Softly they breathed with her, softly they prayed for her. Then the sweetest wisp of a sound floated from their lips and hearts as they sang, "Come, Holy Spirit."

The hymn enveloped Sor María and tenderly moved her.

"Come, come, come," she whispered and gently breathed forth her soul.[14]

PART SEVEN

THE AFTER-STORY:
1665 THROUGH THE PRESENT

CHAPTER 28

Saint María
of Ágreda?

DESIGNATION AS A SAINT IS BY NO MEANS THE ONLY MEASURE
of a person's virtue and ability to inspire spiritual seekers on the path to
union with God. Yet, in a world populated with over 1.1 billion Catholics,
it is surely a powerful way for the Catholic Church to officially multiply
the effect of saintly persons on others, through increased awareness of
their exemplary lives and contributions.

Until the twelfth century, many saints were designated by popular
acclaim, rather than through a set process. Since then, however, the procedure has been formalized by the Vatican, bringing into the mix the
infallible nature of the designation. Saint-making is therefore serious
business, as it carries with it the official endorsement of the church.

All aspects of a saintly candidate's life and works are evaluated, as
well as miracles attributed to his or her intervention after death. The first
step, usually five or more years after death, involves a general review
of the person's life to determine if he or she lived a heroic life of virtue,
most recently clarified in Pope John Paul II's Apostolic Constitution of
January 25, 1983. Having met that criterion, the person is designated
as a venerable of the church, and the formal case for sainthood begins.
A "postulator" is designated in Rome as the Vatican proponent for the
cause, and a "vice postulator" is designated in the person's country of

origin. A neutral "devil's advocate," now called "promoter of the faith," is also appointed to raise pertinent questions about the candidate, and a commission is formed to examine the candidate's legacy of works. In the case of Sor María, multiple commissions have reviewed her works throughout the centuries since her death.

As soon as a miracle can be ascribed to a venerable, the way is usually made clear for the next step—beatification—after which he or she is called "blessed." For centuries, one of the most assured miracles leading to beatification involved the phenomenon of "incorruptibility" of the deceased venerable's body. This state of preservation of the body, without embalming or other measures, was considered a miraculous sign of the person's sanctity. In the latter part of the twentieth century, the church placed less emphasis on this particular form of miracle, allowing that many saints fulfilled the criteria of sainthood without it. One additional miracle, after the candidate's beatification, is then required before formal canonization as an official saint, although the pope on occasion may waive this requirement.

In Sor María's case, apparitions, miracles, and the enduring inspiration of her life and writing have secured her popular legacy through today. As a result, her cause for sainthood is as fascinating as her life. However, just as Sor María was sometimes controversial during her lifetime, the ecclesiastical evaluation of her writing has vacillated over the centuries from condemnation to unbridled praise. Consequently, her cause for sainthood has met obstacles, even as popular veneration surged.

Immediately following her death, a number of people claimed to have briefly seen Sor María's spirit in Ágreda and beyond. Juan Carillo, an Ágreda resident who had just received Communion in a nearby church, testified that he saw her for an instant, radiantly bathed in light. No sooner did she disappear when the convent bells rang out, signifying her death. Ximénez Samaniego also records the testimony of other individuals "of eminent perfection" in various locations distant from Ágreda who—at the hour of her death—saw her spirit rising heavenward.[1]

So compelling was the universal devotion felt for Sor María that prior to interment Ximénez Samaniego advised the nuns to place her corpse in the interior chapel of the lower choir so her remains could be viewed through the Communion grille during hours when the grille's drape was opened.[2] This grille separates the nuns from people in the convent church, including the priest who serves Communion to them through it. Yet the grille faces into the church for all to see.

Soon the constant stream of devotees became so large that in order to maintain decorum the installation of a guard of soldiers became necessary. In their eagerness to obtain relics, people strained to force rosary beads, items of clothing, anything through the bars of the grille. These the nuns then touched to her body on the bier.[3]

On the day of her funeral, the convent church filled to overflowing. Veneration paid to Sor María was so great that Padre Alonso Salizanes, minister general of the Franciscan order, decided not to deliver an oration in her honor for fear that the people would make an unseemly public demonstration of worship forbidden by the church toward anyone or anything except God. With great solemnity, Salizanes conducted the funeral Mass in the teeming convent church. Then Sor María's remains were placed in a simple wood coffin and deposited in the common vaults located in the cellar of the convent.[4]

"Every day," Ximénez Samaniego wrote, "the fame of her sanctity increases, and . . . devotion towards her becomes more fervent. She is called 'the saintly nun, Sor María de Jesús,' from the noblest to the lowest . . . an inspiration from the Lord, the master of human hearts."[5]

Yet, with so many people uplifted by the inspiration of Sor María's life, one very prominent individual considered the loss of his friend as a personal devastation amid the increasing erosion of his nation's power and wealth. News of the king's despair spread throughout Spain like the insidious horrors of the plague. Casting himself to the ground in convulsive grief, without the saintly nun to comfort and advocate for him, he wept in the sight of all, clinging to a bag of relics around his neck and crying out, "Oh God! Thy will be done."[6]

On September 17, 1665, the king himself succumbed to mortality. Church bells rang incessantly for days, as his body lay in state. Among the court's inner circle, Lady Fanshawe, wife of the English ambassador, attended the wake with her husband, noting a grandeur far different from Sor María's simple wooden coffin in Ágreda.[7] She cited a silver coffin atop an elevated platform covered in rich Persian carpet. In it lay Felipe IV with his head on a pillow, wearing a white beaver hat, his hair combed, his beard trimmed, his face and hands painted.[8]

Felipe IV was at peace at last. His long and difficult reign had been doomed since the fall of the Spanish Armada in the era of his grandfather.

He had battled the devaluation of Spain's currency amid the ruthless taxations imposed by his original prime minister, the Count-Duke of Olivares. He had struggled through wars inherited from his father. And he had presided over the inevitable end of Spain's golden age, perhaps incrementally slowing down the country's demise through his own efforts and Sor María's good influence.

The king was succeeded by his sickly four-year-old son, Carlos II, under the supervision of Queen Mariana as regent until Carlos attained his majority. Carlos II was not a strong ruler, and Spain's decline as a world power continued. Yet the young monarch, and indeed all future Spanish royalty, held fast in their reverence for Sor María's saintliness. In 1677 Carlos II honored Sor María's legacy by visiting her remains in Ágreda (see appendix G) with his half brother Don Juan José of Austria and others.

Seventeen years after the death of Felipe IV, Bishop Ximénez Samaniego was able to fulfill what is considered a likely deathbed promise to Sor María regarding the disposition of Felipe IV's copy of *Mystical City of God*. The result of his actions, which did not come to light for a number of years, resulted in one of many complications in her cause for sainthood.

In 1666 the Spanish bishops, as well as many other eminent church officials, gathered to organize the appeal for Sor María's canonization.[9] At the same time, Ximénez Samaniego continued to write his biography of Sor María. It would not move quickly, however, as he was soon to be elevated to the bishopric of one of the four wealthiest dioceses in Spain— Plasencia—a coveted position and one that had recently been filled by the former inquisitor general, Arce y Reynoso.[10]

The following year, ironically, an initial piece of bad news added momentum to the growing enthusiasm for Sor María's cause for sainthood. In September of 1667, the Ágreda nuns reported moisture in the crypt where Sor María's body lay, to the extent that the exterior of the coffin was badly rotted.[11] Their superiors gathered at the convent to inspect the crypt and confirmed a severe overhead drip and humidity. When they opened the coffin, however, they found that Sor María's body was not only intact and incorrupt, but that it gave off a sweet scent, as had the body of Teresa of Avila. Thus bolstered in anticipation of Sor María's path to sainthood, the nuns moved the coffin immediately to a safer location in the crypt.[12]

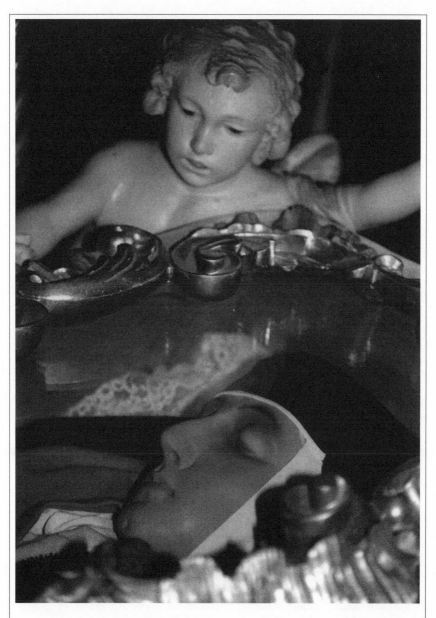

FIGURE 31. Wax face mask placed atop Sor María's face in 1989 to protect small section of bone visible through skin, the only change in corpse since late seventeenth century. Photo by author.

Over the next few years, many testimonies poured in on behalf of Sor María. By June 21, 1672, at the Catholic Congregation of Rites in Rome, the Spanish court formally requested the initiation of her canonization process.[13] Two months later, on August 24, 1672, Pope Clement X agreed to the formation of a commission to introduce her cause for sainthood.[14]

By January 28 of the following year, the first major hurdle in that cause was overcome. In recognition of Sor María's "life of heroic virtue," and of the popular appeal conveyed by many cardinals, princes, noblemen, and King Carlos II of Spain, Pope Clement X signed the decree introducing her cause for beatification and canonization and honoring her with the title of venerable.[15]

September 9, 1675, marked the opening interrogations in the Church of Our Lady of Magaña in Ágreda on behalf of Sor María's cause.[16] Meanwhile her inspiring effect—on laypeople and the religious alike—increased.

Admiration for Sor María, and her deep devotion to the Blessed Mother, inspired the foundation of many more convents in Spain. During her lifetime, these included the convent in Borja, founded in 1652 by nuns from Ágreda, and other convents, although not all of them adopted the same rule of the order of the Immaculate Conception. They are the Augustinian Recoletas of Pamplona (1634), the Conceptionist Convent of Corella (1643), the Convent of Tortosa (1644), the Convent of Lerin–Los Arcos (1650), and the Augustinian Convent of Ágreda (1660), in which Sor María took a kindly interest for its proximity to her ancestral home.[17]

Even after her death, the proliferation of convents continued. These include the Convent of Tafalla, about twenty miles south of Pamplona, founded by nuns from Ágreda in 1671 and dedicated to the Immaculate Conception, and the Conceptionist Convent of Estella, about seventy-five miles north of Ágreda, founded in 1731 by a woman who had visited the convent in Ágreda and been inspired by their rule. Again, nuns from Ágreda journeyed to Estella to assist in the foundation.[18]

Many highly regarded conventual figures wrote about Sor María over the years. These include the abbess María de Jesus of Javea (1612–77) and Spanish writer María de Orozco (1635–1709).[19] Some of these figures write of documented apparitions of Sor María after her death. One of these apparitions occurred in 1755, and one in 1757.

The abbess of the Convent of Santa Clara, Spain, María Francisca Arnedo, interviewed several older nuns in her convent about claims of having seen Sor María in 1755. "There is nothing about this in writing," she wrote, "so in all likelihood it will not qualify for inclusion in the legal documentation." Yet she then included a detailed report of her own interviews with each of the "venerable nuns" independently, because after scrutinizing each account she concluded that their claims were valid and that they had indeed seen Sor María, almost one hundred years after her death.[20]

"My confessor commended the Abbess of Ágreda to me as a masterful teacher," wrote another abbess, María Leocadia, on July 15, 1757, in Guadalajara, Spain. "I invoked her help in cleansing my soul in order to be worthy of the divine presence. Then I felt her at my right-hand side, and she taught me."[21]

Accounts of these apparitions extended—appropriately enough in Sor María's case—to the continents of the New World. "I am compelled to write to you," Abbess Ana María Josefa de San Pantaleón wrote in 1790 to the nuns in Ágreda, from the Convent of the Holy Trinity in the Pueblo of Los Angeles, Mexico. "After reading about the life of the venerable María de Jesús, I see there are better ways than ours to fulfill a perfect Silent Life. . . . We hope to found a Holy Community [like yours]. . . . Please do me the honor of sending me examples of your Constitution immediately."[22]

The resulting convent is operational today, and in all there are twenty-one cloistered convents—monasterios—of the Immaculate Conception now located throughout Mexico.[23]

In the months following Sor María's death, people swarmed to her convent from throughout Spain. They venerated Sor María's memory and remains and, in many cases, supplicated her saintliness for cures of all manner of maladies. A few of those documented by Ximénez Samaniego include:

The daughter of Nicolosa Franco, long afflicted with virulent attacks of epilepsy, was declared instantly cured upon swallowing one sip of water in which had soaked a thread from one of Sor María's cloths. Joseph Oroxio Peralta, a man who had been completely paralyzed and numb for five days, was seen as cured when he touched one of Sor María's rosaries and invoked her assistance.[24]

Another man, Francis Zimeno, was in danger of imminent death. He suffered from extreme fever caused by inflammation of the knee. His doctors despaired after twenty days of treatment that included lancings of four to five inches. Finally taking recourse to a higher power, Zimeno placed a part of Sor María's rosary upon his knee. The next day the physicians not only found him free from fever and pain, but his knee had entirely healed.[25]

So strong was the public's inspiration from Sor María's saintly life and works that over two hundred years after her death another more astounding miracle was attributed to her. On February 20, 1867, Dr. E. Hanon, M.D., of Nivelles, Belgium, wrote the following: "Mary Catherine Plas of Strombeck, [known] in religion [as] Sor M. Colette of the monastery of Conceptionists in this city, aged thirty-two years, has been under my treatment since March 1863."[26]

Dr. Hanon described the progressive inflammation and deterioration of Sor Colette's dorsal vertebrae, resulting in muscle deterioration, grave pain and palpitations, and ultimately complete paralysis. Additionally, the patient vomited blood and could retain no food. By the end of 1866, further treatment was deemed futile, and Sor Colette prayed—unsuccessfully— for an end to her suffering through death.

Then on January 27, 1867, the abbess and all the nuns, including Sor Colette, began a novena in honor of Sor María of Ágreda and her inspiring work in *Mystical City of God*. Each day, for nine consecutive days, they prayed fervently that if it was God's will, Sor Colette would be cured through the merits of Sor María. Throughout the nine days, Sor Colette held in her hands a small image of Sor María.

On Wednesday, February 6, 1867, the convent's spiritual director noted Sor Colette's grievous condition. He heard her confession, believing it to be her last. The abbess, firm in her faith for a cure, nevertheless instructed two nuns on the following day to bring Sor Colette to the choir to give thanks.

On February 7, the two nuns arrived at Sor Colette's room to find her up and fully dressed. Understandably thinking that she would still be weak, the nuns convinced her to sit on a chair, on which they would carry her downstairs to the choir. Soon, however, Sor Colette realized the full extent of her cure. She descended the stairs on her own, walked into the choir, and knelt before the altar fully recovered.

"The Rev. Mother Abbess assured me," wrote Dr. Hanon, "that no remedy had been applied since my treatment had ceased. . . . Sor M. Colette's health was so perfect that on the following day she was able to resume her

FIGURE 32. King Carlos II of Spain (left) and Don Juan of Austria (right) view Sor María's incorrupt body in 1677. Oil painting on canvas, artist unknown. On display in—and image courtesy of—Convent of the Conception, Ágreda.

usual occupations, and to recite the office with her sisters both by day and by night. . . . I am willing to affirm this declaration by a solemn oath."

Hanon's report, alongside the testimony of the abbess, spiritual director, and other nuns, is on record in the diocesan offices of Mechelen, Belgium, and in the Franciscan Curia of Rome. Proponents for her cause hoped that the miraculous cure would propel her into beatification and ultimately canonization as a saint of the Catholic Church. While this was not to be a reality any time soon, other dramatic signs of Sor María's sanctity continued to amass.

The opening of Sor María's coffin in 1667 was the first of fourteen times—through 1989—when her remains were viewed and reported as intact and radiating a pleasant odor. In death, as in life, her visitors represented a veritable who's who of nobility and church greats. They included Spanish kings and queens, French royalty, bishops, cardinals, inquisitors, dukes, princes, ambassadors, and war heroes.[27]

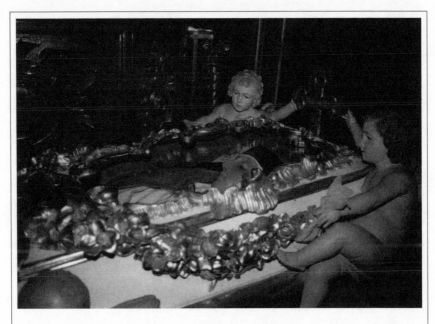

FIGURE 33. Incorrupt body of Sor María of Ágreda, with face protected by a wax likeness, in glass-enclosed casket at side altar of convent church. Photo by author.

On several of these occasions, the inspection of Sor María's corpse constituted an apostolic judicial inspection, headed by the bishop and conducted by doctors and surgeons. During each formal inspection, her corpse was examined and documented as intact and incorrupt. The first of these occurred on October 10, 1757. Then in 1909, 244 years after Sor María's death, her body was moved from the convent cellar to a museum on the second story. At the same time, a reclining statue of her body was installed in the church.

A more recent viewing occurred on May 20, 1989. Forty-six people crowded into the convent's small museum room over the church. These included apostolic delegates, a medical team, and the Ágreda nuns. "The air was filled with reverent silence and expectant emotion as we prepared to open the coffin," wrote the official recorder of the event, Padre Manuel Peña García.[28]

Most of Sor María's body was shielded from the attendees as the doctors examined it. In all anatomical features, suppleness, and size, they pronounced it incorrupt and unchanged since 1909. Reverently, the nuns clothed the body in a new habit, preserving for relics the habit most recently worn. At this time, they also added an artificial mask over Sor María's face, due to visitors' reactions since 1909 at seeing a small section of bone through the skin, the only change in her corpse since the late seventeenth century.[29]

In poignant media coverage of the 1989 event, the contemporary nuns of Ágreda posed for photographs around the open coffin of their beloved founder, now freshly attired. The wooden coffin lid was then replaced with a clear glass covering, and the coffin was moved into the church. The reclining statue was placed atop it.

From then forward, visitors have viewed the body of Sor María through the glass lid, attired in death as she was in life, in the Conceptionist habit. While her face is now covered by a lifelike mask, her hands are visible for all to see. Somewhat darkened with age, they nevertheless appeared to this author as delicate and completely intact, as normal as the hands of any aging person.

In honor of the four hundredth anniversary of Sor María's birth, in 2002 over twelve thousand people visited her remains in Ágreda.[30] Those who are fortunate enough to make this journey come away reporting themselves as feeling blessed. Many, however, also leave perturbed and unable to accept the complex and seeming interminable delays burdening Sor María's cause for sainthood. Because the official rulings on *Mystical City of God* have so impacted that cause, they represent an integral part of her after-story.

Sor María's "Poetic Theology" Banned in Paris

WHETHER ONE'S NAME IS MOTHER TERESA OR OPRAH, NO human eye can see without light, and no seer can penetrate the truth of the spiritual realm without the benefit of inner light. Yet what seers of old saw was not always easily understood by those who stood in judgment of their revelations. Often a seer's visions meant seeing the world through refined, hard-won mystic lenses to which few had applied themselves enough to gain the prescription.

"A flaming light . . . penetrated my brain, heart and breast," wrote Saint Hildegard of Bingen in 1141.[1] Hildegard described what she saw as the dire results of the corruption of her era, as well as the spiritual teaching that could cure it. The painful truth in Hildegard's visions anguished her deeply, causing her much suffering throughout her life. "This vision . . . burns my soul," she wrote.

Like those of Hildegard, the visions of Sor María exacted a price. In seventeenth-century Inquisition-era Spain, in the valley beneath the gentle curves of the Moncayo Mountains, Sor María chronicled the life, teaching, and revelations of Mary, the mother of Jesus. She did so from the light of her inner visions, augmented by the materials available to her.

Visions notwithstanding, the materials available to her were considerable. As outlined in a 2004 treatise on behalf of her sainthood,

Sor María's sources included the Bible, the great classical narratives of Christian theology, ancient Jewish commentaries, apocryphal texts (as distinguished from gnostic materials), and her own intimate, mystical experiences. Sor María's biblical references alone in *Mystical City of God* number close to thirty-two hundred, almost half of which are from the Old Testament.[2] When she expanded the convent in 1630, she made sure to assemble a considerable library on religious subjects and significant religious figures, much of which remains today.[3]

As Antonio Artola Arbiza writes, "Sor María's work was not created from nothing."[4] Yet Artola Arbiza emphasizes that the language of the mystic is often poetic and metaphorical, a thought echoed through the centuries by many who have struggled to understand the visionaries who bequeathed their insights to us in writing.

Following in the footsteps of Teresa of Avila and John of the Cross, Sor María often wrote metaphorically. She described the wound of divine love as "so sweet and attractive that the more it prevails the more it is sought." She portrays Mary as serenading her son in prayers that were like "scarlet lace, with which she bound and secured his love."[5]

"All of *Mystical City of God* is a grand construction of poetic theology," Artola writes, echoing many thoughts expressed by Pope Paul VI extolling the "way of beauty" so distinct from the "way of truth" as pursued by scientists and theologians.[6] Artola Arbiza cites the astonishment following the book's publication, for its subtle concepts of scholastic theology, its noble style and narrative technique, its lucid speculation augmented by spiritual sight, and its pious Marian sentiment. Yet, he concludes, "it is ultimately a poem."[7]

In 1668 King Carlos II of Spain asked two theologians to review the book. These were the eminent Don Diego de Silva, bishop of Guardia and also future general of the order of Saint Benedict, along with Padre Andrew Mendo of the Society of Jesus, a professor at the University of Salamanca.[8] In this study, de Silva wrote the following: "[This book] manifests the treasures of divinity and eternal incarnate Wisdom in the wonderful life of the great Mother of God. . . . I began the examination of this work solely in virtue of obedience, but before I completed it I marveled at its excellence; I began as a critic, but I finished as an admirer."[9] Similarly, Mendo wrote, "Sor María's writing . . . enlightens the mind with a knowledge of the most sublime truths, and inflames the heart with divine love. . . . I think it can be truly said that venerable

María de Jesús of Ágreda surpasses all . . . other members of this order [of Saint Francis]."[10]

Regrettably, Sor María's ardent admirer Pope Clement IX—the former Cardinal Rospigliosi who had granted her only sabbatical, visited her during her lifetime, and eloquently praised her after her death—died in 1669. Nevertheless, to great acclaim, the first edition of *Mystical City of God* was published in Madrid in 1670. Serendipitously, it included Ximénez Samaniego's biography of Sor María, later published independently in Lisbon (1681) and Madrid (1727).[11] Lengthy endorsements of *Mystical City of God* by de Silva and Mendo were published in the foreword. The 1665 letter of praise by Bishop Miguel de Escartín—written just before Sor María's death—served as the church's official approbation.[12]

Rospigliosi's successor, Pope Clement X, approved Sor María's designation as a venerable in 1673 and agreed to the formation of a commission to consider her cause for sainthood.[13] Then, because during Sor María's lifetime the examination of sainthood causes understandably expanded to include any significant body of written works produced by the candidate, *Mystical City of God* was also included in the consideration of her cause.

With the considerable praise that had already been heaped upon *Mystical City of God*, few people anticipated any insurmountable concerns. In a few short years, however, the tables turned and irreparable damage was inflicted on her cause, which haunts it yet today.

Unbeknownst to the Spanish Inquisition, or the Tribunal of the Sacred Congregation of Rites (the office overseeing the sainthood process prior to the Vatican II council),[14] the Spanish opponents of the doctrine of the Immaculate Conception ("Maculists") denounced all Sor María's writings to the Supreme and Universal Roman Inquisition.[15] As a result of the Maculists' accusations, the Roman Inquisition—independently of the Congregation of Rites—placed the book on the church's Index of Forbidden Books on June 26, 1681. Pope Innocent XI announced their decision on August 4, after which all of Spain exploded in an uproar over the conflict.

Sor María's pious narrative of Mary's life had suddenly become a political football. Theological diatribes and classical polemics volleyed back and forth between factions. At the heart of it all was the mystery of the Immaculate Conception, alongside one of its most prominent proponents—Sor María of Ágreda.[16]

Ximénez Samaniego, who knew all Sor María's writings in detail, appealed directly to Pope Innocent XI with a convincing justification of the book's orthodoxy and a review of Sor María's cause to date.[17] The Queen of Spain added her endorsement on September 21, 1681. By October 26, the Vatican's secretary of state wrote that a suspension of the condemnation was likely.[18] By November 9, the decree was indeed lifted.[19] After a temporary gridlock due to all the bureaucratic fumbles between parallel offices, the sainthood commission benignly continued its examination of *Mystical City of God* as a part of Sor María's cause.

Meanwhile, the book's popularity presented logistical problems. Bootlegged copies abounded, appropriated from unapproved copies that were swiftly replicated and distributed to eager readers who longed to read the works of the remarkable Ágreda mystic.

Perhaps worried about the sheer volume of unapproved copies in circulation, and thinking to protect Sor María's reputation from any hint of duplicity regarding her 1650 testimony to the Inquisition, Ximénez Samaniego chose this time to fulfill his deathbed promise to her regarding the king's copy of *Mystical City of God*. In 1682 he burned the entire manuscript, saving only the title page.[20] Ironically, several times in later centuries when Sor María's authorship of the book came into question, the king's copy was fruitlessly sought as a way to prove its authenticity.

Under the leadership of Bishop Ximénez Samaniego, the Spanish Inquisition laboriously recalled all copies of *Mystical City of God* that did not conform to the first approved edition in 1670. Additionally, the Spanish Inquisition met through 1686 in fifty-seven sessions, with experts from sixteen Spanish and foreign universities, to ensure the integrity of the copy of the book.[21]

Any relative calm that temporarily ensued can now be recognized as the eye of the hurricane. Nevertheless, Ximénez Samaniego doggedly persisted on behalf of Sor María. "It is without error, scandal or faulty doctrine," Ximénez Samaniego's team declared on July 3, 1686, to the powers-that-be.[22]

Their work did not go unnoticed in Rome. Yet, a melodrama of misinformation permeates this period in the history of the book, so much so that many ecclesiastical and scholarly experts mistakenly thought—then and today—that the lifting of the decree of condemnation applied only to Spain and its dominions.

In his 2004 treatise, Artola Arbiza clearly shows that it applied to the entire church, pointing out that the Holy See in Rome continued to issue approvals and ecclesiastical licenses for *Mystical City of God*, not only in Spain, but also in France, Germany, Italy, Belgium, and Holland.[23] He also cites Pope Innocent XI's notes about the incident to the secretary of the Index of Forbidden Books, Padre Julio Bianchi, regarding the continuation of the license to publish the book.[24]

Most likely the confusion stemmed from the mistaken inclusion of the book in an appendix of the Index of Forbidden Books published in Venice in 1687. This unfortunate mix-up was finally put to rest on September 26, 1713, when the Roman Inquisition clearly stated that *Mystical City of God* was not forbidden, citing the November 9, 1681, decree of Pope Innocent XI lifting the prohibition on the book.[25]

Before that clarification, however, theologians of the Sorbonne in Paris took it upon themselves to debate the merits of *Mystical City of God*. In 1696, 152 masters of theology reviewed the book in thirty-two sessions from July 2 to July 14.

Anti-Marian sentiment dominated France at the time, and the doctrine of the Immaculate Conception was suspect. While the Sorbonne faculty was then the most prestigious in Europe, their focus in evaluating *Mystical City of God* was pointedly aimed at the overriding Marian nature of the book.[26] After intense deliberation the Sorbonne decried *Mystical City of God* as infected by Spanish nationalism and an exaggerated hypercult of saints and idolatry. They condemned it by eighty-five votes, negating Mary's Immaculate Conception and her titles of Mediatrix and Co-Redemptoress, the latter two dating back to the eighth century.[27]

The Sorbonne's fundamental charges—that Sor María claimed her revelations were greater than the Incarnation and that they were factual rather than private revelations—were based on an interpretive reading of *Mystical City of God* that was later discredited as an inexact translation from Spanish into French.[28] When this was confirmed, Rome's Benedictine cardinal José Sáenz de Aguirre instructed the Sorbonne to annul their censure. King Louis XIV of France, however, would not agree to it. The kings of Austria, Poland, and Portugal backed the King of Spain in petitioning the pope for a definition of the central issue, the doctrine of the Immaculate Conception.[29] It was not forthcoming.

Despite all the official controversy, popular regard in France for Sor María burgeoned. *Mystical City of God* was published in Marseilles and people read it hungrily. The book was openly revered and defended the sainted Louis-Marie Grignion de Montfort. And four universities—Salamanca, Alcalá de Henares, France's own Toulouse, and the Louvain in Belgium—reexamined and approved it in 1729.[30]

However the new approvals, even on the heels of the clarification in 1713, did not completely lift the shadows of doubt left in the wake of the 1681 condemnation and the Sorbonne's censure in 1696. In 1729, therefore, the postulator of Sor María's cause in Rome asked for a new examination of *Mystical City of God*, hoping to finally dispel all misgivings about the book.

Pope Benedict XIII, who had long incorporated material from *Mystical City of God* in sermons dating back to his days as archbishop of Benevento, benignly approved the formation of a new commission from within the College of Cardinals.[31] Benedict XIII died in 1730, and the formation of the commission was left to the new pope, Clement XII. He assigned six cardinals and three consulting theologians to the task on August 9, 1730.[32] Although well meaning, this represented an unfortunate turn of events. For it gave the impression that the book did not already have the church's approbation and therefore that the Congregation of Rites did not have what they would have logically assumed at this point, which is the normal organizational go-ahead to proceed on Sor María's cause for sainthood.[33]

To further exacerbate the situation, the commission did not complete its task, and it was left to the next pope, Benedict XIV, to wend his way through the amassing piles of documentation relevant to Sor María and her devotional history of Mary.

All but two or three popes since Sor María's death have taken some action regarding her sainthood and the status of *Mystical City of God*. All of these popes fell on one side or the other of the issue of the Immaculate Conception of Mary.

"If Sor María had not advanced the doctrine of the Immaculate Conception so much in her books," wrote postulator Padre José Falces prophetically in 1692, "she would be beatified—at least—by now."[34]

While Pope Benedict XIV was not an outright Maculist, he considered the doctrine of the Immaculate Conception, at best, a pious belief and wrote privately that he did not consider it a requirement of faith. Further, he feared that *Mystical City of God* might be embraced by the faithful as a "new Gospel," a thought that would have amazed and horrified Sor María, who took such care to anchor her work with biblical annotations.[35]

Benedict XIV also held the Sorbonne in the highest regard. He was well aware that the Sorbonne had originally ruled against *Mystical City of God* and that the church in France was in great turmoil during his papacy. He feared that an approval on the book would increase that turmoil and wrote of his fears privately to Cardinal Tencin on February 14, 1748, in correspondence that would not come to light until the twentieth century.

"Sor María is a celebrated maidservant of God," he wrote. "A judgment on her book, however, involves advancing an opinion about the Immaculate Conception, which the Franciscans favor and consider the book integral to. A condemnation of it will therefore certainly incense the Franciscans and all her proponents." "In this case," he continued, "I want to examine the book, not relative to her cause for beatification, but to decide if she is the author . . . something very difficult to prove."[36]

Benedict XIV proceeded on two fronts. First, the commission would evaluate *Mystical City of God* for its orthodoxy of belief.[37] To do so, they would address all objections included in the 1681 Maculist accusations. These were forty-two in number and ranged from the sublime to the ridiculous. "Mary's parents cannot be called 'grandparents' of Jesus," they argued. "The vestments of the Virgin were not ashen in color . . . the conception of Christ did not occur from three drops of blood from the Virgin's heart . . . Jesus did not perform any miracles before Cana . . . the praises that *Mystical City of God* pays to Mary are exaggerated."[38] And so on.

Secondly, the commission would address the authenticity of the book's authorship.[39] If Sor María could not be verified as its author, this fact would separate the book from her cause for sainthood and, Benedict XIV hoped, remove it from the influences on the doctrine of the Immaculate Conception. If she were proved to be the author, as turned out indeed to be the case, he would retreat to a position aimed at avoiding turmoil in the church.

The commission's work concluded in 1757, having grown to include all of Sor María's writings. While some advocates sought Felipe IV's destroyed copy of *Mystical City of God*, not knowing of Ximénez Samaniego's action in 1682, this did not prove to be a determining factor.

"The graphology experts completed their examination," Artola Arbiza reported, "and the question [of authenticity] was dissolved." The commission listed twenty-two publications, citing *Mystical City of God* and other writings, including some correspondence, as "authentic works, attributable without a doubt to Mother Ágreda."[40]

Between that decree, and the final examination of the writings for orthodoxy relevant to the 1681 accusations, Benedict XIV died on May 3, 1758.[41] In anticipation of his death before a final resolution, he wrote a confidential document entitled "Judicium"—with instructions that it be read by all future popes—about Sor María's cause for sainthood. He filed it in the Castel Sant'Angelo, a papal fortress just outside the walls of Vatican City in Rome. In this document, he counseled future popes to avoid turmoil in the church by neither approving nor disapproving Sor María's cause or *Mystical City of God*. In 1773 Pope Clement XIV, an advocate for Sor María's cause, opened a session of the Congregation of Rites with hopes to move her cause along, as well as that of the doctrine of the Immaculate Conception. As discussions ensued, however, the votes split when congregants read Benedict XIV's document. Conflicted, Clement XIV decreed a silence on her cause—a decision that was adopted in perpetuity by future popes, effectively condemning her and the book to a perpetual limbo.[42]

"Judicium" was not issued as a document of doctrinal "magisterium," or a directive mandating conformity.[43] If it were, it would have bound future popes irrevocably. Still, it proved an effective strategy. This confidential missive indirectly passed down from pope to pope blocked progress on Sor María's cause until the doctrine of the Immaculate Conception was finally defined and affirmed by Pope Pius IX in 1854.[44]

CHAPTER 30

American "Ágredistas"
Revive Sor María's Cause

AT THE ONSET OF 1854, THE DECREE OF SILENCE FROM 1773 weighed so heavily on the disposition of *Mystical City of God* that even Sor María's loyal proponents considered her cause dead and buried. Only Heaven, they said, could bring about any new interest. Then, with the declaration later that year of the doctrine of the Immaculate Conception by Pope Pius IX, a positive momentum began to build. Two subsequent events were also key: the apparition in 1858 of Our Lady in Lourdes, France, and the miraculous cure of Sor Colette in 1867.[1]

Accounts of the apparition of Our Lady in 1858 to now saint Bernadette Soubirous in Lourdes fueled this momentum when Mary identified herself to Bernadette as Our Lady of the Immaculate Conception. France was now enthusiastically aflame in favor of the new doctrine.

Then, between 1861 and 1863, a French Passionist priest—Serafín del Sagrado Corazón—published a five-volume treatise in Paris praising Sor María and *Mystical City of God*. France—especially Paris—was now abuzz with interest in Sor María.[2] No particular action ensued, however, until the miraculous cure of Sor Colette in Nivelles, Belgium, in 1867. Then Heaven indeed seemed to have spoken.

The miracle of Nivelles (see chapter 28) immediately sparked new interest in Sor María's cause. Whereas before it had primarily been a

Franciscan effort, suddenly it gained a universal appeal. The postulator of her cause, backed by thirty-eight Spanish bishops, requested a new examination of *Mystical City of God*, reasoning that the Nivelles miracle far superseded the 1773 decree of silence. On February 3, 1868, Pope Pius IX decided, however, that first the miracle itself needed further investigation, a process that took several years. He died in 1878 before it was complete and was succeeded by Pope Leo XIII.[3]

After fully documenting the miracle, the Franciscan postulator general and the entire Spanish episcopate appealed to the Congregation of Rites on March 10, 1884, requesting a discussion and vote on behalf of Sor María and the miracle.[4] The promoter of the faith, Monsignor Agustín Caprara, had prepared an exhaustive exegesis, of which the summary pages alone amounted to 515 pages.[5] In it, Monsignor Caprara directed the twenty-eight members of the Congregation of Rites to clearly deliver a positive or negative decision regarding the removal, or not, of the decree of silence.[6]

On March 16, the congregation voted twenty to eight, in favor of removing the silence.[7] A victory at last long last, on behalf of Sor María's cause? Not so, according to Pope Leo XIII, who, when informed of the vote the following week, reserved judgment. Then, a year and a half later, he announced on December 19, 1887, that the decree of silence would remain in effect. His inexplicable announcement painfully dashed hopes for any immediate progress in Sor María's cause.

While many have argued that Popes Benedict XIV and Clement XIV did not invoke papal infallibility in the Judicium of 1758 and the decree of silence of 1773, both actions nevertheless had that effect. Sor María's cause, therefore, again was thwarted.[8] The Franciscans and the Spanish bishops did not lose heart. In light of the strong majority vote in Sor María's favor, they decided to continue with their work on behalf of her cause.

In 1909, because of continued popular admiration of Sor María's inspiring life and works, the bishop of Tarazona received permission to move her corpse to the museum over the convent church, where it might be viewed by the faithful.[9] No further appeals were made for several decades, but Sor María's popularity remained constant, and the number of editions, translations, and publications of *Mystical City of God* multiplied worldwide.

Then in 1954 the jubilant hundred-year anniversary of the declaration of the Immaculate Conception ignited unexpected new hope from the New World.

James A. Carrico (1909–82) operated a small dairy farm in South Bend, Indiana, with his wife Therese and their seven children. Carrico, a devout Catholic, had learned about Sor María of Ágreda from a saintly bearded monk named Solanus Casey (1870–1957), a Capuchin priest of the Franciscan Order of Friars Minor. In the early 1900s, Father Casey had discovered the newly translated English edition of *Mystical City of God.*

Casey, now a venerable of the church himself, was so imbued with love for Our Lady as a result of reading *Mystical City of God* that for fifty-three years until his death, he read it prayerfully each day, on his knees.[10] So infectious was the monk's enthusiasm for this devout treatment of Mary's life that he recommended it to everyone he encountered.

While Father Casey is most often associated with the Friary of Saint Bonaventure in Detroit, Michigan, he also served for many years in Indiana. During those years he regaled James Carrico with praise for Sor María and *Mystical City of God.* When Carrico's devotion to Mary rose exponentially as a result of reading Mary's biography, so did his respect for the book's author.

Casey encouraged Carrico to write about María of Ágreda's life and works, and indeed he did.[11] Artola Arbiza and Mendía's 2004 treatise on Sor María's cause for sainthood aptly credits Carrico for his efforts. "After quite a lapse of time," wrote Artola Arbiza, "a spark of hope kindled [Sor María's] cause, not in Spain, but in America . . . from a group of secular Catholics acting out of great resolve. The principal protagonist was James A. Carrico."[12]

In the shadow of the great University of Notre Dame, which the Carrico farm supplied with eggs, Carrico churned out a storm of correspondence and publications on behalf of Sor María's cause. After the volume of materials and the number of meetings in his home grew considerably, he designated one of his buildings for his Ágreda work—a vacant chicken coop. He painted it red and dubbed it the "Little Red Schoolhouse" in honor of the one-room school of his childhood and in affectionate contrast to the "big schoolhouse" of nearby Notre Dame.

With Solanus Casey's help, Carrico attracted an impressive cadre of American advocates for Sor María. These included Rt. Rev. John S. Sabo, dean of South Bend and president of the Hungarian Catholic League of America; Very Rev. James Keane, editor of *The Age of Mary* periodical (1954–58); Rev. Peter Forrestal, University of Notre Dame author and translator; Walter M. Langford, dean of modern languages at Notre Dame;[13] and Very Rev. Peter Rookey, consultor general of the Servants of Mary.[14]

Keane dedicated much of *The Age of Mary* to articles on the inspiring life and works of Sor María. Sabo contacted the archbishop of Santa Fe, New Mexico, Edwin V. Byrne, who enthusiastically added a second imprimatur to the 1949 English edition of *Mystical City of God*. Byrne traveled to Ágreda and personally conveyed to the nuns the good news of the US efforts on behalf of their founder. Noted Catholic historian Carlos E. Castañeda contributed several articles to *The Age of Mary*.

In Artola Arbiza's 2004 treatise, he cites the dates of two dozen of Carrico's pivotal letters to the Spanish vice postulator of Sor María's cause. In Carrico's collected papers, those letters—and hundreds of others within the United States and internationally—demonstrate his one-pointed dedication and its influence on the American bishops.

The year 1954 was designated the "Year of Mary." In the same period, a group called the "Ágredas" was founded in Beaumont, Texas. Their mission was to pray for religious vocations in honor of Sor María, and for her cause. The Ágredas became part of the National Council of Catholic Women and regularly coordinated their efforts with Carrico.[15] One of its members, Mrs. Dorothy White, painted a scene of Sor María preaching to Native Americans. The painting—featured on the cover of Carrico's short devotional biography of Sor María in 1962—provided the basis for a mural now prominently featured in Saint Anne's Church in Beaumont and is listed in state historical retrospectives.

"These developments so cheered Carrico," wrote Artola Arbiza, "that he initiated an active collaboration between the American and Spanish bishops to promote Sor María's cause."[16] As a result, efforts in Spain and Rome gained a new momentum, and activity in the United States flourished.

In 1958 the former Notre Dame football great, Fr. James Flanagan, founded the Society of Our Lady of the Most Holy Trinity (SOLT) in Texas, patterning its mission and spiritual exercises after inspirations he received through reading *Mystical City of God*. In an era when new vocations to religious orders languished in America, SOLT's membership of priests, nuns, laypeople, and seminarians-in-training flourished. Today, its ecclesiastical work extends throughout the United States, as well as in Belize, Guatemala, China, Haiti, Honduras, Macau, Mexico, Papua New Guinea, the Philippines, Russia, and Thailand.

Carrico spearheaded coordination among the stateside proponents, bringing them together under the umbrella of a newly formed American Council for the Mystical City of God. Flanagan and others from around the country traveled periodically to South Bend to attend its meetings. The American "Ágredistas," as they came to be called, impressed those in Rome and particularly heartened the Franciscan postulator general. "Thanks to the intense correspondence between Carrico and the Postulator General," wrote Artola Arbiza, "a new epoch began in the history of Sor María's cause."[17]

In 1961 the American Ágredistas formed their own commission to study the case and to build a contemporary position on the orthodoxy of *Mystical City of God*. When, by 1970, the results were still indeterminate, Carrico launched a massive letter-writing campaign among the growing number of proponents for Sor María's cause. Artola Arbiza terms it a "veritable SOS."[18] By June 20, 1973, Sor María's advocates submitted a new petition to Rome to lift the decree of silence.[19]

Meanwhile, Franco's regime in Spain—which had ensconced Catholicism as the state religion—was near its end, inevitably clashing with the emerging ecumenical impetus of Vatican II. That Franco supported Sor María's cause during this period need not necessarily have impacted her case adversely, but it certainly didn't help in an era of emerging feminism. Then, young Spanish women might be heard sniping at their regimental pious sisters as "Madre Marías," not directly referring to Sor María, but certainly to the cadre of abbesses among whom she stood.[20]

In Rome, the liberation of Sor María's cause was not immediately forthcoming. In October of that year the only response to the petition was that it required more documentation. Still, the tenor of the response was hopeful. Benito Mendía, Sor María's vice postulator from 1973 to 1983, provided the bulk of necessary analysis by the end of his tenure, which later constituted twelve chapters in Artola Arbiza's 2004 treatise.[21]

Sadly, James A. Carrico died before he could witness several hopeful developments in the late twentieth and early twenty-first centuries. When the Knights of Columbus Solanus Casey chapter of Fort Wayne (Indiana) learned that Casey read *Mystical City of God* on his knees for fifty-three years, they fully embraced Sor María's cause.[22] Today the American Council for the Mystical City of God endures under its aegis.

Then on November 23, 1990, the Congregation of Saints recognized the "heroic virtue" of famed thirteenth-century philosopher-theologian

John Duns Scotus, naming him a venerable of the church. Subsequently, Pope John Paul II beatified Scotus on March 20, 1992. His cause was thought to intimately affect that of Sor María in that his writings on the Immaculate Conception had so influenced her treatment of the doctrine.

In yet one more in a dizzying array of "new" studies on *Mystical City of God*, another commission completed its evaluation in 1995, saying that the book raised some questions about the contrast between Sor María's private revelations and biblical-magisterial treatments of Mary.[23] Undaunted, Sor María's postulators consulted Cardinal Joseph Ratzinger—later elected as Pope Benedict XVI—who served under Pope John Paul II as prefect of the Congregation of Faith. This office has overseen the doctrinal aspects of the sainthood process since the Vatican II council, in conjunction with the Congregation of the Causes for Saints. Ratzinger said that a *nihil obstat* was required in order to reopen the cause, meaning that it must be clearly concluded that *Mystical City of God* contained no error of faith or morals.

The next determination was issued by the Vatican secretary of state on February 19, 1999. It stated that there were neither errors of doctrine nor heresy in *Mystical City of God*. Victory, however, remained elusive.

The 1999 statement went on to declare that Sor María's view of Mary in *Mystical City of God* contrasted with that of sacred Scripture and the Mariology of Vatican II.[24] This was a far cry from a nihil obstat, especially for an author who—had she been able to fast-forward to the time of Vatican II—would have been among the first to herald its Christocentric Mariology. This perplexing conundrum was "ambiguous if not contradictory," wrote Artola Arbiza.[25]

Artola Arbiza attempted to explain the judgment as a result of the labyrinthine divisions within the Vatican, from the Congregation of the Faith, to the Congregation of Saints, to the Congregation of Sacred Rites, to the secretary of state, and more. To deflect the obvious questions that arose, however, was difficult. If *Mystical City of God* had no doctrinal errors, mystified proponents asked, how was the second part of the statement justified in blocking the nihil obstat?[26]

Despite the puzzling stalemate, events in 2000 did much to neutralize the negative effects of the 1999 letter. Cardinal Ángel Suquía, archbishop emeritus of Madrid, headed a special commission in promotion of Sor María's cause. In 2000 he had an extensive meeting with Cardinal Ratzinger to address the terms of the 1999 letter. Cardinal Ratzinger made several helpful suggestions, one of which resulted in Suquía's audience with Pope John Paul II on January 22, 2001.[27]

Later in the year, a strong show of support emerged from the Spanish universities, who celebrated a special week-long congress on Sor María in August at the International University of Alfonso VIII in Soria. Many papers were delivered in honor of the valorous nun, featuring previously unexamined aspects of her life. This paved the way for a wave of enthusiasm surrounding the events in 2002 celebrating the four hundredth anniversary of Sor María's birth.

In 2003 the president of the Spanish Mariological Society and a participating member of the Pontifical International Marian Academy of Rome, Fr. Enrique Llamas, came to Sor María's defense in the wake of the 1999 letter, penning a powerful treatment that would later be translated into English as *Venerable Mother Ágreda and the Mariology of Vatican II*. In it, Llamas lamented the "intellectual myopia" and "anti-feminist obsession" reminiscent of the early critics of Saint Teresa of Avila, now a doctor of the church.[28] In a primarily positive thrust, however, he provided example after example of harmonious similarities between *Mystical City of God* and *Lumen gentium*, a dogmatic constitution of the Catholic Church issued from Vatican II. In doing so, he cautions the reader not to confuse the vast stylistic differences between the two documents—the sparing and theological character of *Lumen gentium* and the repetitive, narrative, and exuberantly baroque style of *Mystical City of God*—with the essential similarity between the two.[29]

Then in 2004, "after several months of seeming inactivity," wrote Artola Arbiza, "an inexplicable interest surged in Rome on behalf of Sor María."[30] It was prompted by the 150th anniversary honoring the doctrinal definition of the Immaculate Conception, and it presented a critical opportunity for Sor María's proponents to petition for the reopening of her cause for sainthood.

On December 6, two days before the feast day of the Immaculate Conception, Sor María's postulators again met with Cardinal Ratzinger. They presented to him an extensive dossier of all the activities promoting Sor María's cause since 1999. The cardinal warmly welcomed the materials.[31]

"He was demonstrably willing to intervene on behalf of reopening the cause," wrote Artola Arbiza.[32]

On the next anniversary of Sor María's birthday, April 2, 2005, Pope John Paul II died. The College of Cardinals elected Cardinal

Joseph Ratzinger to take his place. The new pope assumed the name of Benedict XVI, in honor of his admiration for the papacy of Benedict XV in the early twentieth century. He later appointed a new prefect of the Congregation for the Doctrine of the Faith to take over his work in that capacity. Responsibility for clearing Sor María's cause to proceed thus transferred to Pope Benedict XVI's appointee, American-born cardinal William J. Levada, archbishop emeritus of San Francisco, California, a potentially favorable development for America's own Lady in Blue. In July 2008, Benedict XVI appointed Archbishop Angelo Amato as prefect of the Congregation of the Causes of Saints, within a month of which Amato visited Ágreda to celebrate Mass in the convent church, another encouraging though inconclusive sign regarding Sor María's recognition within her presiding institution.

Whether or not Sor María of Ágreda's future includes the mantle of sainthood, however, her place in history is assured. Her heroic life of virtue stands without question. The citations about the Lady in Blue in US colonial documents remain as historical testimony to her influence on the development of the American Southwest. Her inspiration to countless seventeenth- and eighteenth-century religious figures is found in the lives of celebrated missionaries such as Junípero Serra, founder of the California missions; Antonio Margil de Jesús, foremost Texas missionary;[33] and others. Her literary works, most notably *Mystical City of God*, are studied today worldwide in university language and literature programs.

Sor María's legacy, however, is not relegated to historical archives filled with dusty tomes or academic lectures in ivory towers.

Radio Televisión Española (RTVE) in 1995 inaugurated a new look at women's roles in the history of Spain, entitled "Women in History" (Mujeres en la Historia). Directed by noted journalist María Teresa Alvarez, the series highlighted Sor María of Ágreda as one of the nine most influential women in Spain's history, feting each in a sixty-minute broadcast. Among these impressive women, five of whom were royalty, Sor María stood out as a key political, literary, and religious figure whose influence far exceeded the walls of the cloister. Indeed, because her legacy entwined that of colonial southwest America, the series conducted interviews in the United States as well as Spain.

Clark Colahan moderated much of the American portion of the show on location in New Mexico. Segments included the performance of a

FIGURE 34. Preeminent Texas missionary Padre Antonio Margil, whose biography reflects Sor María's inspiration on his work, and includes texts of Benavides's and Sor María's letters. Wood engraving, artist unknown. Courtesy of Catholic Archives of Texas, Austin.

surviving Native American song about Mother Ágreda of Jesús and the "Mystical City of Light," as well as interviews with a SOLT representative and James Carrico's son who—as Mark Joseph María de Ágreda Anthony Carrico—was actually named after her. The show aired several clips from the performance of *Sor María*, a chamber dance/opera written and directed by award-winning performing artists Joseph Weber (composer) and Michele Larsson (choreographer). The production was sponsored by the Santa Fe Council for the Arts and partially funded by grants from New Mexico Arts and the National Endowment for the Arts.

"We have chosen not to speculate on the degree of reality contained in María's more spectacular claims," Weber wrote in the program. "It is evident from her own and her biographer's writing that she experienced transcendental states . . . not uncommon . . . [when] undergoing transformational experience."[34]

In Spain, as the 1990s progressed into the new millennium, the "Madre María" pejoratives faded into the background as new respect emerged for Sor María among innovative thinkers more likely to entertain the possibility of mystical phenomena, as well as traditionalists willing to take a new look at a figure of such talent and gravitas as Sor María.

Over twelve thousand pilgrims flocked to Sor María's grave in 2002, in honor of the four hundredth anniversary of her birth. That same year, the Spanish Mariological Society endorsed Sor María's cause for sainthood in Rome. Concurrently, the president of the Pontifical International Marian Academy of Rome—Gaspar Calvo—directed a yearlong series of courses on the life and works of Sor María, commenting on the importance of making "more and better known" "such an important figure as Sor María."[35]

In 2002–3, Mel Gibson read *Mystical City of God*, among other works, in preparation for making his 2004 blockbuster film *The Passion of the Christ*. Since Sor María's book is written from Mary's point of view, it touchingly portrays the Blessed Mother's loving presence throughout her son's ordeal. This is an acknowledged element of Mel Gibson's film, and there are other notable similarities between Gibson's and Sor María's treatment of the passion, from the Garden of Gethsemane to the Crucifixion itself. None is more memorable, however, than the unbreakable, most often silent empathic and spiritual ties binding mother and son.

Liturgically, 2004 marked the 150th anniversary of the doctrine of the Immaculate Conception. Even more publications about Sor María poured

FIGURE 35. Convent visiting room (*locutorio*) today features center grille (closed) next to original spiked grille (right) of Sor María's era. Photo by author.

FIGURE 36. Contemporary contemplative nuns of Ágreda allow their photograph to be taken at Convent of the Conception. Photo by author.

out of Spain, most notably *La Venerable M. María de Jesus de Ágreda y la Inmaculada Concepción*, by Antonio Artola Arbiza and Benito Mendía. Throughout the United States, celebrations abounded, especially at the National Shrine of the Immaculate Conception in Washington DC. How gratified Sor María would have been to learn that the Immaculate Conception has—since the Council of Baltimore in 1846—been the patroness of the United States, a country she loved from near and afar.[36]

The following year, in 2005, six handcrafted rosary prototypes were designed by a US firm and dedicated to the inspiring legacy of Sor María, America's Lady in Blue. Appropriately, two of the designs were created from beads of turquoise from the Kingman Mine in Arizona, with crucifixes reminiscent of those from the Spanish colonial era.

"The seeds that Sor María planted in her spiritual journey to the New World have made a great difference in the world not only in the 1600s, but today as well," said Margot Carter-Blair, liturgical artist and designer at the Rosary Workshop.[37] The company's considerable offerings are all custom-made at their headquarters in Stephenson, Michigan, and their sentiments are echoed by many others.

"Sor María is a key cultural phenomenon in the American Southwest," said Miguel Bretos, one of the Smithsonian Institution's curators at the National Portrait Gallery in Washington DC. As such, Bretos had made a particular study of colonial history and art. He cited the mural in Beaumont, Texas, featuring Sor María preaching to the Jumano Native Americans, as well as a full-length portrait on display today in the National Museum of Viceroyalty in Tepotzotlán, Mexico. At the top of the portrait a banner reads, "The Venerable Mother María of Jesús, at the age of twenty years, preached to the Indians of New Mexico."[38]

"Sor María matters fundamentally to us," Dr. Bretos said. "I believe that there are many ways to look at human history, and that her legacy helps us to capture some of the profound spirituality in our history."[39] Contemporary educators are proving Bretos right.

The US Library of Congress (LOC) launched an online and hardcopy research guide for the study of women's history and culture in the United States, safeguarding for future generations the library's comprehensive sources on women's pivotal contributions in our nation's history. In it, Sor María stands out among the notable colonial figures cited from 1580 to 1800, as lauded by Mary Giles in the introduction to *Women in the Inquisition* and highlighted in Clark Colahan's chapter on her in the

FIGURE 37. Turquoise rosary honors Lady in Blue. Designed and crafted in 2005 by the Rosary Workshop of Stephenson, Michigan. Photo by author.

FIGURE 38. Example of decorative missionary trunk used to carry *Mystical City of God* abroad. Images inside trunk cover feature Mary, Saint Francis, Saint John the Evangelist, and Sor María. On display in— and image courtesy of—Convent of the Conception, Ágreda.

same work. The LOC collection "document[s] the efforts of countless . . . women not only to join 'the system' but also to reform and transcend it," writes Janice E. Ruth in the introduction.[40]

Late in 2006 Sor María was included in *Grolier Scholastic*'s new biography series on one thousand influential Hispanic Americans, along-side New Mexico governor Bill Richardson, eminent historian Carlos E. Castañeda, father of California missions Junípero Serra, and others. The series is aimed at educating and inspiring young readers about the many contributions of our country's varied Hispanic leaders, past and pres-ent—certainly a group Sor María deserves to be among.

Inevitably, such a remarkable history would eventually find its way into contemporary performing arts and literature. Javier Sierra's *Da Vinci Code*–like novel *The Lady in Blue* (2007) chronicles more of the investigative reporter's own travels than actually explores the life or experiences of Sor María, and he very creatively ascribes her mystical experiences of bilocation to a type of on-off switch instantaneously triggered by the traditional polyphonic chants sung at the convent. While the nuns in Ágreda may cringe at the whimsical treatment of their revered mystic, the book rightly calls attention to an extraordinary woman and was named the best historical novel of 2008 in English by the International Latino Book Awards.

In 2007 a consortium of cultural and civic organizations in San Angelo, Texas, emerged to encourage artistic works honoring María of Ágreda as the Lady in Blue who taught Christianity to the Jumano Native Americans of West Texas. They particularly note that she is the legendary inspiration behind the origin of the state's flower, the bluebonnet.

"According to one Indian legend," wrote historians at the University of Texas at Austin, "when Mother María last appeared to the natives, she blessed them and then slowly faded away into the hills. The next morning the area was covered with a blanket of strange flowers that were a deep blue in color, like her cloak—the first Texas bluebonnets."[41]

"We're partial to the legend of the bluebonnet, of course," said San Angelo musician Cynthia Jordan, who composed ballads about the Lady in Blue and who works within the consortium to produce annual pageantry commemorating Sor María's legacy. "We want to lead Texas in celebrating one of its most revered pioneer women," Jordan said.[42]

At the same time, "prayer cards"—small two-inch by four-inch cards typically featuring a saintly image on the front and a prayer on the back—are proliferating throughout the Southwest and beyond like bluebonnets raining from above, as Sor María's proponents pray for her beatification and sainthood.

She would be pleased, of course, at one level. Yet she shied away from public attention. She loved the contemplative hush of the cloister, the quiet meditative prayer that the nuns in Ágreda cultivate yet today, the silent inquisition into the divine abyss. There she dilated her heart to hear not only her all too human conscience, but also the heavenly voices that speak to us all, if we but listen.

The Quest to Explain
Mystical Phenomena in a Scientific Age

Mystical phenomena, although esoteric and elusive, may soon be measured scientifically.

While the term *mysticism* often refers to extraordinary spiritual experiences gained through deep meditative prayer, the term *miracle* evokes a particular event of a wondrous nature, one that has no apparent explanation through natural causes. In each case, "ordinary" reality has been transcended, and something unusual has occurred. In many time-honored wisdom traditions, these events are often described as supernatural and attributed to the generous hand of God. Yet, despite the testimony of witnesses regarding some more tangible mystical events, such as levitation or the curing of an illness, most mystical experiences are private and subjective. In more secular venues, they may be termed as paranormal and attributed to the psychic abilities and techniques of the practitioner, or simply debunked as delusion or fiction.[1]

Now, however, scientists are developing the potential to focus the objective measurements of technology on spiritual states of consciousness, just as they have measured the physiological indices of emotional and cognitive states. One of many such promising studies is the ongoing research at the University of Pennsylvania's Division of Nuclear Medicine. In this inquiry, Andrew Newberg (recognized in *Best Doctors in America 2007–2008*) and associates have defined neuroanatomical criteria to quantify a continuum of mystical and prayerful states. In selecting their subjects, they ensured that participants had "no history of medical or neuropsychological problems, or drug abuse" in order to protect their inquiries from contamination of suspect conditions such as temporal lobe epilepsy, schizophrenia, and other pathologies. They then measured neurotransmissions, and even hormone levels, through MRIs, blood work, and PET and SPECT scans in order to track activity in the brain and in the parasympathetic and sympathetic nervous systems.[2]

As a result, Newberg discovered a new range of physical changes that occur during the prayerful practices of Buddhist monks and Catholic Franciscan nuns. With longtime associate Eugene D'Aquili, Newberg developed scientific terminology for these neuropsychological phenomena along an "Aesthetic-Religious Continuum" that includes experiences of transcendent union with God, a sensory "hyperlucidity" not unlike ecstatic trances and visions, and—in terms evocative of María of Ágreda and others—the "intense and progressive certainty" of the knowledge gained in spiritual practice.[3]

At the same time, theoretical and aeronautical physicists are striving to achieve a unified field theory in order to resolve the conflicts between quantum mechanics and relativity. As they do so, various theories have emerged that are strikingly reminiscent themselves of miracles and mystical phenomena: magnetic levitation, quantum nonlocality, and superluminosity in the time-space continuum, all of which have the potential of opening grand new vistas of integrated knowledge previously thought inaccessible.

Scholarship in these arenas promises to be very fertile in the twenty-first century and beyond, offering new hope for the possibility that one day science and religion might sometimes intersect on common ground.

Reference Chronology
for the Lifetime of María of Ágreda

1602   Birth of María Coronel, Ágreda, Spain.

1605   Birth of Spanish Hapsburg prince Felipe, future king of Spain, Portugal, Naples, and Sicily.

1618   Thirty Years' War erupts between Spain, France, Germany, and all major powers.

1620   Nuns witness Sor María levitating in Ágreda; she reports simultaneous bilocation to New World.

1620   Marriage of Prince Felipe to Isabel de Bourbon, daughter of King Henry IV of France.

1621   Death of King Felipe III. Prince Felipe accedes to throne as Felipe IV under thumb of minister Olivares.

1623   Church conducts ecclesiastical investigation of Sor María of Ágreda and exonerates her.

1626   Native Americans inform New Mexico missionaries of repeated apparitions of Lady in Blue.

1627   Sor María is elected abbess of the Convent of the Conception, Ágreda, Spain.

1628   Letters circulate between New World and Spain about Spanish nun's supernatural appearances.

1629   Native American Jumano chieftain, Capitán Tuerto, cites appearances of a Lady in Blue.

1630   New Spain missionary, Alonso Benavides, writes to Felipe IV about the Lady in Blue.

1631   Benavides visits Ágreda for three-week interrogation on Sor María's bilocations and confirms them.

1635	Spanish Inquisition opens case against bilocation experiences of María of Ágreda.
1637	Sor María begins writing controversial biography of Mary as Co-Redemptoress alongside Jesus.
1643	Felipe IV meets Sor María en route to battlefront, begins a twenty-two-year friendship and correspondence.
1644	Death of Isabel, Felipe IV's first wife. He consults Sor María on temporal and spiritual matters.
1645	Sor María completes writing *Mystical City of God*, then burns it on the order of a temporary confessor.
1646	Engagement of Felipe's son to Emperor Ferdinand III's daughter, Mariana of Austria. Death of prince.
1648	Treaty of Westphalia marks end of Thirty Years' War and significant losses for Spain.
1648	Sor María is implicated in a plot against the Crown, adding to the Inquisition's list of concerns about her.
1649	Marriage of King Felipe IV to his son's former fiancée, Mariana of Austria, also Felipe's niece.
1650	Spanish Inquisition interrogates María of Ágreda for eleven days and ultimately acquits her.
1655	Sor María begins second writing of *Mystical City of God*, completed in 1660.
1657	Sor María intervenes with Duke of Gramont, helps to effect the Peace of the Pyrenees with France.
1665	May: death of Sor María de Jesus of Ágreda. September: death of King Felipe IV.

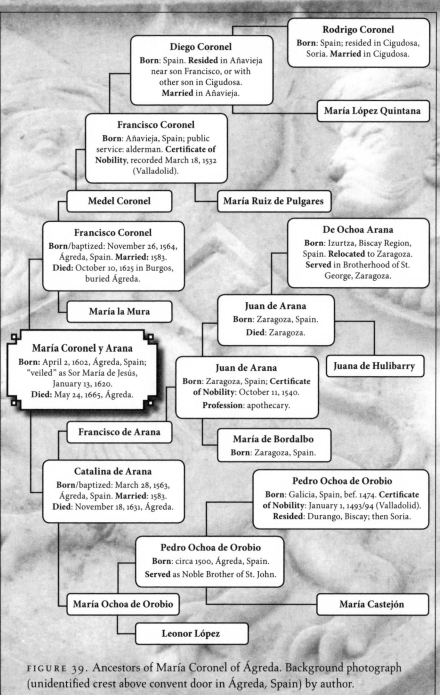

Rodrigo Coronel
Born: Spain; resided in Cigudosa, Soria. **Married** in Cigudosa.

Diego Coronel
Born: Spain. **Resided** in Añavieja near son Francisco, or with other son in Cigudosa. **Married** in Añavieja.

María López Quintana

Francisco Coronel
Born: Añavieja, Spain; public service: alderman. **Certificate of Nobility**, recorded March 18, 1532 (Valladolid).

Medel Coronel

María Ruiz de Pulgares

Francisco Coronel
Born/baptized: November 26, 1564, Ágreda, Spain. **Married**: 1583. **Died**: October 10, 1625 in Burgos, buried Ágreda.

De Ochoa Arana
Born: Izurtza, Biscay Region, Spain. **Relocated** to Zaragoza. **Served** in Brotherhood of St. George, Zaragoza.

María la Mura

Juan de Arana
Born: Zaragoza, Spain. **Died**: Zaragoza.

María Coronel y Arana
Born: April 2, 1602, Ágreda, Spain; "veiled" as Sor María de Jesús, January 13, 1620. **Died:** May 24, 1665, Ágreda.

Juan de Arana
Born: Zaragoza, Spain; **Certificate of Nobility**: October 11, 1540. **Profession**: apothecary.

Juana de Hulibarry

Francisco de Arana

María de Bordalbo
Born: Zaragoza, Spain.

Catalina de Arana
Born/baptized: March 28, 1563, Ágreda, Spain. **Married**: 1583. **Died**: November 18, 1631, Ágreda.

Pedro Ochoa de Orobio
Born: Galicia, Spain, bef. 1474. **Certificate of Nobility**: January 1, 1493/94 (Valladolid). **Resided**: Durango, Biscay; then Soria.

Pedro Ochoa de Orobio
Born: circa 1500, Ágreda, Spain. **Served** as Noble Brother of St. John.

María Ochoa de Orobio

María Castejón

Leonor López

FIGURE 39. Ancestors of María Coronel of Ágreda. Background photograph (unidentified crest above convent door in Ágreda, Spain) by author.

María of Ágreda's Major Writings

YEAR	WORK	MOST RECENT PUBLICATION STATUS
1616 (circa)	"Face of the Earth and Map of the Spheres"	Included in Colahan's *The Visions of Sor María de Agreda,* 1994
1621–26	"Spiritual Garden for the Life of the Soul"	Unpublished
1627	*Ladder to Perfection*	Madrid and Barcelona: 1915 and 1958
1630 (prior to)	*Litany to Our Lady*	Zaragoza: 1630
1634–37	*Laws of the Spouse I*	Barcelona: 1916
1637–45	First writing of *Mystical City of God*	Burned
1641–42	*Laws of the Spouse II*	Barcelona: 1920
1643–65	*Correspondence with Felipe IV*	Madrid: 1991
1647–50	*Spiritual Exercises for Retreats*	Madrid: 1975
1652–55	"Sabbaticals"	Excerpted in vol. 5 of *Mística Ciudad de Dios,* Madrid: 1914, 1985
1655–60	Second writing of *Mystical City of God*	80+ editions 1670–2007
1660	*Some Doctrinal Events and Teachings for the Soul (I)*	Leon: 1993

YEAR	WORK	MOST RECENT PUBLICATION STATUS
1665	*Some Doctrinal Events and Teachings for the Soul (II)*	Leon: 1993
Last years	Autobiography of the early years	Included in vol. 5 of *Mística Ciudad de Dios*, Madrid: 1914, 1985

Note: Sor María wrote a number of other tracts, some of which were burned ("Grace," and "Celestial Glory"); some of which were published in journals or other books ("The Six Angels," her 1650 letter to Manero, "The Passion of Our Lord Jesus Christ," and the accounts of her visions of Queen Isabel and Prince Baltasar Carlos); and some of which yet reside in the convent's archives, such as *Daily Exercises* (Barcelona: 1879), "Mystical Theology," "Laws of the Spouse III," and "Sighs of the Soul," as well as numerous reflections on prayer, perfection, contrition, celestial union, God's love, and various events in her life. There are also folios with an additional eight hundred letters to a variety of commoners and nobility.

María of Ágreda's Daily Schedule

2:00–4:00 a.m.	Matins (community morning prayers)
4:00–6:00 a.m.	Sleep/rest for most of community (for Sor María—private devotions)
6:00–8:00 a.m.	Choir, recitation of canonical prayers, Mass, Communion
8:00–9:30 a.m.	Private meditation
9:30–12:00 (noon)	Convent chores, administrative/abbess duties
12:00–1:00 p.m.	Angelus prayers, followed by lunch
1:00–5:00 p.m.	Works of charity, administration, writing, confession, meetings with priests and confessors
5:00–6:00 p.m.	Choir, community prayers
6:00–7:00 p.m.	Dinner
7:00–8:00 p.m.	Compline (community evening prayers)
8:00–9:00 p.m.	Return to cell; private confession and recitation of Miserere in expiation
9:00–11:00 p.m.	Sleep/rest
11:00 p.m.–2:00 a.m.	Private devotions, including Way of the Cross as follows:
11:00–12:30 a.m.	*Meditation on Jesus*
	thirty minutes: kneeling with cross on shoulders; thirty minutes: kneeling with arms cruciform, hands pressed on iron nails; thirty minutes: prostrate on cross meditating on seven last words of Christ
12:30–2:00 a.m.	*Meditation on fruits of Christ's passion*

She often attended breakfast and lunch meals but only ate dinner (vegetarian) unless instructed otherwise.

She fasted on bread and water three times per week: Tuesday, Thursday, Saturday; on Fridays, she took no water, in memory of Christ's thirst during his passion.

Sor María's Southwest American
Presence after Her Death

TEXAS CHIEFTAIN CITES LEGEND OF LADY IN BLUE   1690

A Nabedache chieftain in a Texas village near San Antonio tells Padre
Damian Manzanet that the Lady in Blue visited his mother and others
frequently around the year 1630.[1]

NEW MEXICO NATIVES RECALL WOMAN IN BLUE   FEBRUARY 1699

Elder Indians at Gila River (New Mexico), along Camino del Diablo, tell
Capt. Juan Mateo Mange and Padre Eusebio Kino of a beautiful white
woman dressed in blue with a black head covering, and a cross, who spoke
to them and left through the air. Having heard the same story five days
earlier from Indians in Sonoita (Arizona), they conclude it was Sor María
of Ágreda.[2]

NATIVE AMERICANS HONOR MEMORY OF LADY IN BLUE   CIRCA 1710–14

Native Americans near present-day Nacogdoches, Texas, ask the French
explorer St. Denise for blue cloth to bury their dead. When asked why,
they state it is in memory of the Lady in Blue who came to them years
ago, teaching baptism and the Christian ways.[3]

FATHER OF CALIFORNIA MISSIONS INSPIRED BY SOR MARÍA AUGUST 18, 1772

Father Junípero Serra tells his biographer that Sor María's writings drew
him to his missionary work in the New World. Supposedly he brought
only two books with him to California—the Bible and *Mystical City of
God*.[4] Of the twenty-one missions founded by eighteenth-century Spanish
priests in California, nine are inspired by *Mystical City of God*.[5]

Father Antonio Margil de Jesús founded Our Lady of the Immaculate
Conception in present-day San Antonio. The "Conception" mission—
earlier named Conception of Ágreda, in honor of Sor María of Ágreda—
is considered Texas's best preserved Spanish mission.[6]

TEXAS STATE FLOWER RECALLS SOR MARÍA   CONTEMPORARY

Legend has it that after Sor María's last visit to the Jumano Indians, she
disappeared in the air, and blue flowers blanketed the countryside in her
wake. The flowers, called bluebonnets, became Texas's official state flower.

NEW MEXICO OPERA CELEBRATES MYSTICAL LADY IN BLUE   1986

Performing artists Joseph Weber and Michele Larsson compose and
produce a chamber dance/opera entitled *Sor María,* first performed in
1986 with support of the Santa Fe Council for the Arts, New Mexico Arts,
and the National Endowment for the Arts.[7]

SPAIN'S RADIO TELEVISIÓN ESPAÑOLA COVERS LADY IN BLUE IN   1995
NEW MEXICO

Spanish television hosts a series on the nine most influential women in
Spain's history, filming the history of one of its honorees—Sor María—
on location in Spain and New Mexico. *El País,* Spain's largest newspaper
with a daily readership of over two million, covered the series with a
prominent portrait of Sor María above the fold.[8]

SOR MARÍA HONORED AS ONE OF ONE THOUSAND INFLUENTIAL   2006
HISPANIC AMERICANS

In recognition of her widespread influence and inspiration to countless
colonial Southwest missionaries in the seventeenth and eighteenth
centuries, Sor María is featured in the *Grolier Scholastic* series alongside one thousand influential Hispanic Americans, past and present.

POPULAR AWARENESS BUILDS   2008

Awareness proliferates in Texas, New Mexico, and beyond, as San Angelo
consortium builds artistic repertoire on María of Ágreda and Javier
Sierra's novel on the Lady in Blue is lauded by the International Latino
Book Awards as the year's best English-edition historical novel.

BLUEBONNET EVOKES LADY IN BLUE TO CONTEMPORARY JUMANOS   2008

Sighting in 2006 of the tallest bluebonnet to date in West Texas history,
at 5' 2" tall, evokes to contemporary Jumano descendants the presence and
blessing of the Lady in Blue in their past history, their survival, and their
current efforts toward tribal recognition.[9]

Popes and Their Terms during and after
Sor María's Lifetime

Clement VIII	(1592–1605)
Leo XI	(1605)
Paul V	(1605–21)
Gregory XV	(1621–23)
Urban VIII	(1623–44)
Innocent X	(1644–55)
Alexander VII	(1655–67)
Clement IX	(1667–69)
Clement X	(1670–76)
Blessed Innocent XI	(1676–89)
Alexander VIII	(1689–91)
Innocent XII	(1691–1700)
Clement XI	(1700–21)
Innocent XIII	(1721–24)
Benedict XIII	(1724–30)
Clement XII	(1730–40)
Benedict XIV	(1740–58)
Clement XIII	(1758–69)
Clement XIV	(1769–74)
Pius VI	(1775–99)
Pius VII	(1800–23)
Leo XII	(1823–29)
Pius VIII	(1829–30)
Gregory XVI	(1831–46)

Blessed Pius IX	(1846–78)
Leo XIII	(1878–1903)
St. Pius X	(1903–14)
Benedict XV	(1914–22)
Pius XI	(1922–39)
Pius XII	(1939–58)
Blessed John XXIII	(1958–63)
Paul VI	(1963–78)
John Paul I	(1978)
John Paul II	(1978–2005)
Benedict XVI	(2005–)

Fourteen Inspections of Sor María's Incorrupt Corpse (1667–1989)

SOR MARÍA'S COFFIN OPENED FOR FIRST TIME   SEPTEMBER 10, 1667

Nuns discover excess moisture in the crypt area beneath the Convent of the Conception, as well as damage to the exterior of Sor María's coffin. Yet upon opening it, they find her body fully supple and intact and move it to a safer area in the crypt.[1]

SPANISH KING INSPECTS BODY   JUNE 5, 1677

King Carlos II inspects Sor María's corpse in Ágreda, reporting her face as pleasant and agreeable, and that a beautiful odor emanated from her body. Other witnesses present include his brother Serenísimo, his uncle Don Juan José of Austria, and others.[2]

SPANISH QUEEN VIEWS REMAINS   JUNE 27, 1702

Wife of Spain's King Felipe V, Doña María Luisa Gabriela de Saboya, views Sor María's incorrupt remains in Ágreda with huge entourage. Furtive poaching in the crypt results in the extraction of both feet and a shinbone. The perpetrators are not discovered until 1737.[3]

RELICS OF SOR MARÍA FOUND IN MADRID   APRIL 10, 1737

The feet and shinbone of Sor María's corpse are discovered among the queen's possessions in Madrid.[4] Church officials issue a "most elevated citation" to acknowledge the incorrupt condition of the corpse.[5]

CORPSE CERTIFIED AS INCORRUPT   OCTOBER 10, 1757

Sor María's corpse is unanimously certified as intact, pleasant smelling, and incorrupt by an apostolic judicial inspection, headed by Bishop Don Esteban Vilanova of Tarazona, along with three doctors and three surgeons.[6]

RELICS DISBURSED   OCTOBER 10, 1757

Prior to or on the same occasion, other "modest disbursements" are made
from Sor María's corpse: a shinbone to the Duke of Alburquerque, a toe
bone to the Discalced Carmelites of San José in Zaragoza, a toe to José
Tudela of Tudela, and five small bones to the Convento de Concepcionistas
de Estella in Navarra.[7]

CRYPT SACKED DURING FRENCH INVASION   NOVEMBER 24, 1808

Ágreda and surrounding area is sacked when twenty-five thousand soldiers
under Napoléon's General Ney invade Spain. Nuns flee to caves in Mount
Moncayo. Soldiers crush the locks and search Sor María's crypt for jewels.
Nuns verify on their return that there was no damage to her body.[8]

CRYPT REINFORCED AFTER INVASION   JANUARY 10, 1809

Sor María's crypt and body are reinspected after the departure of the
French. Because of the forced opening, a tapeworm had invaded the coffin
lid and made a ten-centimeter hole in the wood. This is repaired, and three
locks are installed.[9]

CORPSE AGAIN DOCUMENTED AS INTACT   OCTOBER 6, 1813

Vice general of Ágreda, Don Raimundo Oria, who had distinguished
himself in battle against the French, with bishop of Tarazona's permission
inspects Sor María's body to check on problems noted in 1809. He places
documentation in crypt verifying intact condition and relocks.[10]

BISHOPS AND ECCLESIASTICS CERTIFY CORPSE   MAY 14, 1849

Sor María's body is again inspected to the satisfaction of bishop of
Tarazona Don Vicente Ortiz y Labastida and various ecclesiastics on
pastoral visit to convent. Corpse and documents are all certified as stable
and intact.[11]

CORPSE INSPECTED   JULY 10, 1886

Bishop of Cartagena, Don Tomas Bryam, visits convent and inspects Sor
María's incorrupt body with Don Francisco Silvela, Silvela's wife, and the
Marquesa de la Casa de Loring, Doña Amalia Heredia.[12]

FRENCH DIGNITARY VISITS TOMB   JULY 11, 1908

French royalty Doña Isabel de Bourbon and her distinguished retinue visit
Sor María's sepulcher and pray before her intact remains.[13]

BODY MOVED TO MUSEUM   SEPTEMBER 13, 1909

Bishop of Tarazona, Ozcoidi y Udave, visits Sor María's body and moves
coffin to convent museum in second-story room over church. A reclining

statue of her body is installed in the church. A complete anatomical examination of the body, and a review of the enclosed documents, again verifies that all is intact.[14]

COFFIN OPENED AFTER 312 YEARS   1977

Bishop of Tarazona diocese places a pillow under the head of Sor María's corpse. Again it is found intact and sweet smelling.[15]

COFFIN MOVED AFTER FOURTEENTH INSPECTION   MAY 20, 1989

Doctors and technicians conduct the fourteenth inspection of Sor María's body, and again it is found incorrupt. They move her corpse to a platform in the church, under the reclining statue.[16]

CHAPTER 1

1. Alonso de Benavides, "Tanto que se sacó de una carta," as translated by Carlos E. Castañeda and quoted in *Our Catholic Heritage in Texas, 1519–1936*, vol. 1, *The Mission Era: The Finding of Texas, 1519–1693* (Austin, TX: Von Boeckmann-Jones, 1936), 197. María of Ágreda's "Letter to the Missionaries," May 15, 1631, as cited by Francisco Palou in *Life and Apostolic Labors of the Venerable Father Junípero Serra*, trans. C. Scott Williams (Pasadena, CA: George Wharton James, 1913), 332. María of Ágreda's "Report to Father Manero," 1650, translated by Clark A. Colahan, *The Visions of Sor María de Agreda: Writing Knowledge and Power* (Tucson: University of Arizona Press, 1994), 123.

2. Felipe IV's letter to Sor María, October 4, 1643, in Martin Hume, *The Court of Philip IV, Spain in Decadence* (New York and London: G. P. Putnam's Sons and Eveleigh Nash, 1907), 382.

3. María of Ágreda and Felipe IV, *María de Jesús de Ágreda: Correspondencia con Felipe IV, religión y razón de estado*, intro. and notes by Consolación Baranda (Madrid: Editorial Castalia, 1991), e.g., 55, 63, 88, 103, 216; hereinafter cited simply as *Correspondencia* unless crediting editorial notes, in which case Baranda's name will appear. All translations from this and other works are mine unless otherwise noted.

4. Hume, *The Court of Philip IV*, 417.

5. José Ximénez Samaniego, *Life of Venerable Mary of Jesus de Ágreda: Poor Clare Nun*, trans. Ubaldus [Pandolfi] da Rieti (Evansville, IN: Keller-Crescent Printing and Engraving, 1910), 49, 87–88.

6. Ibid., 111, 77.

7. Mention of mystical phenomena will, of course, permeate this treatment of María of Ágreda's life, as she was after all a mystic.

In striving to understand the possibility of such unusual experiences, I encountered a variety of accounts, ranging from that of Sor María's own countrywoman, Saint Teresa of Avila (1515–82), to contemporary commentators on spiritual and paranormal phenomena. Teresa described her own experience of levitation in her autobiography (*The Life of St. Teresa of Jesus of the Order of Our Lady of Carmel, Written by Herself*, trans. David Lewis [London: Thomas Baker, 1904], 155). "A rapture is absolutely irresistible . . . you see and feel yourself carried away, you know not whither . . . my soul was carried away . . . and then the whole body as well, so that it was lifted up from the ground," she wrote, foreshadowing Sor María's comments in *Mystical City of God*, where she writes about the powerful effects of her prayerful moments: "Even the body becomes spiritualized during such times, free[d] from its weight" (María de Ágreda, *Mystical City of God*, vol. 1, books 1–2, *The Conception*, trans. George J. Blatter [Chicago: Theopolitan Company of Chicago, 1914; Albuquerque, NM: Corcoran, 1949], 38, hereinafter cited as *MCOG-GJB*, to indicate Blatter's translation, alongside the volume name and page). Additionally, regarding the phenomena of bilocation, or appearing in two separate geographic locations at the same time, there are a number of recorded incidents. See C. Bernard Ruffin, *Padre Pio, the True Story* (Huntington, IN: Our Sunday Visitor, 1991), 329–30.

8. María de Jesús de Ágreda, *Mística Ciudad de Dios: Vida de María,* ed. Angel Martínez Moñux, Celestino Solaguren, and Luis Villasante (Madrid: Fareso, 1970), 3:167, 172.

9. William S. Fulco (Ancient Mediterranean Studies faculty, Loyola Marymount University, Los Angeles; translator of Latin and Aramaic portions of Mel Gibson's film *The Passion of the Christ*). In e-mail interviews with author, January 2004, Fulco said Gibson relied primarily on the biblical accounts of Christ's death when writing the actual script, but he did read Ágreda's work and many others during his early research.

10. Evaluation of the "heroic exercise of virtue" is the initial stage in the Catholic Church's designation process for sainthood. The resultant honorific, that is, being named a "venerable" of the church, clears the path for proponents of the candidate's cause to pursue his or her beatification and ultimate canonization. The comment about *Mystical City of God* was made in 1668 by Andrew Mendo of the University of Salamanca (Salamanca, Spain), as quoted in Ximénez Samaniego, *Life of Venerable Mary of Jesus,* 144–45.

11. In "The Blessed Virgin Mary," *The Catholic Encyclopedia* cites references for Mary's role as Divine Mother dating back to the first century (New Advent, 2007, www.newadvent.org/cathen/15464b.htm [accessed December 1, 2007]).

1. María de Jesús de Ágreda, *Autenticidad de la* Mística Ciudad de Dios *y biografía de su autora* (Barcelona: Heredos de Juan Gili, Editores, 1914; Madrid: Heredos de Juan Gili, Editores, 1985), 41–42, 44; a volume supplementing the text of *Mística Ciudad de Dios* with autobiographical and biographical selections of its author, and hereinafter referred to as *MCDD y biografía de su autora*.

2. Teresa of Avila, *The Life of St. Teresa*, 156.

3. Author's e-mail correspondence with Concepcionista Ágredista archivist, regarding María of Ágreda's library and breviary, June 21, 2008.

4. Ágreda, *MCDD y biografía de su autora*, 81.

5. Author's site inspection, Ágreda, Spain, October 1998; regarding change of street name: Manuel Peña García, *Sor María de Jesús de Ágreda* (Ágreda: El Burgo de Osma, 1997), 43, 73.

6. Ximénez Samaniego, *Life of Venerable Mary of Jesus*, 6–7. Ximénez Samaniego—a longtime family friend and one who evinced a common propensity of the times to overendow events even hinting of the miraculous—could hardly be deemed an impartial judge of character. He nevertheless serves as a valuable source of many details of Sor María's life by simple fact of his having been there, as Thomas Downing Kendrick (*Mary of Ágreda: The Life and Legend of a Spanish Nun* [London: Routledge & Kegan Paul, 1967], 23) and Colahan (*Visions of Sor María de Agreda*, 31, 43) acknowledge. He also would have felt a great responsibility to document aspects of her life that would enhance her cause for sainthood (Augustine Esposito, La Mistica Cuidad de Dios *[1670] Sor María de Jesús de Ágreda* [Potomac, MD: Scripta Humanistica, 1990], 6). With this in mind, I have worked to limit his firsthand testimony to those instances when it provides a salient fact, flavor, or quote.

7. Peña García, *Sor María de Jesús de Ágreda*, 44, 46.

8. Ágreda, *MCDD y biografía de su autora*, 37.

9. Peña García, *Sor María de Jesús de Ágreda*, 46.

10. Ágreda, *MCDD y biografía de su autora*, 38; Peña García, *Sor María de Jesús de Ágreda*, 291.

11. Peña García, *Sor María de Jesús de Ágreda*, 289–90.

12. Implicit in Pérez's testimony was the common understanding at the time that the lower classes supported the Crown with taxes, the religious orders supported the Crown with prayers, and the nobility supported the Crown on the battlefield with their swords. Referencing Antonio Dominguez Ortiz, *The Golden Age of Spain, 1516–1659*, trans. James Casey (London: Weidenfeld and Nicolson, 1971), 116.

13. Peña García, *Sor María de Jesús de Ágreda*, 289–90.

14. In contrast to those who cite Senior's Christian name as "Fernando Nuñez Coronel," Carroll B. Johnson attributes that name to an in-law of Senior's, Rabí Mayor (Mair) Meldamet and clearly cites Senior as "Ferrad [*sic*] Perez Coronel." Carroll B. Johnson. "El Buscón: D. Pablos, D. Diego y D. Franciso," *Hispanofila* (May 1974): 14.

15. Ibid., 12.

16. J. H. Elliott, *Imperial Spain: 1469–1716* (New York: St. Martin's Press, 1966), 104–5; also Henry Charles Lea, *A History of the Inquisition of Spain* (New York and London: Macmillan, 1922), 2:310.

17. Daniel C. Matt, *The Essential Kabbalah, the Heart of Jewish Mysticism*, intro. Huston Smith (New York: HarperSanFrancisco, 1998), 5–6, 15.

18. Clark Colahan, "Mary of Agreda, the Virgin Mary, and Mystical Knowing," *Studia Mystica* 3, no. 3 (1988): 55; Colahan, *Visions of Sor María de Agreda*, 38, comparing the Christian Kabbalah's influence on both Teresa of Avila and María of Ágreda.

19. Catherine Swietlicki, *A Spanish Christian Cabala: The Works of Luis de León, Santa Teresa de Jesús, and San Juan de la Cruz* (Columbia: University of Missouri Press, 1986), 28, 44, 50, 69n88.

20. Ágreda, *MCDD y biografía de su autora*, 47.

21. Ibid., 41–42.

22. Ibid., 44.

23. Ibid., 44–46.

24. Ibid., 82.

25. Ibid., 82–85.

26. Ibid., 82–83, 86.

27. Ximénez Samaniego, *Life of Venerable Mary of Jesus*, 7–8.

28. Ibid., 9.

29. Ágreda, *MCDD y biografía de su autora*, 83.

30. Peña García, *Sor María de Jesús de Ágreda*, 292.

31. Kendrick, *Mary of Ágreda*, 4.

32. Margaret Thompson Schrepfer, *17th Century Games* (Haslett, MI: Penny Books, 1993), 10–12.

33. Ximénez Samaniego, *Life of Venerable Mary of Jesus*, 13.

34. Sor María references her spiritual understanding as an inner vision or perception illuminated by "infused knowledge" (Ágreda, *MCOG-GJB: Conception*, 26–27, 36), for which I have adopted the phrase "interior knowing."

35. Ágreda, *MCDD y biografía de su autora*, 99.

36. Peña García, *Sor María de Jesús de Ágreda*, 293.

37. Ibid.

38. Ibid.

39. Colahan's translation, *Visions of Sor María de Agreda*, 115.

40. Ágreda, *MCDD y biografía de su autora*, 99; Peña García, *Sor María de Jesús de Ágreda*, 67–68, 293.

41. Ximénez Samaniego, *Life of Venerable Mary of Jesus*, 17.

42. Ágreda, *MCDD y biografía de su autora*, 100.

43. Colahan's translation, *Visions of Sor María de Agreda*, 115–16.

44. Kendrick, *Mary of Ágreda*, 7.

45. Ágreda, *MCDD y biografía de su autora*, 102.

CHAPTER 3

1. Peña García, *Sor María de Jesús de Ágreda*, 45.

2. Sor María writes in her autobiography (*MCDD y biografía de su autora*, 48) that her father was sixty years old at the time the plan emerged to convert their ancestral home into a convent. As a result, this was reported in Ximénez Samaniego's biography of her, as well as Carrico's, Kendrick's, and others. She wrote the work in her own later years, however, and cited his age incorrectly. Based on baptismal records and convent archives, Francisco Coronel was baptized as an infant in 1564. Peña García (*Sor María de Jesús de Ágreda*, 44) further documents his age at thirty-eight years when Sor María was born in 1602, making him just over fifty years old in 1615. Her mother, baptized in March of 1563, was twenty months older than her father, making Catalina also in her early fifties at the time. See "Ancestors of María Coronel of Ágreda," appendix B.

3. Ágreda, *MCDD y biografía de su autora*, 47.

4. Ibid.

5. Ibid., 40. These references to good blood (*buena sangre*) might simply have reflected a partiality for nobility or a deep devotion for the Christian faith. Yet, they also likely reflected a posture of self-preservation in reaction to prejudicial social tensions still prevalent at the time in Spain as a result of Inquisition pronouncements mandating purity of blood (*limpieza de sangre*—a phrase María actually uses later in this passage—i.e., *Christian* blood, without any trace of Jewish heritage) in order to qualify for certain secular and religious posts and even university programs (see Elliott, *Imperial Spain*, 104, 217–20, 305). The irony of its use here is the strong probability of the Coronel converso heritage.

6. Ágreda, *MCDD y biografía de su autora*, 39–40.

7. Ibid., 48.

8. Ibid.

9. Ibid., 48, 49.

10. Ibid., 49, 50.

11. Concepcionista Ágredista archivist, interview by author, Ágreda, Spain, October 21, 1998.

12. Colahan, *Visions of Sor María de Agreda*, 21, 25.

13. "Tratado del grado de la luz," of which the "Mapa" is a part, is one of Sor María's apocryphal writings, that is, one that is not acknowledged as hers by the Vatican, despite scholarly opinion to the contrary. Author's e-mail correspondence with Concepcionista Ágredista archivist, January 13–14, 2006.

14. Colahan's translation, *Visions of Sor María de Agreda*, 48–49.

15. Ibid., 65.

16. Ibid., 50.

17. Peña García, *Sor María de Jesús de Ágreda*, 47–48.

18. Colahan's translation, *Visions of Sor María de Agreda*, 50, 63.

19. Ibid., 52.

20. Ibid., 69, 62, with minor sentence inversion.

21. Ibid., 69.

22. Ibid., 69–70.

23. Ortiz, *The Golden Age of Spain*, 124.

24. Kendrick, *Mary of Ágreda*, 8–9; Elliott, *Imperial Spain*, 318–19.

25. Ágreda, *MCDD y biografía de su autora*, 55.

26. Ibid., 56.

CHAPTER 4

1. Ágreda, *MCDD y biografía de su autora*, 57.

2. Author's March 7, 2005, e-mail correspondence with Concepcionista Ágredista archivist, clarifying the gift of the final one thousand ducats from the outlying towns.

3. Agustín Rubio Semper, "Agreda en el Siglo XVII," in *El papel de sor María Jesús de Ágreda en el barroco español* (Soria: Universidad Internacional Alfonso VIII, 2002), 54.

4. Concepcionista Ágredista archivist, February 19, 2005, e-mail correspondence with the author.

5. Ágreda, *MCDD y biografía de su autora*, 59.

6. Ágreda, *MCOG-GJB: Conception*, 178.

7. Thomas A. Thompson, director of the Marian Library, International Marian Research Institute, University of Dayton, Ohio. Phone interview by author, November 21, 2004.

8. Ágreda, *MCDD y biografía de su autora*, 62.

9. Ibid., 63n2.

10. Ibid., 63n1; Kendrick, *Mary of Ágreda*, 9.

11. Peña García, *Sor María de Jesús de Ágreda*, 294.

12. Named Monasterio Purísima Concepción in contemporary diocesan structure, the convent is most properly called Monasterio de la Concepcionistas Franciscanas. Informally, it is also referred to as Convento de la Concepción and the nuns as Concepcionistas Ágredistas.

13. Peña García, *Sor María de Jesús de Ágreda*, 78, 79.

14. Ibid., 87.

15. Kendrick, *Mary of Ágreda*, 12; Ximénez Samaniego, *Life of Venerable Mary of Jesus*, 66.

16. Ágreda, *MCDD y biografía de su autora*, 116–18.

17. Ximénez Samaniego, *Life of Venerable Mary of Jesus*, 49; Kendrick, *Mary of Ágreda*, 15.

18. Ximénez Samaniego, *Life of Venerable Mary of Jesus*, 87–88.

19. Kendrick, *Mary of Ágreda*, 16.

20. Ximénez Samaniego, *Life of Venerable Mary of Jesus*, 88.

21. Ágreda, *MCDD y biografía de su autora*, 120.

22. Kendrick, *Mary of Ágreda*, 12–13, 58.

23. Ibid., 16.

24. Ximénez Samaniego, *Life of Venerable Mary of Jesus*, 51–52.

25. Kendrick, *Mary of Ágreda*, 18; Peña García, *Sor María de Jesús de Ágreda*, 297.

26. Kendrick, *Mary of Ágreda*, 17–18.

27. Ximénez Samaniego, *Life of Venerable Mary of Jesus*, 67, 71.

28. Kendrick's translation, *Mary of Ágreda*, 18.

29. Ibid., 20.

30. Ximénez Samaniego, *Life of Venerable Mary of Jesus*, 49, 53–54.

31. Kendrick's translation, *Mary of Ágreda*, 19.

32. Peña García, *Sor María de Jesús de Ágreda*, 298.

33. Ibid.; Kendrick, *Mary of Ágreda*, 56; author's March 7, 2005, e-mail correspondence with Concepcionista Ágredista archivist, who confirmed that Sor María's election was "at the request of her peers, the nuns" and presented notes extracted from a convent history documenting all appointments of abbesses since the date of its foundation.

34. Ágreda, *MCOG-GJB: Conception*, 5–6.

35. Ibid., 39.

36. Ibid., 7.

37. Ibid., 6–7.

38. Ibid., 7.

39. Ibid., 8.

40. Kendrick, *Mary of Ágreda*, 20.

CHAPTER 5

1. Ágreda, *MCOG-GJB: Conception*, 175–76.
2. Colahan's translation, *Visions of Sor María de Agreda*, 119.
3. While several authorities attribute the Jumanos' motivation to a legitimate desire for the protection from Apaches that might result if a mission route patrolled by soldiers connected the Santa Fe area with missions in their own encampments, Hickerson offers the most detailed rationale of how they might have manipulated events to this end without ever having seen the Lady in Blue. Citing documentation that the Jumanos arrived in Isleta days prior to the arrival of Perea's caravan and had time to assess the missionaries' interest in potentially miraculous apparitions, she speculates that they would have had ample time to invent a compatible account that would help them to obtain a mission. See Nancy P. Hickerson, *The Jumanos: Hunters and Traders of the South Plain* (Austin: University of Texas Press, 1994), 94–96. While this is a viable premise, it also need not dispute Sor María's testimony.
4. Ibid., A34, 420.
5. Ibid., 420.
6. Hickerson, *The Jumanos*, map 6 (Jumano locations, 1535–1700), 65.
7. Frederick Hodge, ed., *Handbook of American Indians North of Mexico*, part 1 (New York: Pageant Books, 1959), 636.
8. Hickerson, *The Jumanos*, xvii–xviii.
9. Per author's phone interview with Jumano-Apache tribal historian Enrique Madrid (Redford, Texas) on July 4, 2008, there are several hundred—and the number is growing—official tribal registrants on file at the US Bureau of Indian Affairs, many with mitochondrial DNA records.
10. Frederick Hodge, *The Jumano Indians* (Worcester, MA: Davis Press, 1910), 4; Castañeda, *Our Catholic Heritage in Texas*, 200.
11. Hodge, *The Jumano Indians*, 6.
12. Ibid., 7; Hickerson, *The Jumanos*, 68.
13. Hickerson, *The Jumanos*, xxiii–xxiv, 203; Handbook of Texas Online, s.v. "Jumano Indians," www.tshaonline.org/handbook/online/articles/JJ/bmj7.html (accessed May 18, 2000).
14. Castañeda, *Our Catholic Heritage in Texas*, 105–6; Hickerson, *The Jumanos*, 25.
15. The distance of one league is an archaic unit measured at about three of today's miles. Four hundred leagues, as cited later in Padre Marcilla's letter to the archbishop of Mexico, would describe a distance of about twelve hundred miles.

16. Gus Clemens, *Legacy: The Story of the Permian Basin Region of West Texas and Southeast New Mexico* (San Antonio, TX: Mulberry Avenue Books, 1983), 17.

17. Gus Clemens, *The Concho Country* (San Antonio, TX: Mulberry Avenue Books, 1980), 27.

18. Hickerson, *The Jumanos*, 216.

19. Alonso de Benavides, *A Harvest of Reluctant Souls: The Memorial of Fray Alonso de Benavides, 1630*, ed. and trans. Baker H. Morrow (Niwot: University Press of Colorado, 1996), 79.

20. Hubert Bancroft, *History of the Pacific States of North America: Arizona and New Mexico, 1530–1888* (San Francisco: History Company Publishers, 1888), 12:159.

21. Kendrick, *Mary of Ágreda*, 34.

CHAPTER 6

1. Kendrick, *Mary of Ágreda*, 34.

2. Ibid., 31, 34.

3. José Antonio Pichardo, "The Miraculous Journeys of Mother María de Jesús de Ágreda to La Quivira," in *Pichardo's Treatise on the Limits of Louisiana and Texas*, trans. Charles W. Hackett (Austin: University of Texas Press, 1931–46), 2:469.

4. Hickerson, *The Jumanos*, 21–22, 24, 101. Quivira is first mentioned in Coronado's exploration accounts as being in the vicinity Manso now considered. It is distinct, however, from the pueblo currently named "Gran Quivira," which is located in the Salinas pueblo complex south of Albuquerque and which was originally called "Las Humanas" until the eighteenth century.

5. While later analyses show Sor María's geographic knowledge to be vague, and the kingdoms of the Chillescas and Carbucos were never found, the directions in Marcilla's letter to Manso seem to point to the Jumanos in the area of the Palo Duro Canyon trading center (Hickerson, *The Jumanos*, 25) identified by Castañeda as Quivira (*Our Catholic Heritage in Texas*, 105–6, 201). This is near present-day Amarillo (Texas), which is about 1,213 miles from Mexico City, or approximately 400 leagues.

6. Edgar L. Hewett and Reginald G. Fisher, *Mission Monuments of New Mexico* (Albuquerque: University of New Mexico Press, 1943), 84, 86, 245.

7. Castañeda, *Our Catholic Heritage in Texas*, 197.

8. Alonso de Benavides, *Fray Alonso de Benavides' Revised Memorial of 1634*, ed. and trans. Frederick Webb Hodge (Albuquerque: University of New Mexico Press, 1945), 94; and 30–33 for lineage of this memorial.

9. Hickerson, *The Jumanos*, 94; Hewett and Fisher, *Mission Monuments of New Mexico*, 84, 86, 245.

10. Benavides, *A Harvest of Reluctant Souls*, xxiv.

11. David Weber, *The Spanish Frontier in North America* (New Haven, CT: Yale University Press, 1992), 92.

12. Hodge, *The Jumano Indians*, 9.

13. Benavides, *A Harvest of Reluctant Souls*, Morrow's translation, 79.

14. Ibid., *Fray Alonso de Benavides' Revised Memorial of 1634*, ed. Hodge, 315n135, citing Agustín Vetancurt, *Teatro Mexicano: Croníca de la Provincia del Santo Evangelio de Mexico* (Mexico: María de Benavides, 1697), 311.

15. Benavides, *Fray Alonso de Benavides' Revised Memorial of 1634*, Hodge's translation, 94.

16. Hickerson, *The Jumanos*, 95.

17. Benavides, *Fray Alonso de Benavides' Revised Memorial of 1634*, Hodge's translation, 94.

18. Ibid., *A Harvest of Reluctant Souls*, Morrow's translation, 80; Ibid., *Fray Alonso de Benavides' Revised Memorial of 1634*, Hodge's translation, 94; Ibid., *A Harvest of Reluctant Souls*, Morrow's translation, 80.

19. Ibid., *Fray Alonso de Benavides' Revised Memorial of 1634*, Hodge's translation, 94.

20. Ibid.

21. Hodge, *The Jumano Indians*, 10.

22. Hickerson, *The Jumanos*, 106.

23. Ibid., 108–9.

24. Marion Habig, interview by Jane Wilmer for the Institute of Texan Cultures, University of Texas–San Antonio, Salado, Texas, June 21, 1982.

25. Benavides, "Tanto que se sacó," in Hodge's translation of Benavides, *Fray Alonso de Benavides' Revised Memorial of 1634*, 136.

26. Bancroft, *History of the Pacific States of North America*, 162.

27. Ibid., 163.

28. Benavides, *A Harvest of Reluctant Souls*, ed. Morrow, xi; Bancroft, *History of the Pacific States of North America*, 102.

29. Hickerson, *The Jumanos*, 91.

30. Benavides, *A Harvest of Reluctant Souls*, Morrow's translation, 79.

31. Hodge, *The Jumano Indians*, 9.

32. Benavides, *A Harvest of Reluctant Souls*, Morrow's translation, 80–81.

33. Ibid., 80–83.

34. Clemens, *The Concho Country*, 22.

35. Benavides, *A Harvest of Reluctant Souls*, Morrow's translation, 83.

36. Ibid.

37. Habig interview by Jane Wilmer, June 21, 1982.

38. Ibid.

39. Mark Carrico's unpublished master's thesis and accompanying map regarding the Moqui ("On the Path of Blue Flowers," University of New Mexico, 1975); Donald C. Cutter's article "With a Little Help from Their Saints," *Pacific Historical Review* 53, no. 2 (May 1984): 123–40, regarding the Hopi.

40. Colahan, *Visions of Sor María de Agreda,* 104.

41. Kendrick, *Mary of Ágreda,* 34

42. Ágreda, *Mística Ciudad de Dios: Vida de María,* 1:362.

43. For more on mystical experiences and neuroscience, please see the afterword.

44. Ágreda, *MCDD y biografía de su autora,* 119–20.

CHAPTER 7

1. Weber, *The Spanish Frontier in North America,* 95.

2. Ibid., 23, 81, 88, 94.

3. Ibid., 84–86, 87, 88, 95.

4. Benavides, "Tanto que se sacó de una carta," trans. Castañeda, *Our Catholic Heritage in Texas,* 197; also see 197n6, wherein Castañeda clarifies *pardo* as brown, in contrast to other versions that incorrectly term the Franciscan robe as gray although that is technically a legitimate translation option.

5. Colahan's translation, Manero report, *Visions of Sor María de Agreda,* 121.

6. Ibid., 120. For more on the legitimizing effect of Sor María's bilocations on colonization efforts, see Katie MacLean, "María de Agreda, Spanish Mysticism and the Work of Spiritual Conquest," *Colonial Latin American Review* (June 2008): 41–43.

7. María of Ágreda's letter to the missionaries: Palou, *Life and Apostolic Labors,* trans. Williams, 332.

8. Colahan's translation, Manero report, *Visions of Sor María de Agreda,* 123.

9. Ibid., 122, 124.

10. Ibid., 123.

11. Benavides's letter to the missionaries: Palou, *Life and Apostolic Labors,* trans. Williams, 329.

12. María of Ágreda's letter to the missionaries: Palou, *Life and Apostolic Labors,* trans. Williams, 332.

13. Ibid.

14. Ibid., 331.

15. Colahan's translation, Manero report, *Visions of Sor María de Agreda*, 121.
16. Ibid.
17. María of Ágreda's letter to the missionaries: Palou, *Life and Apostolic Labors*, trans. Williams, 331.
18. Benavides's letter to the missionaries: Palou, *Life and Apostolic Labors*, trans. Williams, 329.
19. Ximénez Samaniego, *Life of Venerable Mary of Jesus*, 85.

CHAPTER 8

1. Ximénez Samaniego, *Life of Venerable Mary of Jesus*, 68–73.
2. Peña García, *Sor María de Jesús de Ágreda*, 295, 300; Kendrick, *Mary of Ágreda*, 161–62.
3. Ximénez Samaniego, *Life of Venerable Mary of Jesus*, 59–61.
4. Ibid.; author's February 19, 2005, correspondence with Concepcionista Ágredista archivist.
5. Ágreda, *MCOG-GJB: Conception*, 8.
6. Ximénez Samaniego, *Life of Venerable Mary of Jesus*, 55.
7. Peña García, *Sor María de Jesús de Ágreda*, 156; "her initiative" per author's correspondence with Concepcionista Ágredista archivist, March 7, 2005.
8. Pedro Luis Echeverría Goñi, "La Madre Ágreda y la construcción de su convento," in *Monografías universitarias* (Soria, Spain: Universidad Internacional Alfonso VIII, 2002), 84; author's March 7, 2005, correspondence with Concepcionista Ágredista archivist.
9. Peña García, *Sor María de Jesús de Ágreda*, 298.
10. Ágreda, *MCDD y biografía de su autora*, 165.
11. Echeverría Goñi, "La Madre Ágreda," 85.
12. Ágreda, *MCDD y biografía de su autora*, 165, quoting Padre Fuenmayor.
13. Echeverría Goñi, "La Madre Ágreda," 75, 85, 89n60.
14. Sor María Josefa de San Juan Evangelista Camargo, *Testificación sobre la vida, virtudes y milagros de la V. Sor María de Jesús, para los Procesos*, as quoted by Peña García, *Sor María de Jesús de Ágreda*, 156.
15. Echeverría Goñi, "La Madre Ágreda," 98; Peña García, *Sor María de Jesús de Ágreda*, 156–157.
16. Echeverría Goñi, "La Madre Ágreda," 80. Note: following Vatican II, the curtain might be opened during Mass, but the iron grille remained.
17. Antonio Artola Arbiza and Benito Mendía, *La venerable M. María de Jesús de Ágreda y la Inmaculada Concepción: El proceso eclesiástico a la Mística Ciudad de Dios* (Soria, Spain: La Heras, 2004), 20.
18. Echeverría Goñi, "La Madre Ágreda," 82.
19. Ibid., 86–87.

20. Ibid., 86n49.
21. Peña García, *Sor María de Jesús de Ágreda*, 157.
22. Echeverría Goñi, "La Madre Ágreda," 86.
23. Ibid., 87n50–51.
24. Peña García, *Sor María de Jesús de Ágreda*, 158.
25. Echeverría Goñi, "La Madre Ágreda," 88.
26. Ibid.
27. Ximénez Samaniego, *Life of Venerable Mary of Jesus*, 111.
28. Echeverría Goñi, "La Madre Ágreda," 95–96.
29. Ibid., 94n73, quoting José Ximénez Samaniego, *Prólogo galeato: Relación de la vida de la venerable Madre Sor María de Jesús* (Madrid: En la Imprenta de la Causa de la V. Madre, 1765), 110.
30. Echeverría Goñi, "La Madre Ágreda," 97.
31. Ágreda, *MCDD y biografía de su autora*, 151–53.
32. Ibid., 153, per parish records dated November 28, 1626.
33. Echeverría Goñi, "La Madre Ágreda," 85, 97, 88; author's correspondence with Concepcionista Ágredista archivist, March 7, 2005.
34. Echeverría Goñi, "La Madre Ágreda," 97.
35. Peña García, *Sor María de Jesús de Ágreda*, 300; Echeverría Goñi, "La Madre Ágreda," 98.

CHAPTER 9

1. Ágreda, *MCOG-GJB: Conception*, 12.
2. Clark Colahan, "María de Jesús de Ágreda, The Sweetheart of the Holy Office," in *Women in the Inquisition*, ed. Mary E. Giles (Baltimore, MD: Johns Hopkins University Press, 1999), 159.
3. Ibid., 160.
4. Ágreda, *MCOG-GJB: Conception*, 6.
5. Kendrick, *Mary of Ágreda*, 21.
6. Ricardo Fernández Gracia, *Arte, devoción y política, La promoción de las artes en torno a sor María de Ágreda* (Soria, Spain: Diputación Provincial de Soria, 2002), 21.
7. Ágreda, *MCOG-GJB: Conception*, 12.
8. Ibid., 10, 11.
9. Ibid., 13–14.
10. Peña García, *Sor María de Jesús de Ágreda*, 301.
11. Ágreda, *MCOG-GJB: Conception*, xv.
12. Ibid., 12–13, 43.
13. Ibid., 23.
14. Ibid., 35.
15. Ibid.

16. Ibid., 36.

17. Ibid.

18. In his article "Visions and Apparitions" in volume 15 of *The Catholic Encyclopedia* (New York: Robert Appleton, 1912), Lucian Roure outlines traditional Catholic teaching on visions as initially defined by Saint Augustine in the fourth century and later expanded by eighteenth-century pope Benedict XIV and others. Sor María defines her visions within this framework.

19. Ágreda, *MCOG-GJB: Conception*, 43–44.

20. Ágreda, *MCDD y biografía de su autora*, A56, 423, 424.

21. Ágreda, *MCOG-GJB: Conception*, 25; for more by Sor María on angels, see Clark Colahan and Celia Weller's translation of Sor María's tract on angels, "An Angelic Epilogue," *Studia Mystica* 13, no. 4 (1990): 50–59.

22. Ágreda, *MCOG-GJB: Conception*, 42, 44.

23. Ibid., 39.

24. Ibid., 44.

25. Ibid., 34. For an additional note on the element of certainty, see afterword.

26. Ibid., 25.

27. Ibid., *Coronation*, 665.

28. Ibid., *Conception*, 34.

29. Ibid., title page.

CHAPTER 10

1. Ágreda, *MCOG-GJB: Conception*, 27.

2. Ibid.

3. This shared symbolism of Mary as the "New Jerusalem" (Ágreda, *Mystical City of God: Conception*, 197, 201–2) was memorialized by multiple engravings in early editions of the work, most notably by Pedro Villafranca (1668) for the frontispiece of the first Spanish edition, featuring Duns Scotus across from Sor María (see figure 21). Later, in the painting entitled *St. John the Evangelist and Mother María de Jesús de Agreda*, Cristobal de Villalpando (1649–1714) portrays Sor María and Saint John together contemplating a vision combining Mary and the city of Jerusalem (oil on canvas, 74"h x 50"w, on display at the Regional Museum of Guadalupe in Zacatecas, Mexico).

4. Ágreda, *MCOG-GJB: Conception*, 202.

5. Ibid., 199.

6. Thomas A. Thompson, phone interview by author, November 20, 2004.

7. Ágreda, *MCOG-GJB: Conception*, 203.

8. Ibid., 173–74.

9. Ibid., 174.

10. Ibid.
11. Ibid.
12. Ibid., 176.
13. Ibid., 174.
14. Ibid., 175.
15. Ibid., 174, 175.
16. Ibid.
17. Ibid., 179–80.
18. Ibid., 180–81.
19. Ibid., 181–82.
20. Ibid., 184, 185, 187, 220.
21. Ibid., *Transfixion*, 71, 472, 70.
22. Ibid., 488.
23. Ibid., *Coronation*, 307.
24. Richard P. McBrien, "Mary and the Church," in *Catholicism*, vol. 2, XXIV (Minneapolis, MN: Winston Press, 1980), 881.
25. Ágreda, *MCOG-GJB: Transfixion*, 69, 70.
26. Ibid., *Conception*, 221.
27. Ibid., *Coronation*, 306.

CHAPTER 11

1. Ágreda, *MCOG-GJB: Transfixion*, 126. Ibid., *Conception*, 534; Ibid., *Coronation*, 386. Ibid., *Transfixion*, 142, 699. Ibid., 707. Ibid. Ibid., *Conception*, 34. Ibid., 17; Ibid., *Incarnation*, 29; Ibid., *Coronation*, 408. Ibid., *Coronation*, 103. Ibid., *Incarnation*, 199. Ibid., 122. Ibid., 80.
2. Ibid., *Transfixion*, 177, 126; Ibid., *Incarnation*, 187; Ibid., *Coronation*, 415.
3. Ibid., *Coronation*, 387; Ibid., *Transfixion*, 784.
4. Ibid., *Incarnation*, 177, 158; Ibid., *Coronation*, 416, 427, 519; Ibid., *Incarnation*, 158, 328.
5. Ibid., *Incarnation*, 143; Ibid., *Coronation*, 441.
6. Ibid., *Incarnation*, 391–92.
7. "Por qué Sor María es 'santa,'" published by Concepcionistas de Ágreda in *La venerable madre María de Jesús de Ágreda: Publicación para promover su beatificación* (Ágreda: Purísima Concepción, 2004), 6.
8. Ibid.
9. Ágreda, *MCOG-GJB: Incarnation*, 359, 361.
10. Ibid., *Conception*, 193.
11. Ibid., *Incarnation*, 135–36.
12. Ibid., *Conception*, 492.
13. Ibid., 483–86.

14. Ibid., *Incarnation*, 136.
15. Ibid., 7–8; Ibid., *Transfixion*, 537.
16. Ibid., *Transfixion*, 450.
17. Ibid., *Conception*, 586.
18. Teresa of Avila, *The Life of St. Teresa*, 242.
19. Evelyn Underhill, *Mystics of the Church* (Ridgefield, CT: Morehouse, 1925), 184–85, quoting from John of the Cross's "Spiritual Canticle."
20. Ágreda, *MCOG-GJB: Coronation*, 303.
21. Ibid., *Transfixion*, 225; Ibid., *Conception*, 253. Ibid., *Incarnation*, 27.
22. Ibid., *Conception*, 499, 544; Ibid., *Incarnation*, 557, and others.
23. Saint Francis de Sales, *Treatise on the Love of God*, trans. John K. Ryan, 6:1 (Rockford, IL: Tan Books, 1975), 1:270–71; sermon by Pope John Paul II, June 28, 1984, preached at Gemelli Polyclinic and Faculty of Medicine, Rome, as published in *L'Ossevatore Romano* 843:9, English weekly edition.
24. Ágreda, *MCOG-GJB: Conception*, 544.
25. Ángel Martínez Moñux, *María*, Mística Ciudad de Dios: *Una mariología interactive* (Burgos, Spain: Monte Carmelo, 2001), 25; Concepcionistas de Ágreda, *Publicación para promover su beatificación* (Ágreda: Purísima Concepción, 2003), 1.
26. Lea, *A History of the Inquisition of Spain*, 2:133–34.
27. Hume, *The Court of Philip IV*, 347–49.

CHAPTER 12

1. Ágreda, *MCOG-GJB: Conception*, 245–46.
2. Elliott, *Imperial Spain*, 330.
3. Hume, *The Court of Philip IV*, 338, 340.
4. Ágreda, *MCOG-GJB: Conception*, 245.
5. Ibid., 246.
6. Ibid., *Coronation*, 332.
7. Elliott, *Imperial Spain*, 319.
8. Hume, *The Court of Philip IV*, 363–68.
9. Ibid., 365.
10. Ibid., 367.
11. Ibid., 368.
12. Ibid., 54, 370.
13. Elliott, *Imperial Spain*, 346.
14. Lea, *A History of the Inquisition of Spain*, 2:137–38.
15. Elliott, *Imperial Spain*, 346.
16. Ibid.; *Correspondencia* (Baranda), 52n6.

1. Elliott, *Imperial Spain*, 346; Hume, *The Court of Philip IV*, 397.
2. Lea, *A History of the Inquisition of Spain*, 4:39.
3. Jacques Damase, *Carriages*, trans. William Mitchell (New York: G. P. Putnam's Sons, 1968), 21, 27, 101.
4. Hume, *The Court of Philip IV*, 379.
5. Ibid.
6. Comunidad de Castilla y León, *Ágreda y su tierra: Fiestas en honor de Ntra. Sra. de los Milagros, 1947–1997. Cincuenta Aniversario de su Coronacion* (Ágreda: Comisión de Cultura y Festivos, 1997), 7.
7. Ibid., 30–34.
8. Ágreda, *MCOG-GJB: Incarnation*, 291.
9. María de Jesús de Ágreda, Philip IV, and Francisco Silvela, *Cartas de la venerable Madre Sor María de Ágreda y del Señor Rey Don Felipe IV: Precididas de un bosquejo histórico por D. Francisco Silvela* (Madrid: Purísima Concepción de Ágreda, 1885–86), 1:1. Hereinafter cited as *Cartas 1* and *Cartas 2*.
10. *Cartas 1*, 411–12, from an early letter that predates the formal collection of correspondence.
11. Ibid., 412.
12. Kendrick, *Mary of Ágreda*, 97.
13. *Cartas 1*, 412.
14. Ibid., 412–13.
15. Ibid., 414.
16. Ibid., 413.
17. *Correspondencia* (Baranda), 53n9.
18. *Cartas 1*, 413.
19. Ágreda, *MCOG-GJB: Coronation*, 329.
20. Ibid., 326.
21. Fernández Gracia, *Arte, devoción y política*, 18.
22. Ximénez Samaniego, *Life of Venerable Mary of Jesus*, 57.
23. Colahan's translation, *Visions of Sor María de Agreda*, 126.

CHAPTER 14

1. Hume's translation, *Court of Philip IV*, 381–84. In this and other quotations from the correspondence, the citation will appear at first mention of the letter's date; additional endnotes related to a letter, if any, will indicate supplementary sources as noted.
2. *Cartas 1*, 4–7.
3. Ibid., 7–8.
4. Ibid., 8–10.

5. *Correspondencia* (Baranda), 67n31.
6. Hume's translation, *Court of Philip IV*, 389–90.
7. Ibid., 390n1.
8. Ibid.
9. *Correspondencia*, 90–95, from Sor María's notes as preserved in manuscript form at the Convent of Santo Domingo de la Calzada, Madrid.
10. Hume's translation, *Court of Philip IV*, 395.
11. Ibid., 392–94.
12. *Cartas 1*, 20–22.
13. Ibid., 22–24.
14. Ibid., 23.
15. Hume's translation, *Court of Philip IV*, 395–96.

CHAPTER 15

1. Peña García, *Sor María de Jesús de Ágreda*, 303.
2. Kendrick, *Mary of Ágreda*, 72.
3. Ágreda, *MCOG-GJB: Conception*, 12.
4. Ibid., *Incarnation*, 4.
5. Peña García, *Sor María de Jesús de Ágreda*, 303; Kendrick, *Mary of Ágreda*, 74.
6. Kendrick, *Mary of Ágreda*, 72.
7. *Cartas 1*, 90–91.
8. *Correspondencia* (Baranda), 89n52.
9. *Cartas 1*, 104–5.
10. *Correspondencia*, 89, 89n52, 91, 95, written outside the correspondence proper, per extant manuscript preserved in Santo Domingo de Calzada.
11. Kendrick, *Mary of Ágreda*, 72–73.
12. Hume, *Court of Philip IV*, 398–99.
13. Ibid., 399–400.
14. *Cartas 1*, 128–29.
15. Kendrick, *Mary of Ágreda*, 72.
16. Ibid., 73.
17. Ibid.
18. Hume's translation, *Court of Philip IV*, 400.
19. *Cartas 1*, 163.
20. Ibid., 164.
21. Ibid., 165–66.
22. Hume, *Court of Philip IV*, 207.
23. *Cartas 1*, 166–67.
24. *Correspondencia* (Baranda), 104n59.

CHAPTER 16

1. Ágreda, *MCOG-GJB: Conception*, 16.
2. Kendrick, *Mary of Ágreda*, 73–74.
3. *Correspondencia*, 109.
4. Ibid., 110.
5. Ibid., 111, 117.
6. *Cartas 1*, 183–87.
7. *Correspondencia* (Baranda), 121n80.
8. Hume, *Court of Philip IV*, 403.
9. *Cartas 1*, 187.
10. Ibid., 188–92.
11. Kendrick, *Mary of Ágreda*, 74.
12. *Correspondencia* (Baranda), 129n91.
13. Ágreda, *MCOG-GJB: Conception*, 5.
14. Kendrick, *Mary of Ágreda*, 20; Ximénez Samaniego, *Life of Venerable Mary of Jesus*, 120; Peña García, *Sor María de Jesús de Ágreda*, 298, 304.
15. Ágreda, *MCOG-GJB: Incarnation*, 6.
16. This is one of Sor María's signature maxims, quoted through today in Ágreda, and noted by Ximénez Samaniego, Peña García, and others.
17. Ágreda, *MCOG-GJB: Coronation*, 268.
18. Kendrick, on page 74 of *Mary of Ágreda*, writes that de la Torre died on March 19, 1647. However, Baranda in *Correspondencia* (129n91) puts the date at March 20, 1647. Peña García (*Sor María de Jesús de Ágreda*, 304) merely cites the year, 1647.
19. *Cartas 1*, 201–2.
20. Ibid., 203.
21. Kendrick, *Mary of Ágreda*, 75.
22. *Cartas 1*, 229.
23. Kendrick, *Mary of Ágreda*, 74.
24. *Correspondencia*, 258–59, 259n204.
25. Esposito, *La Mistica Cuidad de Dios*, 9.
26. *Cartas 1*, 308.
27. Kendrick's translation, *Mary of Ágreda*, 103.
28. *Cartas 1*, 331.
29. Ibid., 333.
30. Ibid., 349 (December 18, 1649).
31. Hume, *Court of Philip IV*, 411.
32. Kendrick, *Mary of Ágreda*, 120–22.
33. Kendrick's translation, *Mary of Ágreda*, 75.
34. Ibid., 75n1.

CHAPTER 17

1. Kendrick, *Mary of Ágreda*, 122.
2. *Cartas 1*, 346–50.
3. Ibid., 350–51.
4. Colahan, "Sweetheart of the Holy Office," 161.
5. Ibid., Colahan's translation, 161.
6. Ibid.
7. Ibid., 161–62.
8. *Cartas 1*, 403–4.
9. Kendrick, *Mary of Ágreda*, 76.
10. Ibid., Kendrick's translation, 76.
11. Hume, *Court of Philip IV*, 412.
12. *Cartas 2*, 4 (November 26, 1649).
13. Hume's translation, *Court of Philip IV*, 417.
14. Ibid.
15. Kendrick, *Mary of Ágreda*, 76.
16. Colahan, *Visions of Sor María de Agreda*, 94
17. *Cartas 2*, 3–5.
18. *Cartas 1*, 407.
19. *Cartas 2*, 5–6, with inversions.
20. Ibid., 7–9, with inversions.
21. Kendrick, *Mary of Ágreda*, 76.

CHAPTER 18

1. Felipe—in his December 29, 1648, letter to Sor María—assures her of his trust in her, his belief in her character, and his certainty that she had nothing to do with the Hijar plot. See *Cartas 1*, 350–51, and Kendrick, *Mary of Ágreda*, 123–24.
2. Ágreda, *MCDD y biografía de su autora*, 414.
3. Ibid., 417.
4. In the citations to follow, questions are labeled with Q preceding the number (e.g., "Q11"), and replies are paired with A (e.g., "A11"). Only the first instance of a specific question and answer are annotated, and all immediately ensuing quotes are inclusive to that reference, unless other citations intervene, or there are identifiable multiple parts to a question. In some instances I used Colahan's translation on the related question, as noted.
5. Ibid., Q12, 418.
6. Ibid., A12, 418.
7. Colahan, *Visions of Sor María de Agreda*, 123.
8. Ágreda, *MCDD y biografía de su autora*, Q28, 418.

9. Ibid., A28, 419.
10. Ibid., Q29, 419.
11. Ibid., A29, 419.
12. Ibid., Q32, 419.
13. Ibid., A32, 419–20.
14. Colahan, *Visions of Sor María de Agreda*, 124.
15. Ibid., Colahan's translation, 124–25.
16. Ibid., 122.
17. Ágreda, *MCDD y biografía de su autora*, Q34, 420.
18. Ibid., A34, 420.
19. Colahan's translation, *Visions of Sor María de Agreda*, 126.
20. Ágreda, *MCDD y biografía de su autora*, question between 34 and 35, 420–21.
21. Ibid., response between 34 and 35, 421.
22. Ibid., 417n1.
23. Ibid., Q35, 421 .
24. Ibid., A35, 421.
25. Ibid., Q37, 421.
26. Colahan, *Visions of Sor María de Agreda*, 111, 119.
27. Ágreda, *MCDD y biografía de su autora*, A37, 421.
28. Ibid., Q39, 422.
29. Ibid., A39, 422.
30. Ibid., Q63, 425.
31. Ibid., A63, 420.
32. Ibid.
33. Colahan, *Visions of Sor María de Agreda*, 122.

CHAPTER 19

1. Benavides, in Palou, *Life and Apostolic Labors*, trans. Williams, 330.
2. Ágreda, *MCDD y biografía de su autora*, Q62, 424.
3. Ibid., A62, 425.
4. Ibid., Q63, 425.
5. Ibid., A62, 425.
6. Ibid., A63, 425.
7. Ibid., Q42, 422.
8. Ibid., A42, 422–23.
9. Colahan's translation, *Visions of Sor María de Agreda*, 69.
10. Palou, *Life and Apostolic Labors*, trans. Williams, 332.
11. Colahan, *Visions of Sor María de Agreda*, 121.
12. Ágreda, *MCDD y biografía de su autora*, A42, 422–23.

13. Ibid., Q59, 424.

14. Colahan's translation, *Visions of Sor María de Agreda*, 119.

15. Ágreda, *MCDD y biografía de su autora*, A59, 424.

16. Ibid., Q56, 423.

17. Ibid., A56, 423.

18. Ágreda, *MCOG-GJB: Conception*, 84.

19. Ágreda, *MCDD y biografía de su autora*, Q66, 426.

20. Ibid., A66, 426.

21. Ibid., Q77-1, 427.

22. Ibid., A77-1, with inversions, 427–28.

23. Ibid., Q77-2, 427.

24. Ibid., A77-2 and additional response between Q77 and Q78, 427–28.

CHAPTER 20

1. Ágreda, *MCDD y biografía de su autora*, Q77-3, 427.

2. Ibid., A77-3, 428.

3. Ximénez Samaniego, *Life of Venerable Mary of Jesus*, 128.

4. Ágreda, *MCDD y biografía de su autora*, A77-3, 429.

5. Ibid., A77-4, 429.

6. Ibid., Q78-1, 430.

7. Ibid., A78-1, 430.

8. Kendrick, *Mary of Ágreda*, 159.

9. Ibid., 162; Ágreda, *MCDD y biografía de su autora*, A78-1, 430.

10. Ágreda, *MCDD y biografía de su autora*, Q78, 430.

11. Ibid., supplement to A78, 430–31.

12. Ibid., Q78-1, 431.

13. Ibid., A78-1, 431.

14. Ibid., Q78-2, 431.

15. Ibid., A78-2, 431.

16. Ibid., Q78-3, 431.

17. Ibid., A78-3, 431.

18. Ibid., 432.

CHAPTER 21

1. Ágreda, *MCDD y biografía de su autora*, 432.

2. Ibid., 432–33.

3. Ibid., 433–36.

4. Ibid., 436.

5. Kendrick's translation, *Mary of Ágreda*, 107.

6. Ibid., 108.
7. Ibid.
8. Ágreda, *MCDD y biografía de su autora*, 437.
9. Colahan, "Sweetheart of the Holy Office," 166.
10. Ágreda, *MCDD y biografía de su autora*, 436–37.
11. *Cartas 2*, 13–15, with inversions.

CHAPTER 22

1. Lea, *A History of the Inquisition of Spain*, 2:134.
2. Ibid., 137.
3. Ibid., 143.
4. Ibid., 137.
5. Ibid., 140.
6. Ibid., 147.
7. Ibid., 150.
8. *Cartas 2*, 15.
9. Ibid., 16–17.
10. Kendrick, *Mary of Ágreda*, 77–78.

CHAPTER 23

1. Peña García, *Sor María de Jesús de Ágreda*, 112.
2. Ibid., 307.
3. Ibid.
4. In section III of his article "Novices," Arthur Vermeersch covers the confessional exercises of novices. *The Catholic Encyclopedia*, vol. 11 (New York: Robert Appleton, 1911).
5. Ágreda, *MCDD y biografía de su autora*, 214–17.
6. Ibid., 203–4.
7. *Cartas 2*, 155.
8. Ibid., 156; *Correspondencia* (Baranda), 170n127.
9. *Cartas 2*, 157–59.
10. Ibid., with inversions, 160–61.
11. Peña García, *Sor María de Jesús de Ágreda*, 307; Elliott, *Imperial Spain*, 349.
12. Hume, *Court of Philip IV*, 403, 418, 487, 506.
13. Ibid., 420, 420n1.
14. Ibid., 421, 397; Elliott, *Imperial Spain*, 346.
15. *Cartas 2*, 161–64.
16. Ximénez Samaniego, *Life of Venerable Mary of Jesus*, 140.

CHAPTER 24

1. Ágreda, *MCDD y biografía de su autora*, 220.
2. Ibid., 218; Peña García, *Sor María de Jesús de Ágreda*, 307.
3. Ágreda, *MCDD y biografía de su autora*, 231.
4. Ibid., 222.
5. Ibid., 235–36.
6. Ibid., 236, 231.
7. Ibid., 237.
8. Ibid., 237, 241.
9. Ximénez Samaniego, *Life of Venerable Mary of Jesus*, 140.
10. Colahan, *Visions of Sor María de Agreda*, 135 on "self-scorn," and 133 on "strategies of empowerment."
11. Ximénez Samaniego, *Life of Venerable Mary of Jesus*, 136–38.
12. Ágreda, *MCOG-GJB: Incarnation*, 15.
13. Ximénez Samaniego, *Life of Venerable Mary of Jesus*, 138.
14. Ágreda, *MCDD y biografía de su autora*, 253, 255; these angels are identified in Clark A. Colahan and Celia Weller, "An Angelic Epilogue," *Studia Mystica* 13, no. 4 (1990): 50–59.
15. Ágreda, *MCDD y biografía de su autora*, 255.
16. Ibid., 234.
17. Kendrick, *Mary of Ágreda*, 101.
18. Hume, *Court of Philip IV*, 452.
19. Elliott, *Imperial Spain*, 352.
20. Hume's translation, *Court of Philip IV*, 452.
21. *Cartas 2*, 290–93.
22. Ibid., 324.
23. Ibid., 325–27.
24. Hume's translation, *Court of Philip IV*, 439–40.
25. *Cartas 2*, 381.
26. Kendrick, *Mary of Ágreda*, 103–4.
27. Ágreda, *MCOG-GJB: Incarnation*, 340.
28. *Cartas 2*, 391.

CHAPTER 25

1. Ximénez Samaniego, *Life of Venerable Mary of Jesus*, 128.
2. Artola Arbiza and Mendía, *La venerable M. María de Jesús*, 25.
3. Ágreda, *MCOG-GJB: Conception*, 17.
4. Ibid., 17, 18.
5. *Cartas 2*, 741.
6. Ágreda, *MCOG-GJB: Incarnation*, 257.

7. Ibid.

8. *Cartas 2*, 411.

9. Kendrick, *Mary of Ágreda*, 78.

10. Don Luis Méndez de Haro y Guzmán, *Letters from the Pyrenees, July to November 1659*, ed. Lynn Williams (Exeter: University of Exeter Press, 2000), ix.

11. Hume, *Court of Philip IV*, 465–66.

12. Méndez de Haro, *Letters from the Pyrenees*, x.

13. Kendrick, *Mary of Ágreda*, 133.

14. *Cartas 2*, 474–75.

15. Kendrick, *Mary of Ágreda*, 134.

16. Elliott, *Imperial Spain*, 352; Méndez de Haro, *Letters from the Pyrenees*, x.

17. Ágreda, *MCDD y biografía de su autora*, 394.

18. Hume, *Court of Philip IV*, 456; *Correspondencia* (Baranda), 221n165.

19. Hume's translation, *Court of Philip IV*, 457–58.

20. *Correspondencia* (Baranda), 52n6.

21. Kendrick's translation, *Mary of Ágreda*, 135–36.

22. Hume, *Court of Philip IV*, 471–73.

23. Peña García, *Sor María de Jesús de Ágreda*, 309; Hume, *Court of Philip IV*, 466, 473–74.

24. *Cartas 2*, 537, 538.

25. Kendrick's translation, *Mary of Ágreda*, 78–79.

26. Hume, *Court of Philip IV*, 476–77.

27. Ibid., 482–85.

28. Ibid., 485.

29. *Cartas 2*, 621–22, note that the king cited Sor María's letter of the twenty-third, while her text in this volume dates it as June 22, 1660; Hume, *Court of Philip IV*, 484.

30. *Cartas 2*, 623.

CHAPTER 26

1. Ágreda, *MCDD y biografía de su autora*, 375–76.

2. Ximénez Samaniego, *Life of Venerable Mary of Jesus*, 111.

3. Ágreda, *MCDD y biografía de su autora*, 374.

4. Ágreda, *MCOG-GJB: Conception*, 40.

5. Ximénez Samaniego, *Life of Venerable Mary of Jesus*, 159–62.

6. Ágreda, *MCOG-GJB: Conception*, 41.

7. Ágreda, *MCDD y biografía de su autora*, 379–83, from the recorded account.

8. Kendrick, *Mary of Ágreda*, 57, 112.

9. *Cartas* 2, 665.

10. Hume, *Court of Philip IV,* 487.

11. Hume's translation, *Court of Philip IV,* 491–92.

12. *Cartas* 2, 669–71.

13. Ibid., 675.

14. Peña García, *Sor María de Jesús de Ágreda,* 311.

15. *Cartas* 2, 677.

16. Ibid., 678.

CHAPTER 27

1. Kendrick, *Mary of Ágreda,* 149.

2. *Cartas* 2, 731.

3. Ibid., 732.

4. Kendrick's translation, *Mary of Ágreda,* 151.

5. Ibid.

6. Peña García, *Sor María de Jesús de Ágreda,* 311, 129.

7. Ximénez Samaniego, *Life of Venerable Mary of Jesus,* 143–44.

8. Ibid., 175.

9. Ibid., 176–77.

10. Ibid., 179, 181.

11. Ibid., 181.

12. Ibid., 182.

13. Ibid., 182–83.

14. Ibid., 183.

CHAPTER 28

1. Ximénez Samaniego, *Life of Venerable Mary of Jesus,* 183–84.

2. Ibid., 185–86.

3. Ibid.

4. Ibid.

5. Ibid., 186–87.

6. Hume, *Court of Philip IV,* 507, 508–9.

7. Ibid., 498, 512.

8. Ibid., 512–13.

9. Fiscar Marison (George J. Blatter), ed. and trans., *MCOG-GJB: Conception,* xxi.

10. Kendrick, *Mary of Ágreda,* 157; Lea, *A History of the Inquisition of Spain,* 1:558.

11. Peña García, *Sor María de Jesús de Ágreda,* 314.

12. Ibid.

13. In his article "María de Ágreda," T. J. Campbell cites this date in volume 1 of *The Catholic Encyclopedia* (New York: Robert Appleton, 1907), 229.

14. Peña García, *Sor María de Jesús de Ágreda*, 316.

15. Ximénez Samaniego, *Life of Venerable Mary of Jesus*, 189; Peña García, *Sor María de Jesús de Ágreda*, 316; James A. Carrico, *Life of Venerable Mary of Ágreda: Author of* The Mystical City of God, *the Autobiography of the Virgin Mary* (San Bernardino, CA: E. J. Culligan, 1962), 82.

16. Peña García, *Sor María de Jesús de Ágreda*, 316.

17. Ibid., 170, 172, 175, 176, 177.

18. Ibid., 166–69.

19. Ibid., 178, 179.

20. Ibid., 181.

21. Ibid., 181–82.

22. Ibid., 183.

23. Author's correspondence with Concepcionista Ágredista archivist, January 14, 2006.

24. Ximénez Samaniego, *Life of Venerable Mary of Jesus*, 187–88.

25. Ibid., 188.

26. Ibid., 194–98.

27. Artola Arbiza and Mendía, *La venerable M. María de Jesús*, 32; appendix D, this work.

28. Concepcionistas de Ágreda, *Publicación para promover su beatificación* (August 1989), 1–2.

29. Ibid.

30. *Diario de Soria*, daily newspaper in Soria, Spain, October 12, 2002.

CHAPTER 29

1. Underhill, *Mystics of the Church*, 78–79.

2. Artola Arbiza and Mendía, *La venerable M. María de Jesús*, 42, 169, 49n30.

3. Consolación Baranda, in "Sor María, la dama azul," *Mujeres en la historia*, dir. María Teresa Álvarez (Madrid: RTVE Servicios Comerciales, 1995), segment in sixty-minute videocassette.

4. Artola Arbiza and Mendía, *La venerable M. María de Jesús*, 38.

5. Ágreda, *MCOG-GJB: Conception*, 303; Ibid., *Transfixion*, 225; Ibid., *Conception*, 253; Ibid., *Incarnation*, 27.

6. Artola Arbiza and Mendía, *La venerable M. María de Jesús*, 42, more literally translated as "a grand poetical-theological construction" (una gran construcción poético-teológica); in the 1995 RTVE production, he described it similarly, calling it a "theological poem." Enrique Llamas, *Venerable Mother Agreda and the Mariology of Vatican II*, trans. Peter D. Fehlner (New Bedford, MA: Academy of the Immaculate, 2006), 5, 8, 10.

7. Artola Arbiza and Mendía, *La venerable M. María de Jesús*, 35.

8. Ximénez Samaniego, *Life of Venerable Mary of Jesus*, 144.

9. Ibid., 144–45.

10. Ibid., 145–46.

11. Kendrick, *Mary of Ágreda*, 157.

12. Peña García, *Sor María de Jesús de Ágreda*, 315.

13. Ximénez Samaniego, *Life of Venerable Mary of Jesus*, 189; Peña García, *Sor María de Jesús de Ágreda*, 316; Carrico, *Life of Venerable Mary of Ágreda*, 82.

14. The second Vatican Council (1962–65: opened by Pope John XXIII and closed by his successor, Pope Paul VI) constituted a worldwide assembly of Catholic bishops and representatives, convened to explore ecumenical unity and the role of the church in the modern world.

15. Artola Arbiza and Mendía, *La venerable M. María de Jesús*, 66; author's correspondence with Artola Arbiza, April 2–4, 2008.

16. Artola Arbiza and Mendía, *La venerable M. María de Jesús*, 84.

17. Ibid., 73–74.

18. Ibid., 75.

19. Ibid., 81.

20. Kendrick, *Mary of Ágreda*, 77n2.

21. Artola Arbiza and Mendía, *La venerable M. María de Jesús*, 85.

22. Ibid., 85, 91.

23. Ibid., 81.

24. Ibid., 87n3.

25. Ibid., 98.

26. Ibid., 106.

27. Peña García, *Sor María de Jesús de Ágreda*, 320; Eamon R. Carroll, "Mariology," in *New Catholic Encyclopedia* (Washington, DC: Gale Cengage, 2003), 169.

28. Artola Arbiza and Mendía, *La venerable M. María de Jesús*, 107, 108, 110.

29. Ibid., 111.

30. Campbell, "María de Ágreda," 1:229.

31. Artola Arbiza and Mendía, *La venerable M. María de Jesús*, 100, 123.

32. Ibid., 125, 127.

33. Ibid., 127.

34. Peña García, *Sor María de Jesús de Ágreda*, 319; Artola Arbiza and Mendía, *La venerable M. María de Jesús*, 94.

35. Artola Arbiza and Mendía, *La venerable M. María de Jesús*, 144, 156n30.

36. Pope Benedict XIV, *Correspondance de Benoit XIV*, ed. Emile de Heeckeren (Paris: Plon-Nourrit, 1912), 1:384–85.

37. Artola Arbiza and Mendía, *La venerable M. María de Jesús,* 133.

38. Ibid., 136–37.

39. Ibid., 133.

40. Ibid., 140, 154n14.

41. Ibid., 140.

42. Ibid., 142, 208–11.

43. Ibid., 151.

44. Ibid., 163.

CHAPTER 30

1. Artola Arbiza and Mendía, *La venerable M. María de Jesús,* 115, 243.

2. Ibid., 244.

3. Ibid., 246.

4. Ibid., 247.

5. Ibid., 250.

6. Ibid., 249.

7. Ibid., 251.

8. Ibid., 252.

9. Ibid., 259.

10. Carrico, *Life of Venerable Mary of Ágreda,* 8.

11. Ibid., 95.

12. Artola Arbiza and Mendía, *La venerable M. María de Jesús,* 260.

13. Carrico, *Life of Venerable Mary of Ágreda,* 84.

14. Ibid., 11.

15. James Carrico collected papers, 1953–61, copied to the author by Michael J. Carrico.

16. Artola Arbiza and Mendía, *La venerable M. María de Jesús,* 261.

17. Ibid., 262.

18. Ibid., 263.

19. Ibid.

20. Author's e-mail correspondence from Clark Colahan, March 31, 2008.

21. Artola Arbiza and Mendía, *La venerable M. María de Jesús,* 264.

22. The Knights of Columbus is a lay organization of 1.6 million American Catholic men and was founded in 1882 and consecrated to the Blessed Virgin Mary.

23. Artola Arbiza and Mendía, *La venerable M. María de Jesús,* 269.

24. Ibid., 272.

25. Ibid., 273.

26. Ibid., 270–73.

27. Ibid., 275, 282n79.

28. Llamas, *Venerable Mother Agreda,* trans. Fehlner, 12.

29. Ibid.
30. Artola Arbiza and Mendía, *La venerable M. María de Jesús*, 276.
31. Ibid., 276–77.
32. Ibid., 277.
33. Palou, *Life and Apostolic Labors*, trans. Williams, 8, 134, 327–34; Eduardo Enrique Rios, *Life of Fray Antonio Margil O.F.M.*, trans. Benedict Leutenegger (Washington, DC: Academy of American Franciscan History, 1959), 63; *Handbook of Texas Online*, s.v., "Nuestra Señora de la Purísima Concepción de Acuña Mission," www.tsha.utexas.edu/handbook/online/articles/NN/uqn9.html (accessed December 5, 2005).
34. Author's copy of the program, courtesy of the Knights of Columbus Solanus Casey Chapter.
35. *Heraldo de Soria*, daily newspaper in Soria, Spain, August 7, 2001. Note: after retiring from the Marian Academy of Rome, and following the death of Ángel Martínez Moñux in 2006, Calvo returned to Spain and assumed responsibilities as Sor María's vice postulator.
36. Wilton Gregory, *Mary in the Church: A Selection of Teaching Documents* (Washington, DC: USCCB, 2003), 48.
37. Concepcionistas de Ágreda, *Publicación para promover su beatificación* (August 2005), 6–7.
38. Ricardo Fernánde Gracia, *Iconografía de Sor María de Ágreda* (Soria, Spain: Caja Duero, 2002), 115.
39. Miguel A. Bretos, e-mail and phone interviews by author, September 23, 2004, November 4, 2004, and following.
40. *American Women: A Library of Congress Guide for the Study of Women's History and Culture in the United States*, ed. Sheridan Harvey (Washington, DC: Library of Congress and University Press of New England, 2002), as accessed online at memory.loc.gov/ammem/awhhtml/index.html (search by keyword *Agreda* from this page), and memory.loc.gov/ammem/awhhtml/awmss5/index.html (accessed March 3, 2008).
41. Donald E. Chipman and Harriett Denise Joseph, *Explorers and Settlers of Spanish Texas* (Austin: University of Texas Press, 2001), 43.
42. Author's phone interview with Cynthia Jordan, March 2, 2007.

AFTERWORD

1. Andrew B. Newberg, Michael Pourdehnad, Abass Alavi, and Eugene G. D'Aquili, "Cerebral Blood Flow during Meditative Prayer: Preliminary Findings and Methodological Issues," *Perceptual and Motor Skills* 97 (2003): 626.
2. Andrew B. Newberg, "The Measurement of Regional Cerebral Blood Flow during the Complex Cognitive Task of Meditation: A Preliminary SPECT Study," *Psychiatry Imaging: Neuroimaging* (2001): 106.

3. Eugene G. D'Aquili and Andrew B. Newberg, "The Neuropsychology of Aesthetic, Spiritual, and Mystical States," *ZYGON: Journal of Religion and Science* 35, no. 1 (March 2000): 45–48.

APPENDIX E

1. "Carta de Don Damian Manzanet," trans. Lilia M. Casis, *Spanish Exploration in the Southwest, 1542–1706*, ed. Herbert E. Bolton (New York: Charles Scribner's Sons, 1916), 387.
2. Herbert E. Bolton, *Rim of Christendom: A Biography of Eusebio Francisco Kino, Pacific Coast Pioneer* (New York: Macmillan, 1936), 417–18.
3. Pichardo, "The Miraculous Journeys," 498.
4. Carrico, *Life of Venerable Mary of Ágreda*, 53–54, 98n25.
5. Colahan, "Presencia agredana histórica y actual en Norteamérica," in *Actas del I Congreso Internacional* (Leon: La Orden Concepcionista, 1990), 2:267.
6. Rios, *Life of Fray Antonio Margil*, trans. Leutenegger, 63.
7. Radio Televisión Española (RTVE), "Sor María, la dama azul," in *Mujeres en la Historia*, dir. María Teresa Álvarez (Madrid: RTVE Servicios Comerciales, 1995), sixty-minute videocassette.
8. Ibid.; *El País*, "TVE recrea la vida de nueve mujers tan influyentes como desconocidas," April 2, 1995.
9. Author's phone interviews with Jumano-Apache tribal historian Enrique Madrid (Redford, Texas), July 4, 2008, and Jumano-Apache chieftain Gabriel Carrasco (El Paso, Texas), July 7, 2008.

APPENDIX G

1. Peña García, *Sor María de Jesús de Ágreda*, 314.
2. Ibid., 316–17.
3. Ibid., 321.
4. Ibid.
5. Ibid., 324.
6. Ibid., 327–28.
7. Ibid.
8. Ibid., 334.
9. Ibid.
10. Ibid.
11. Ibid.
12. Ibid., 339.
13. Ibid., 341.
14. Ibid.
15. Ibid., 348.
16. Ibid., 349.

Ágreda, María de Jesús de. *Autenticidad de la* Mística Ciudad de Dios *y biografía de su autora.* Barcelona: Heredos de Juan Gili, Editores, 1914. Reprint, Madrid, 1985.

———. *Correspondencia con Felipe IV: Religión y razón de estado.* Introduction and notes by Consolación Baranda. Madrid: Editorial Castalia, 1991.

———. *Mística Ciudad de Dios: Vida de María.* Edited by Angel Martínez Moñux, Celestino Solaguren, and Luis Villasante. Madrid: Fareso, 1970.

———. *Mystical City of God.* Vol. 1, Books 1–2, *The Conception.* Vol. 2, Books 3–4, *The Incarnation.* Vol. 3, Books 5–6, *The Transfixion.* Vol. 4, Books 7–8, *The Coronation.* Translated by George J. Blatter as Fiscar Marison. Chicago: Theopolitan Company of Chicago, 1914. Reprint, Albuquerque, NM: Corcoran, 1949.

———, Philip IV, and Francisco Silvela. *Cartas de la venerable Madre Sor María de Ágreda y del Señor Rey Don Felipe IV: Precididas de un bosquejo histórico por D. Francisco Silvela,* Vols. 1–2. Madrid: Purísima Concepción de Ágreda, 1885–86.

Álvarez, María Teresa, director. "Sor María, La Dama Azul." *Mujeres en la historia.* Madrid: Radiotelevisión Española (RTVE), Servicios Comerciales, 1995. Sixty-minute videocassette.

Artola Arbiza, Antonio M., and Benito Mendía. *La venerable M. María de Jesús de Ágreda y la Inmaculada Concepción: El proceso eclesiástico a la* Mística Ciudad de Dios. Soria, Spain: La Heras, 2004.

Bancroft, Hubert Howe. *History of the Pacific States of North America: Arizona and New Mexico, 1530–1888,* Vol. 12. San Francisco: History Company, 1888.

Benavides, Alonso de. *A Harvest of Reluctant Souls: The Memorial of Fray Alonso de Benavides, 1630.* Translated and edited by Baker H. Morrow. Niwot: University Press of Colorado, 1996.

————. *Fray Alonso de Benavides' Revised Memorial of 1634.* Translated and edited by Frederick Webb Hodge, George P. Hammond, and Agapito Rey. Albuquerque: University of New Mexico Press, 1945.

Benedict XIV, Pope. *Correspondance de Benoit XIV.* Edited by Emile de Heeckeren. Paris: Plon-Nourrit, 1912.

Blanshard, Paul. *Freedom and Catholic Power in Spain and Portugal, An American Interpretation.* Boston: Beacon Press, 1962.

Bolton, Herbert E. *Rim of Christendom: A Biography of Eusebio Francisco Kino, Pacific Coast Pioneer.* New York: Macmillan, 1936.

————, ed. *Spanish Exploration in the Southwest, 1542–1706.* New York: Charles Scribner's Sons, 1916.

Brandon, William. *Quivira: Europeans in the Region of the Santa Fe Trail, 1540–1820.* Athens: Ohio University Press, 1990.

Carrico James A. *Life of Venerable Mary of Ágreda: Author of* The Mystical City of God, *the Autobiography of the Virgin Mary.* San Bernardino, CA: E. J. Culligan, 1962.

Carrico, Mark J. "On the Path of Blue Flowers." Paper submitted to Dr. Donald Cutter as part of course work in History of the Southwest, University of New Mexico, November 25, 1975.

Castañeda, Carlos, E. *Our Catholic Heritage in Texas, 1519–1936.* Vol. 1, *The Mission Era: The Finding of Texas, 1519–1693.* Austin, TX: Von Boeckmann-Jones, 1936.

Clemens, Gus. *The Concho Country.* San Antonio, TX: Mulberry Avenue Books, 1980.

————. *Legacy: The Story of the Permian Basin Region of West Texas and Southeast New Mexico.* San Antonio, TX: Mulberry Avenue Books, 1983.

Colahan, Clark A. "María de Jesús de Ágreda, The Sweetheart of the Holy Office." In *Women in the Inquisition: Spain and the New World,* edited by Mary E. Giles, 155–70, 336–38. Baltimore, MD: Johns Hopkins University Press, 1999.

————. "Mary of Agreda, the Virgin Mary, and Mystical Knowing." *Studia Mystica* 3, no. 3 (1988): 53–65.

————. *The Visions of Sor María de Agreda: Writing Knowledge and Power.* Tucson: University of Arizona Press, 1994.

————, and Celia Weller. "An Angelic Epilogue." *Studia Mystica* 13, no. 4 (1990): 50–59.

Comunidad de Castilla y León. *Ágreda y su tierra: Fiestas en honor de Ntra. Sra. de los Milagros, 1947–1997. Cincuenta aniversario de su coronacion.* Ágreda: Comisión de Cultura y Festejos, 1997.

Concepcionistas de Ágreda. *La Venerable Madre María de Jesús de Ágreda: Publicacion para promover su beatificación,* Vols. 1–47. Edited by

Manuel Pena Garcia, 1988–98, and Ángel Martínez Moñux, 1998–2007. Ágreda: Purísima Concepción, 1988–2007.

Cruz, Joan Carroll. *The Incorruptibles*. Rockford, IL: Tan Books, 1977.

Cutter, Donald C. "With a Little Help from Their Friends." *Pacific Historical Review* (a publication of the American Historical Association) 53, no. 2 (May 1984): 123–40.

Damase, Jacques. *Carriages*. Translated by William Mitchell. New York: G. P. Putnam's Sons, 1968.

Davies, R. Trevor. *Spain in Decline: 1621–1700*. London: Macmillan, 1957.

Driver, Harold E. *Indians of North America*. 2nd ed. Chicago and London: University of Chicago Press, 1961, 1969.

Echeverría Goñi, Pedro Luis. "La Madre Ágreda y la construcción de su convento." In *Monografias universitarias: El papel de sor María Jesús de Ágreda en el barroco español*, edited by Yolanda Martínez Hernando and Carlos de la Casa Martínez, 75–103. Soria, Spain: Universidad Internacional Alfonso VIII, 2002.

Elliott, J. H. *Imperial Spain: 1469–1716*. New York: St. Martin's Press, 1966.

Esposito, Augustine M. La Mistica Cuidad de Dios *(1670) Sor María de Jesús de Ágreda*. Potomac, MD: Scripta Humanistica, 1990.

Fernández Gracia, Ricardo. *Arte, devoción y política, La promoción de las artes en torno a sor María de Ágreda*. Soria, Spain: Diputación Provincial de Soria, 2002.

———. *Iconografía de Sor María de Ágreda*. Soria, Spain: Caja Duero, 2002.

Froehle, Virginia Ann, *Called into Her Presence: Praying with Feminine Images of God*. Notre Dame, IN: Ave María Press, 1992.

Gindely, Anton. *History of the Thirty Years' War: With an Introductory and a Concluding Chapter by the Translator*, Vols. 1 and 2. Translated from the German by Andrew Ten Brook. New York: G. P. Putnam's Sons, 1884.

Gregory, Wilton. Foreword to *Mary in the Church: A Selection of Teaching Documents*. Washington, DC: USCCB, 2003.

Handbook of Texas Online. "Ágreda, María de Jesús de," "Jumano Indians," "Nuestra Señora de la Purísima Concepción de Acuña Mission." Texas State Historical Association: www.tshaonline.org (accessed May 18, 2000, and December 5, 2005).

Hewett, Edgar L., and Reginald G. Fisher. *Mission Monuments of New Mexico*. Albuquerque: University of New Mexico Press, 1943.

Hickerson, Nancy Parrott. *The Jumanos: Hunters and Traders of the South Plains*. Austin: University of Texas Press, 1994.

Hodge, Frederick Webb, ed. *Handbook of American Indians North of Mexico*, Part 1. New York: Pageant Books, 1959.

———. *The Jumano Indians*. Reprinted from a presentation to the American Antiquarian Society. Worcester, MA: Davis Press, 1910.

Hume, Martin. *The Court of Philip IV: Spain in Decline.* New York: G. P. Putnam's Sons, 1907.

Johnson, Carroll B. "El Buscón: D. Pablos, D. Diego y D. Francisco." *Hispanofila* (May 1974): 1–26.

Josephy, Alvin M., Jr. *500 Nations: An Illustrated History of North American Indians.* New York: Alfred A. Knopf, 1994.

Kamen, Henry. *Empire: How Spain Became a World Power, 1492–1763.* New York: HarperCollins, 2003.

———. *The Spanish Inquisition: A Historical Revision.* New Haven, CT: Yale University Press, 1997.

Kendrick, Thomas Downing. *Mary of Ágreda: The Life and Legend of a Spanish Nun.* London: Routledge & Kegan Paul, 1967.

Kessell, John L. "María de Ágreda's Ministry to the Jumano Indians of the Southwest in the 1620s." In *Great Mysteries of the West,* edited by Ferenc Morton Szasz, 121–44. Golden, CO: Fulcrum, 1993.

Kubler, George. *The Religious Architecture of New Mexico in the Colonial Period and since the American Occupation.* Albuquerque: University of New Mexico Press, 1940.

Lea, Henry Charles, LL.D. *A History of the Inquisition of Spain,* Vols. 1, 2, 3, 4. New York: Macmillan, 1922.

Llamas, Enrique. *Venerable Mother Ágreda and the Mariology of Vatican II.* Translated by Peter Damian Fehlner. New Bedford, MA: Academy of the Immaculate, 2006.

MacLean, Katie. "María de Agreda, Spanish Mysticism and the Work of Spiritual Conquest." *Colonial Latin American Review* (June 2008): 29–48.

Martínez Moñux, Ángel. *María, Mística Ciudad de Dios: Una mariología interactiva.* Burgos, Spain: Monte Carmelo, 2001.

Matt, Daniel C. *The Essential Kabbalah, the Heart of Jewish Mysticism.* Introduction by Huston Smith. New York: HarperSanFrancisco, 1998.

McBrien, Richard P. "Mary and the Church." In *Catholocism,* Vol. 2, 865–901. Minneapolis, MN: Winston Press, 1980.

McNamara, Jo Ann Kay. *Sisters in Arms: Catholic Nuns through Two Millennia.* Cambridge, MA: Harvard University Press, 1996.

Méndez de Haro y Guzmán, Don Luis. *Letters from the Pyrenees.* Edited by Lynn Williams. Exeter: University of Exeter Press, 2000.

North American Indian Tribal Groups. "1653." As reproduced from the Fletcher Boeselt Collection by Carto-Graphic Galleries of San Antonio, Texas.

O'Connell, Rev. John P., ed. *The Holy Bible: Holy Trinity Edition.* Chicago: Catholic Press, 1951.

Ortiz, Antonio Dominguez. *The Golden Age of Spain, 1516–1659.* Translated by James Casey. London: Weidenfeld and Nicolson, 1971.

Palou, Francisco. *Life and Apostolic Labors of the Venerable Father Junípero Serra.* Translated by C. Scott Williams. Pasadena, CA: George Wharton James, 1913.

Parsons, Francis B. *Early 17th Century Missions of the Southwest.* Tucson, AZ: Dale Stuart King, 1966.

Peele, William T. "Indians of North America." *National Geographic* (December 1972): 739A.

Peña García, Manuel. *Sor María de Jesús de Ágreda.* Ágreda, Spain: El Burgo de Osma, 1997.

Pichardo, José Antonio. "The Miraculous Journeys of Mother María de Jesús de Ágreda to La Quivira." In *Pichardo's Treatise on the Limits of Louisiana and Texas,* Vol. 2, 465–509. Translated by Charles W. Hackett. Austin: University of Texas Press, 1931–46.

Rios, Eduardo Enrique. *Life of Fray Antonio Margil O.F.M.* Translated by Benedict Leutenegger. Washington, DC: Academy of American Franciscan History, 1959.

Rubio Semper, Agustín. "Ágreda en el Siglo XVII." In *Monografías universitarias: El papel de sor María Jesús de Ágreda en el barroco español,* edited by Yolanda Martínez Hernando and Carlos de la Casa Martínez, 43–60. Soria, Spain: Universidad Internacional Alfonso VIII, 2002.

Smith, Huston. *The World's Religions: The Wisdom Traditions.* New York: Harper Collins, 1991.

Swanton, John R. *The Indian Tribes of North America.* Washington, DC: Smithsonian Institution Press, 1952. Reprint ed., 1962.

Swietlicki, Catherine. *A Spanish Christian Cabala: The Works of Luis de León, Santa Teresa de Jesús, and San Juan de la Cruz.* Columbia: University of Missouri Press, 1986.

Teresa of Avila, Saint. *The Life of St. Teresa of Jesus of the Order of Our Lady of Carmel, Written by Herself.* Translated by David Lewis. London: Thomas Baker, 1904.

Terrell, John Upton. *American Indian Almanac.* New York: World, 1971.

Underhill, Evelyn. *Mysticism.* New York: E. P. Dutton, 1961.

———. *Mystics of the Church.* Harrisburg, PA: Morehouse, 1925.

Vecsey, Christopher. *American Indian Catholics: On the Padres' Trail.* Notre Dame, IN: University of Notre Dame Press, 1996.

Weber, David J. *The Spanish Frontier in North America.* New Haven, CT: Yale University Press, 1992.

Wright, Muriel H. *A Guide to the Indian Tribes of Oklahoma.* Norman: University of Oklahoma Press, 1951.

Ximénez Samaniego, José. *Life of Venerable Mary of Jesus de Ágreda: Poor Clare Nun.* Translated by Ubaldus [Pandolfi] da Rieti. Evansville, IN: Keller-Crescent Printing and Engraving, 1910.

Page numbers in italics indicate illustrations. The letter *n* following a page number indicates a note on that page.

Ágreda, María de Jesús of (María Coronel y Arana): appearance of, 3, 63–64; austerities of, 33–34, 37, 69; as author, 5, 25–26, 70, 89–90, 95–97, 110–11, 256–57; character of, 37–38, 73, 90, 112, 167, 179; confessors and, 61, 73, 64–65, 136, 142, 171, 198; converso heritage of, 15, 295n5; death of, 234–36, 240–41, 242, 247–49; early years of, 12, 17–21, 32–35; ecstasies of, 4, 33–36, 46, 88; education of, 17–19, 20; exterioridades of, 35, 37, 40, 46, 168; on God, 17, 19, 26, 110, 181–82, 214, 234; health of, 20–21, 70, 164, 205, 217; iconography of, 1–3, 6, 145, 270, 304n3; Inquisition and, 88, 164, 169–74, 177–79, 189–93; legacy of, 5–6, 262, 265, 267, 270, 272, 273; levitation of, 4, 34–37; library of, 11, 15, 25–26, 251; light imagery and, 16–17, 19, 21, 91–94, 172, 181, 206; meditative

prayer and, 20, 21, 34, 35, 91, 93, 98, 110; miracles and, 229–30, 245–47; missionary zeal of, 4, 20, 25–26, 44, 66; as mystic, 3–5, 15, 21, 34, 61, 93–94, 291–92n7; Peace of Pyrenees and, 223–24; personal struggles of, 6, 19, 35–36, 89, 154–57, 178; prescience of, 4, 228, 235; sainthood case of, 6, 240, 242–47, 252, 255–59, 265, 320n35; self-concept of, 38, 71, 95, 110, 145, 182, 214, 314n10. *See also under* bilocations of María of Ágreda; Felipe IV; *Mystical City of God*; visions of María of Ágreda

Ágreda (Spain), village of, 10, 11; administrative role of, 128; culture of, 16; support for convent, 29, 71

Ágredas, the (Beaumont, Texas), 261
Aguirre, Cardinal José Sáenz de, 254
Alexander VII, Pope, 100, 223–24, 232
American Southwest, 50, 51; colonization of, 10, 54, 63, 115; María of Ágreda's legacy in, 1, 3, 5, 48, 265, 270. *See also* missions, New World

ACKNOWLEDGMENTS

This may be the most daunting part of the book to write because the support in producing it has been so generous. First thanks go, of course, to Sor María for her outstanding intelligence and bravery in living a life and leaving a legacy so worthy of sharing. If I have fallen short in the portrayal, it is not attributable in any way to the subject, nor to those I recognize below for their contributions, but rather to my own limitations. I would like to recognize:

Clark Colahan, whose scholarly guidance and relentless honesty have vastly helped the final version of this work. Mary Giles, who before she died read my earlier treatment of Sor María's life and wholeheartedly encouraged me to publish. Nancy Hickerson, whose definitive scholarship on the Jumano Native Americans has helped these stalwart people to regain their tribal identity and helped me to appreciate their history. Katie MacLean, who generously shared her expertise and insight on seventeenth-century Spanish linguistics, culture, and colonial history.

Mª Consolación Campos Martínez, teacher, linguist, and advocate—among many—for Sor María's beatification, who tirelessly advised me from Spain and facilitated the acquisition of so many of the fine photographs displayed within. Pedro Antonio Calavia Calvo, talented governmental press adviser and avocational photographer, who gallantly climbed the hill across from the convent to photograph its entire length for the *autora* from America, when her own camera failed.

Most Rev. Michael D. Pfeifer, bishop and spiritual leader of the San Angelo Catholic diocese of Texas; composer-performer Cynthia Jordan; the entire community of San Angelo for their ongoing enthusiasm in recognizing Sor María's unique contributions in Texas history; and all Jumanos and Jumano-Apache Native Americans for such longstanding loyalty and love for their Lady in Blue, particularly contemporary chieftain Gabriel Carrasco, tribal historian Enrique Madrid, and artist-activist Margo Tamez.

Padre Ángel Martínez Moñux (in memoriam), Padre Antonio Artola Arbiza, and the kindhearted Conceptionist nuns of Ágreda, for their tireless correspondence, guidance, and access to precious archival material; Alex Fiato, Michael Carrico, and the entire Carrico family, Knights all; Patrick O'Brien, CEO of *Faith Magazine*, for his excellent strategic advice on publishing; agent Molly Lyons of Joëlle Delbourgo Associates; and editor Lisa Pacheco and designer Melissa Tandysh, of the University of New Mexico Press, for their exceptional expertise and creativity in bringing this work to fruition.

The insightful encouragement of my early readers, especially Colette Coomes, Msgr. Robert Lunsford, Msgr. Michael Murphy, and Jeanne Kendall, artist, photographer, and dear friend, who not only contributed her photographs of Saint Augustine's at Isleta Pueblo, but who sat on her back deck as the first outside reader of each of my iterations on the life of my favorite mystic.

Kristine Scarff and Mary-Ellen Wyard for exuding unfailing daughterly enthusiasm; my cherished Fab-Four friends (Patricia Cammarata, Jo Sauve, and Diane Davis); the peerless Sandra Wicker—who comprises an unwavering one-woman cheering squad; all of my friends, who have indulged my Ágreda interests for so long that I'm sure they wonder if I can talk about anything else; and, with tenderness, the late Agnes Fedewa, who initially led me to read *Mystical City of God*.

Finally, I acknowledge Stanley Christopher Fedewa, the sweetest and brightest star in my galaxy, my first reader and editor, a wonderful writer in his own right, and a serious student of mysticism, without whose tireless encouragement, perception, and love—and yes, food slipped under the door—this would be a much poorer work.

ABOUT THE AUTHOR

With a background in literature, communications, and political science, Marilyn Fedewa held directorial and cabinet-level positions through 1997 in higher education administration at Pepperdine University, Michigan State University, and Olivet College. Since then she has coauthored the official biography of a prominent Michigan political figure (*Man in Motion*, 2003) and published many articles about María of Ágreda for a popular audience. She lives and works in Lansing, Michigan, with her husband, S. C. Fedewa. Photo by Edwards Studios.